# Political Economy of Development and Environmental Degradation in India

## About the Author

**Manasranjan Dashmishra** is presently Reader in Economics, Post Graduate Department of Management, at Shri Vaishnav Institute of Management, Indore (MP). He has a brilliant research and academic career. He has to his credit B.A. (Hons.) from Fakir Mohan University, Orissa, M.A., M.Phil., and Ph.D. in Economics from Devi Ahilya University, Indore (MP). Previously he has served School of Economics, Devi Ahilya University as a Project Fellow (UGC-SAP) and Visiting Faculty. He has delivered several lectures in various teaching departments such as International Institute of Professional Studies, Institute of Management Studies of Devi Ahilya University. He has contributed many research papers on various economic issues and also presented papers at various national and international seminars. He has contributed to leading academic journals, edited books and newspapers.

# Political Economy of Development and Environmental Degradation in India

**Manasranjan Dashmishra**

**CONCEPT PUBLISHING COMPANY PVT. LTD.**
**NEW DELHI-110059**

**ISBN-13: 978-81-8069-722-7**

First Published 2011

*Published and Printed by*

Concept
Since 1974

**Concept Publishing Company Pvt. Ltd.**
**Regd. Office:**
A/15-16, Commercial Block, Mohan Garden
New Delhi-110059 (India)
*Phones* : 25351460, 25351794, *Fax* : 091-11-25357109
*Email* : publishing@conceptpub.com
*Website*: www.conceptpub.com

**Editorial Office:**
H-13, Bali Nagar, New Delhi-110 015, India.

Cataloging in Publication Data--*Courtesy:* D.K. Agencies (P) Ltd. <docinfo@dkagencies.com>

**Dashmishra, Manasranjan.**
Political economy of development and environmental degradation in India / Manasranjan Dashmishra.
p. cm.
Includes bibliographical references (p. ) and index.
ISBN 9788180697227

1. Economic development--Environmental aspects--India. 2. Environmental degradation--India. 3. Agriculture--Environmental aspects--India. 4. Industries--Environmental aspects--India. I. Title.

DDC 338.954 22

**Dedicated to**

My revered teacher who enlightened me

**Professor Ganesh Kawadia**

and

My dear beloved parents

**Shri Bhimsen Dash & Smt. Puspita Dash**

**Dr. Satendra Kumar**
B. Tech. (Hons.) MBA, Ph.D.
**Director**

**Shri Vaishnav℠ Institute of Management**
(ISO 9001-2001 Certified)

# Foreword

Environmental issues such as natural hazards, particularly cyclones and annual monsoon floods, population growth, increasing individual consumption, industrialization, infrastructural development, poor agricultural practices, and resource mal-distribution, are gaining utmost importance in the political agenda of developing countries with high industrial and modern agricultural activities. The growth expectations in these economies are still high to accommodate unsolved social and poverty problems. These generate heavy pressure on land, land degradation, forests, habitat destruction and loss of biodiversity. Changing consumption pattern has led to rising demand for energy. The final outcomes of this are air pollution, global warming, climate change, water scarcity and water pollution. As a result, the environmental concern in policy making is becoming more complex. When ecological degradation costs are not paid by those generating it, then there are externalities to the economic system. Economic activities are then planned without taking into account these environmental externalities and so people's consumption pattern are forged without any internationalization of environmental cost. In this process, future generation will be left with degraded natural capital stock. Therefore, growth strategies should have proper government intervention for better utilization of environmental resources.

Government intervention is faced with challenges of balancing cost and benefit among the contemporary and future generation to justify policy action in a way to maximize social welfare. In the context of developing countries, where growth expectation are high, least cost environmental policies are crucial since they reduce the conflict with the environmental issues. Therefore, policy makers in the region must be aware of the specific issues of the relationship between economic aspects and environmental phenomena to offer policy initiatives, which can increase efficiency and provide equity.

The other important aspect of economic development of the developing countries is related to high level of poverty and poor social sector development. Under these situations, there is lack of awareness in the public demand for quality of environments. This also creates pressure on quality of natural resources. Therefore, growth and poverty create two-way pressures on environmental resources. Thus, there is a need for appropriate growth strategies and government intervention to optimize growth with better quality of environment. With this view Dr. Manasranjan Dashmishra has made an excellent effort to unravel the role of political economy in development and the resulting environmental degradation in India.

In his book, the subject matter has been presented in ten chapters. The first chapter includes the introductory part of environmental concerns and its economic significance which highlights on sustainable development, the club of Rome, Rio conference on environment and development, the Kyoto Protocol, United Nations Environment Programme, global warming, Pachauri's thought on climate change and environmental laws in India. In the second chapter, he has given insights into four major aspects such as environmental issues, political issues of development, interlink between development strategies and environmental degradation and literature survey. The third chapter gives details about the models and theoretical framework of this book. The fourth chapter engraves the aspects related to economics of development in India, which includes various aspects of economic development during successive five year plans and new economic reforms era. The fifth chapter elucidates various environmental issues in India. These issues include land resources, forest resources, water resources and air pollutions in India. The chapter sixth tries to empirically interlink between economic development and environmental degradation. In the seventh, eighth and ninth chapter, Dr. Dashmishra has attempted to establish a trade-off between agricultural growth, industrial growth and trade liberalization and environmental degradation in India. The tenth chapter gives the summary of conclusions and suggestions regarding the role of political economy in development and environmental degradation in India.

The author has tackled this very vital aspect of economic development in relation to India very lucidly in a manner so as to make readers not only grasp the concepts which link economic development with environmental degradation but also to enable them to appreciate the phenomenon of environmental degradation as it holds the key of social and economic safety of our future generation. Very little has been attempted by authors in this area of economic development and I am sure that this piece of academic work will be very useful and significantly enrich the readers' understanding about safer physical environment and how to achieve it.

July 28, 2010

**Dr. Satendra Kumar**
Director
Shri Vaishnav Institute of Management, Indore (Madhya Pradesh)
Formerly Professor and Head
Department of Business and Industrial Management,
South Gujarat University, Surat (Gujarat)

Scheme No. 71, Gumasta Nagar, INDORE - 452 009 (M.P.) Phone : 0731-2382963 (Direct Line)
Telefax: 0731-2789926, Reception : 2780011, 2789925 Cel: 9425900016, Res. 2389014
E-mail: director@svimi.org, satendrakumark@yahoo.com

# Preface

In the pace of rapid economic development, we have exploited our natural resources at a rapid rate. It has disturbed the ecological balance, and the environment has become unfriendly. With the process of development, the quality of environment is deteriorating. If such a process continues, then in the near future, we will not get good quality of environment, which is very essential for welfare of the people. This will adversely influence the process of economic growth as well as socio-economic life. Further, environmental issues are gaining importance in the political and economic agenda of developing countries like India with high industrial and modern agricultural and sophisticated trade activity.

Since independence, the Government of India has been formulating many plans and developing strategies for rapid overall development of the country and removing the country from the shackles of poverty. For this, various plans have been made and modified from time to time. Emphasis has been given to raise the productivity, remove poverty and avoid unemployment problems, etc. Not only this, economic reforms has been introduced in 1991, in which the motto of privatization, liberalization and globalization was fixed, but no consideration has been given to protect the environment so that economic development can be achieved at a faster rate without exploiting the environmental resources. As a result, the planning process in India has focused mainly on the maximization of growth with the given resources. This makes environmental concern in policy making more complex and difficult. When environmental degradation costs are not paid by those generating it, then they are externalities to the economic system. If economic activity are planned without taking into consideration these environmental externalities, then consumption patterns are forged without any internationalization of environmental cost. In this process, future generations will be left with degraded natural capital stock. The main objective of this book is to critically synthesize and interpret the relationship between the process of economic development and environmental issues. Will our country be able to sustain economic growth indefinitely without running into resource constraints or spoiling the environment beyond repair? What is the relationship between steadily increasing economic activity and environmental quality?

In compending this book, I owe thanks to a number of persons. First of all, my sincere regards are extended to the revered teachers, Dr. Ganesh Kawadia, Professor and Head, School of Economics and Dr. S. Mahalati (my spiritual mother), Professor and Head, Department of BAHA'I Chair for Studies in Development, Devi Ahilya University, Indore (MP), who provided all academic and sympathetic support to carry out my higher studies. Boundless regards are due for Dr. R.K. Sharma, Professor and Director, Prestige Institute of Management and Research (Under-graduate Courses), Indore, Maj. Gen. Dr. J.R. Bhatti, Ex-Director, Shri Vaishnav Institute of Management, Indore, and Dr. Govind Singh Saun, Director, Indian Council of Social Science Research, New Delhi, for their valuable suggestions for the present book.

I would like to extend my sincere gratitude to Dr. Balbir Singh Butola, Associate Professor, Centre for the Study of Regional Development, School of Social Science, Jawaharlal Nehru University, New Delhi who showered knowledge and blessings on me. He generated academic inquisitiveness in me and went through the manuscript and many aspects dealt in this book have been modified through a series of interactions and debate.

My special thanks are due for Mr. Netranand Rout, Mr. Khirod Kumar Kesh, Mr. Pradosh Kumar Dash, Dr. Gyanprakash, Dr. Nirupama Nagar, Dr. Kanhaiya Ahuja, Dr. Rekha Acharya, Dr. Hitendra Bargal, Dr. Ajay Kumar Singh, Dr. Anand Shrivastava, Dr. Kaushlendra Vikram Mishra, Mr. Manohar Kapse, Mrs. Anuradha Pathak, Mrs. Sonal Chaudhry, Mr. Sakharam Mujalde and many for their efforts to shape my academic acculturation.

I am very much indebted to my beloved parents for their blessings, encouragement and support. I am really appreciative of my elder brother Dr. Chittaranjan Dash, OFS-I, Orissa, now holding the position of Deputy Director, in Madhusudan Das Regional Academy of Financial Management, Bhubaneswar, Orissa, who has really struggled and sacrificed a lot to cultivate my career, sister-in-law Sangeeta, loving sister Padmaja (Nani) and brother-in-law Dr. Rajib Lochan Sahoo, Archivist, Reserve Bank of India, Central Records and Documentation Centre, Pune. I have no word to express my gratitude to my wife Mrs. Pooja Pateria (Dashmishra) and our children Padmamurty, Ishaan, Shaswat, Saurish, and Padmasambhab encouraged my research pursuits with a lot of patience and forbearance.

Last but not the least I am highly thankful to the Librarians and Staff of different libraries from where I have collected research material for this study. My sincere thanks to my colleagues, the authors of different texts and researchers whose works and ideas I have significantly used and analyzed while doing my literary exercise.

Indore **Manasranjan Dashmishra**

# Contents

# List of Tables

# List of Figures

# 1

# Introduction

> *"It shall be the duty of every citizen... (g) to protect the forests and improve the natural environment, forests, lakes, rivers and wild life and to have compassion for living creatures."*
>
> *Article 51A, Constitution of India*

Before the early 1990s, the "political economy[1] of India" was a protected and strictly regulated economy, both internally and externally. It was in a state of sorry affairs. The staged and sensible shuffle in reforms started taking place from 1991 onwards. It was marked with rapid reforms and its subsequent successful implementation. The government took several actions, which were more coherent than their previous ones. Its paradigm shift from strong state economy to market economy (mixed economy) led to the "Revival of Indian Economy". Although there were some hurdles, the process of globalization and liberalization gathered its momentum.[2]

After independence, the Planning Commission was set up with the Prime Minister as its Chairperson in 1950. India adopted the path of planned development for fast balanced economic growth with social justice. The focus of the planning was to create better employment opportunities and removal of poverty and regional disparity. At the time of independence, Indian economy was in a very poor shape in terms of low per capita income, poor industrialization and lack of capital for modernization and transformation of the economy.[3] The planners therefore adopted the strategies by which the focus was on supply side of economics with complete control on demand pattern. The fiscal policy was used to mobilize resources for economic development. The planners planned for self-reliance in the economy by overall control in import propensity of the country. Thus, they used the planning process to mobilize saving and to develop a strong capital goods base by providing heavy industrialization in the economy.[4]

The structure of political economy of India covers both internal and external ground. The steps of economic reforms, which were initiated, gave significant results internally as well as externally. Some of these results are as follows: rupee was sharply devalued by about 20 per cent and made fully convertible on the current account but not on capital account. Licensing was almost abolished for imports and tariffs were substantially curtailed. FDI was allowed to the tune of 51 per cent which resulted in influx of wide range of industries and portfolio investments. Banking system was overhauled. Number of industries reserved for the public sector was reduced to six.[5] Taxation system was rationalized and tax rates were made at par with ASEAN countries. Anti-trust legislation was amended to facilitate expansion and diversification. And industrial licence was abolished except in the case of 15 industries of strategic or environmental importance.

## ENVIRONMENTAL CONCERNS AND ITS ECONOMIC SIGNIFICANCE

Environmental protection as part of the economic development process can be characterized by a continuum of institutional quality that guides and sustains economic activity. There are supply and demand sides to the quality of institutions protecting the environment, and both are influenced by the trade orientation of an economy. On the demand side, economic growth implies higher income and increasing demand for environmental protection and standards. This process is a political one because, in most instances, environmental protection cannot be purchased readily on the market by decentralized agents. This demand for environmental protection is multifaceted like the environment. Economic agents care first about their immediate environment (water, air) or about environmental factors that directly affect their health. At much higher levels of income, environmental problems that are more remote in space and time eventually become prominent; this typically occurs after graduation from the developing economy stage. The "global village" is an industrialized-country notion. Free trade reinforces the demand for effective environmental institutions by fostering the income prospects of economic agents through a greater pie and unfettered knowledge flows. On the supply side, governments in developing economies have scarce amount of resources and human capital to allocate to the provision of competing institutional functions, including environmental protection. These governments are accumulating policy and institutional experience, and some stylized facts are emerging. Institutional knowledge can be transferred across industries and borders. Hence, the free movement of institutional knowledge reinforces the sustainability of economic development. This is a robust conclusion. Environmental side-acceptance to trade agreements could facilitate such knowledge transfer.

A decade after the 1972 Stockholm Conference, the UN-sponsored Stockholm Environmental Conference held just over 10 years later was the first successful attempt to achieve global recognition of environmental issues. Indicative of the lack of concrete involvement in environmental protection to that time was the fact that only 15 nations had a department or ministry responsible for environmental affairs compared to 143 in 1984. Many governments were uncertain of what were the most serious or pressing problems in their country. There was obviously a need to identify those issues and to determine how to manage them once identified. At the same time, the public at large was becoming more critically aware that environmental protection had been neglected by government and often ignored by industry. It soon became evident that a large amount of money would have to be spent to redress some of the more evident problems. However, many developing nations were reluctant to slow down the much-needed industrial growth by imposing costly environmental controls on industry. In fact, some waived environmental control altogether as an incentive to attract industry. In some sectors, it was often stated that industrial development and environmental protection were mutually exclusive activities. The need of an awareness, commitment and dedication by all sectors of society to protect their environment was just beginning to develop, replacing the rather simplistic view that all environmental problems were caused by greedy industry.[6]

The situation is alarming all over the globe. The developed countries have the resources to address these concerns, but with our weak infrastructure and poverty, we are facing serious problems in our country. Population growth is our major problem. Our population is growing at a rate that is simply unacceptable and its impact on our ecology is devastating. Unless we give it the same national consensus and priority that we accord to our national security and defence, our burgeoning population will do irreversible damage to the environment.

Our forests are already reeling under its adverse impact. Our annual rate of deforestation is massive and our tropical forests, rich source of world's bio-diversity, are rapidly disappearing. Deforestation will adversely affect the rainfall pattern, as trees are primarily a source of water and only secondarily producers of timber.

Industrialization is essential for our economic development, but industrialization without regard for environmental factors is counterproductive not only in the long run but almost immediately. Thoughtless industrialization can destroy the ecological balance of a region very quickly. Many concerned persons have focused on this aspect of economic development. Paul Kennedy in his book, *Preparing for the 21st Century* and Club of Rome's study, *The First Global Revolution* highlight the challenge of balance between economic growth and the environment. They clearly spell out that the nations that are not able to resolve the dichotomy between the environment and development may ultimately disintegrate and disappear.

Thus, there is a need for a realistic assessment of the impact of economic development on environmental pollution and ecosystem degradation. To achieve a realistic assessment, we must go beyond impressionistic statements, to qualitative and quantitative estimates on the impact of economic development on environmental pollution and ecosystem degradation. However, converting this need into a reality presents a daunting challenge, even for affluent countries with traditions of good statistical services and a growing interest in environmental matters. Needless to say, attempting to quantify the impact of economic development in the form of human actions on the long-term environment in India, a country abounding in dubious statistics and unverifiable claims, and peopled by masses of uncooperative bureaucrats prone to treat any unflattering statistics as a deep state secret, is a far more complicated task. And yet, no such study was attempted in India. Among the earliest attempts of its kind, this study estimated the impact of quantum of economic development on environmental degradation in the form of forest and land degradation, air pollution and water pollution in India.

## The Club of Rome (1971)

The Club of Rome[7] elevated significant public interest with its report *Limits to Growth,*[8] which pointed out 'The Population Bomb' would come true within a century. Published in 1972 and presented for the first time at the International Students' Committee (ISC) Annual Management Symposium in St. Gallen, Switzerland, it predicted that economic growth could not continue indefinitely because of the limited availability of natural resources, particularly oil. In the 1970s oil price shocks led to sharp price increases for many commodities. At that time many became alarmed at the rate of utilization of natural resources by mankind. It seemed that in just a few years real scarcity would become a major global problem. A clear reason for this alarm was the concept that certain natural resources are inherently limited in nature, and that current rates of use, or even the likely future rates of use would surely use them all up in the foreseeable future. The voice of this movement was the "Club of Rome", so named because they felt that Western society, like ancient Rome, was doomed.[9]

However, even before *Limits to Growth* was published, Eduard Pestel and Mihajlo Mesarovic of Case Western Reserve University had begun work on a far more elaborate model (it distinguished ten world regions and involved 200,000 equations compared with 1000 in the Meadows model). The research had the full support of the Club and the final publication, *Mankind at the Turning Point* was accepted as the official Second Report to the Club of Rome in 1974. In addition to providing a more refined regional breakdown, Pestel and Mesarovic had succeeded in integrating social as well as technical data. The Second Report revised the predictions of the original, *Limits to Growth,* and gave a more optimistic prognosis for the future of the environment, noting that many of the factors were within human control and therefore that environmental and economic catastrophe were preventable or avoidable, hence the title.[10]

**Sustainable Development**

According to *Brundtland Commission,*[11] sustainable development is a pattern of resource use that aims to meet human needs while preserving the environment so that these needs can be met not only in the present, but in the indefinite future, which has become the most often-quoted definition of sustainable development as development that meets the needs of the present without compromising the ability of future generations to meet their own needs.[12] Sustainable development holds together concern for the '*carrying capacity*'[13] of natural systems with the social challenges facing humanity. As early as the 1970s 'sustainability' was employed to describe an economy '*in equilibrium with basic ecological support systems*'.[14] Ecologists have pointed to the '*limits of growth*'[15] and presented the alternative of a 'steady state economy'[16] in order to address environmental concerns.

The concept of sustainable development can be conceptually broken into three constituent parts: environmental sustainability, economic sustainability and socio-political sustainability (Fig 1.1).[17] Sustainable development does not focus solely on environmental issues. The United Nations' '*2005 World Summit*'[18] Outcome Document refers to the 'interdependent and mutually reinforcing pillars' of sustainable development as economic development, social development, and environmental protection.[19]

## Environmental Sustainability

It is the process of making sure that the current processes of interaction with the environment are pursued with the idea of keeping the environment as pristine as naturally possible based on ideal-seeking behaviour. An 'unsustainable situation' occurs when natural capital (the sum total of nature's resources) is used up faster than it can be replenished. Sustainability requires that human activity only uses nature's resources at a rate at which they can be replenished naturally. Inherently the concept of sustainable development is intertwined with the concept of carrying capacity. Theoretically, the long-term result of environmental degradation is the inability to sustain human life. Such degradation on a global scale could imply extinction for humanity.

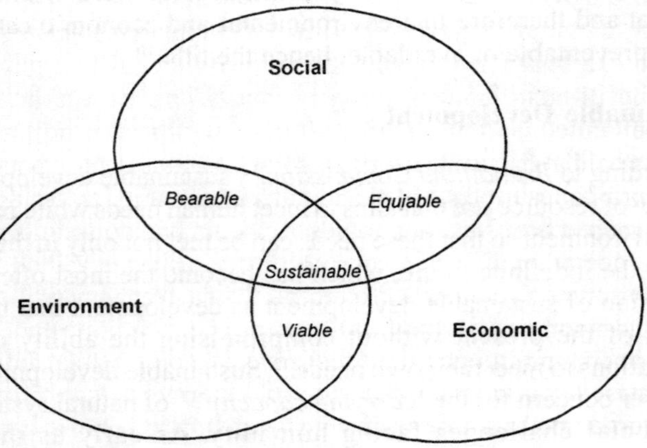


**Fig. 1.1:** Constituent Parts of Sustainable Development

**Economic Sustainability**

According to *'Agenda 21'*,[20] information, integration, and participation are clearly identified as key building blocks to help countries achieve development that recognises these interdependent pillars. It emphasises that in sustainable development everyone is a user and provider of information. It stresses the need to change from old sector-centred ways of doing business to new approaches that involve cross-sectoral coordination and the integration of environmental and social concerns into all development processes. Furthermore, Agenda 21 emphasizes that broad public participation in decision making is a fundamental prerequisite for achieving sustainable development.[21]

**Socio-political Sustainability**

According to *Hasna*, socio-political sustainability is a process which tells of a development of all aspects of human life affecting sustenance. It means resolving the conflict between the various competing goals, and involves the simultaneous pursuit of economic prosperity, environmental quality and social equity famously known as three dimensions (triple bottom line) with the resultant vector being technology. Hence, it is a continually evolving process; the 'journey' (the process of achieving sustainability) is of course vitally important, but only as a means of getting to the destination (the desired future state).[22]

**Rio Conference on Environment and Development**

The United Nations Conference on Environment and Development was held at Rio de Janeiro, Brazil from 3 to 14 June 1992. Statement of principles for the Sustainable Management of Forests was adopted by more than 178 countries at this conference. It was held to confirm the declaration of the United Nations Conference on the Human Environment, adopted at Stockholm on 16 June 1972, and seeking to build upon it. The goal was to establish a new and equitable global partnership through the creation of new levels of cooperation among States, key sectors of societies and people through working towards international agreements which respect the interests of all and protect the integrity of the global environmental and developmental system by recognizing the integral and inter-dependent nature of the Earth.

It proclaims[23] that

1. Human beings are at the centre of concerns for sustainable development. They are entitled to a healthy and productive life in harmony with nature.
2. States have, in accordance with the Charter of the United Nations and the principles of international law, the sovereign right to exploit their own resources pursuant to their own environmental and developmental policies, and the responsibility to ensure that activities within their jurisdiction or control do not cause damage to the environment of other States or of areas beyond the limits of national jurisdiction.
3. The right to development must be fulfilled so as to equitably meet developmental and environmental needs of present and future generations.
4. In order to achieve sustainable development, environmental protection shall constitute an integral part of the development process and cannot be considered in isolation from it.
5. All States and all people shall cooperate in the essential task of eradicating poverty as an indispensable requirement for sustainable development, in order to decrease the disparities in standards of living and better meet the needs of the majority of the people of the world.
6. The special situation and needs of developing countries, particularly the least developed and those most environmentally vulnerable, shall be given special priority. International actions in the field of environment and development should also address the interests and needs of all countries.
7. States shall cooperate in a spirit of global partnership to conserve, protect and restore the health and integrity of the Earth's ecosystem. In view of the different contributions to global environmental degradation, States have common but differentiated responsibilities. The developed countries acknowledge the responsibility that they bear in the international pursuit to sustainable development in view of the pressures their societies place on the global environment and of the technologies and financial resources they

command.

8. To achieve sustainable development and a higher quality of life for all people, States should reduce and eliminate unsustainable patterns of production and consumption and promote appropriate demographic policies.
9. States should cooperate to strengthen endogenous capacity-building for sustainable development by improving scientific understanding through exchanges of scientific and technological knowledge, and by enhancing the development, adaptation, diffusion and transfer of technologies, including new and innovative technologies.
10. Environmental issues are best handled with participation of all concerned citizens, at the relevant level. At the national level, each individual shall have appropriate access to information concerning the environment that is held by public authorities, including information on hazardous materials and activities in their communities, and the opportunity to participate in decision-making processes. States shall facilitate and encourage public awareness and participation by making information widely available. Effective access to judicial and administrative proceedings, including redress and remedy, shall be provided.
11. States shall enact effective environmental legislation. Environmental standards, management objectives and priorities should reflect the environmental and development context to which they apply. Standards applied by some countries may be inappropriate and of unwarranted economic and social cost to other countries, in particular developing countries.
12. States should cooperate to promote a supportive and open international economic system that would lead to economic growth and sustainable development in all countries, to better address the problems of environmental degradation. Trade policy measures for environmental purposes should not constitute a means of arbitrary or unjustifiable discrimination or a disguised restriction on international trade. Unilateral actions to deal with environmental challenges outside the jurisdiction of the importing country should be avoided.

Environmental measures addressing transboundary or global environmental problems should, as far as possible, be based on an international consensus.

13. States shall develop national law regarding liability and compensation for the victims of pollution and other environmental damage. States shall also cooperate in an expeditious and more determined manner to develop further international law regarding liability and compensation for adverse effects of environmental damage caused by activities within their jurisdiction or control to areas beyond their jurisdiction.
14. States should effectively cooperate to discourage or prevent the relocation and transfer to other States of any activities and substances that cause severe environmental degradation or are found to be harmful to human health.
15. In order to protect the environment, the precautionary approach shall widely be applied by States according to their capabilities. Where there are threats of serious or irreversible damage, lack of full scientific certainty shall not be used as a reason for postponing cost-effective measures to prevent environmental degradation.
16. National authorities should endeavour to promote the internalization of environmental costs and the use of economic instruments, taking into account the approach that the polluter should, in principle, bear the cost of pollution, with due regard to the public interest and without distorting international trade and investment.
17. Environmental impact assessment, as a national instrument, shall be undertaken for proposed activities that are likely to have a significant adverse impact on the environment and are subject to a decision of a competent national authority.
18. States shall immediately notify other States of any natural disasters or other emergencies that are likely to produce sudden harmful effects on the environment of those States. Every effort shall be made by the international community to help States so afflicted.
19. States shall provide prior and timely notification and relevant information to potentially affected States on activities that

may have a significant adverse transboundary environmental effect and shall consult with those States at an early stage and in good faith.

20. Women have a vital role in environmental management and development. Their full participation is therefore essential to achieve sustainable development.
21. The creativity, ideals and courage of the youth of the world should be mobilized to forge a global partnership in order to achieve sustainable development and ensure a better future for all.
22. Indigenous people and their communities and other local communities have a vital role in environmental management and development because of their knowledge and traditional practices. States should recognize and duly support their identity, culture and interests and enable their effective participation in the achievement of sustainable development.
23. The environment and natural resources of people under oppression, domination and occupation shall be protected.
24. Warfare is inherently destructive of sustainable development. States shall, therefore, respect international law providing protection for the environment in times of armed conflict and cooperate in its further development, as necessary.
25. Peace, development and environmental protection are inter-dependent and indivisible.
26. States shall resolve all their environmental disputes peacefully and by appropriate means in accordance with the Charter of the United Nations.
27. States and people shall cooperate in good faith and in a spirit of partnership in the fulfilment of the principles embodied in this Declaration and in the further development of international law in the field of sustainable development.

## The Kyoto Protocol

The Kyoto protocol[24] is an international environmental treaty intended to achieve stabilization of greenhouse gas concentrations in the atmosphere at a level that would prevent dangerous anthropogenic interference with the climate system.[25] It establishes legally binding commitments for the reduction of four greenhouse gases (GHGs—carbon dioxide, methane, nitrous oxide, sulphur hexafluoride), and two groups of gases (hydrofluorocarbons and perfluorocarbons) produced by industrialized nations, as well as general commitments for all member countries. As of 2008, 183 countries have ratified the protocol,[26] which was initially adopted for use on 11 December 1997 in Kyoto, Japan and which entered into force on 16 February 2005. Under Kyoto protocol, industrialized countries agreed to reduce their collective GHG emissions by 5.2 per cent compared to the year 1990. National limitations range from 8 per cent reductions for the European Union and some others to 7 per cent for the United States, 6 per cent for Japan, and 0 per cent for Russia. The treaty permitted GHG emission increases of 8 per cent for Australia and 10 per cent for Iceland.[27] One of the provisions of the Kyoto Protocol, known as the Clean Development Mechanism (CDM), establishes a framework within which the industrialised countries can meet a part of their carbon dioxide emission reduction requirements by purchasing Certified Emission Reductions (CERs) from India and other developing countries. These CERs are generated through an international process that continuously monitors and verifies that clean energy projects in developing countries are indeed leading to lower carbon dioxide emissions than would occur otherwise.[28]

**United Nations Environment Programme (UNEP)**

The UNEP coordinates United Nations environmental activities, assisting developing countries in implementing environmentally sound policies and encourages sustainable development through sound environmental practices. It was founded as a result of the United Nations Conference on the Human Environment in June 1972 and has its headquarters in Nairobi, Kenya. The UNEP is the designated authority of the United Nations system in environmental issues at the global and regional level. Its mandate is to coordinate the development of environmental policy consensus by keeping the global environment under review and bringing emerging issues to the attention of governments and the international community for action. The mandate and objectives of UNEP emanate from United Nations General Assembly resolution 2997 (XXVII) of 15 December 1972 and subsequent amendments adopted at UNCED in 1992, the Nairobi Declaration on the Role and Mandate of UNEP, adopted at the

Nineteenth Session of the UNEP Governing Council, and the Malmö Ministerial Declaration of 31 May 2000.[29]

Its activities cover a wide range of issues regarding the atmosphere, marine and terrestrial ecosystems. It has played a significant role in developing international environmental conventions, promoting environmental science and information and illustrating the way those can work in conjunction with policy, working on the development and implementation of policy with national governments and regional institution and working in conjunction with environmental Non Governmental Organizations (NGOs). UNEP has also been active in funding and implementing environmentally related development projects. UNEP has aided in the development of guidelines and treaties on issues such as the international trade in potentially harmful chemicals, transboundary air pollution, and contamination of international waterways. The World Meteorological Organization and the UNEP established the Intergovernmental Panel on Climate Change (IPCC) in 1988. UNEP is also one of several Implementing Agencies for the Global Environment Facility (GEF).[30]

## Global Warming

Global warming is the increase in the average temperature of the Earth's near-surface air and oceans since the mid-twentieth century and its projected continuation. Global surface temperature increased 0.74 ± 0.18 °C (1.33 ± 0.32 °F) during the 100 years ending in 2005.[31] The Inter-governmental Panel on Climate Change (IPCC) concludes that the temperature increase since the mid-twentieth century is 'very likely' due to the increase in anthropogenic greenhouse gas concentrations.[32] Natural phenomena such as solar variation and volcanoes probably had a small warming effect from pre-industrial times to 1950 and a small cooling effect from 1950 onward.[33] These basic conclusions have been endorsed by at least 30 scientific societies and academies of science,[34] including all of the national academies of science of the major industrialized countries. While a small minority has voiced disagreement with these findings,[35] the overwhelming majority of scientists working on climate change agree with the IPCC's main conclusions.

The major cause of global warming is the emission of greenhouse gases like carbon dioxide, methane, nitrous oxide, etc. into the atmosphere. The major source of carbon dioxide is power plants.

These power plants emit large amount of carbon dioxide produced from burning of fossil fuels for the purpose of electricity generation. About twenty per cent of carbon dioxide emitted in the atmosphere comes from burning of gasoline in the engines of vehicles. This is true for most of the developed countries. Buildings, both commercial and residential, represent a larger source of global warming pollution than cars and trucks.

Building of these structures requires a lot of fuel to be burnt which emits a large amount of carbon dioxide in the atmosphere. Methane is more than 20 times as effectual as $CO_2$ at entrapping heat in the atmosphere. Methane is obtained from resources such as rice paddies, bovine flatulence, bacteria in bogs and fossil fuel manufacture. When fields are flooded, anaerobic situation builds up and the organic matter in the soil decays, releasing methane to the atmosphere. The main sources of nitrous oxide include nylon and nitric acid production, cars with catalytic converters, the use of fertilizers in agriculture and the burning of organic matter. Another cause of global warming is deforestation that is caused by cutting and burning of forests for the purpose of residence and industrialization.

Climate model projections indicate that global surface temperature will likely rise a further 1.1 to 6.4 °C (2.0 to 11.5 °F) during the twenty-first century. The uncertainty in this estimate arises from use of differing estimates of future greenhouse gas emissions and from use of models with differing climate sensitivity. Some other uncertainties include how warming and related changes will vary from region to region around the globe. Although most studies focus on the period up to 2100, warming is expected to continue, even in the absence of new emissions, because of the large heat capacity of the oceans and the lifespan of $CO_2$ in the atmosphere.[36] Increasing global temperature will cause sea levels to rise and will change the amount and pattern of precipitation, likely including an expanse of the subtropical desert regions.[37] Other likely effects include Arctic shrinkage and resulting Arctic methane release, increases in the intensity of extreme weather events, changes in agricultural yields, modifications of trade routes, glacier retreat, species extinctions and changes in the ranges of disease vectors.

Political and public debate continues regarding the appropriate response to global warming. The available options are: mitigation to reduce further emissions; adaptation to reduce the damage caused by warming; and geoengineering to reverse global warming. Most national governments have signed and ratified the Kyoto Protocol aimed at reducing greenhouse gas emissions.

## Pachauri on Climate Change

According to *Dr. Rajendra K. Pachauri,*[38] climate change is taking place. This is the clear finding of the report of IPCC Working Group-1. "Business-as-usual" greenhouse gas emissions are going to go up in the near future with increases in temperature and an increase in extreme events. He has advised to use low carbon technologies, including renewable energy (bio-fuels, nuclear, etc.) so as to meet the global challenge, considering that there will be a much greater consumption of energy in the future.

According to him, climate change is expected to exacerbate current stresses on water resources. On a regional scale, mountain snow pack, glaciers, and small ice caps play a crucial role in fresh water availability. Widespread mass losses from glaciers and reductions in snow cover over recent decades are projected to accelerate throughout the twenty-first century, reducing water availability, hydropower potential and the changing seasonality of flows in regions supplied by melt water from major mountain ranges, such as the Hindu-Kush, the Himalaya, the Andes, where more than one-sixth of the world's population currently live. There is also high confidence that many semi-arid areas such as the Mediterranean Basin, western United States, southern Africa, and north-eastern Brazil will suffer a decrease in water resources due to climate change. In Africa, by 2020, between 75 and 250 million people are projected to be exposed to increased water stress due to climate change. Climate change could further adversely affect food security and exacerbate malnutrition at low latitudes, especially in seasonally dry and tropical regions, where crop productivity is projected to decrease for even small temperature increases, such as one to two degrees Celsius. By 2020, in some African countries, yields from rain-fed agriculture could be reduced by up to 50 per cent. Agricultural production, including access to food, in many African countries is projected to be severely compromised.[39]

Therefore, he has suggested that there is a need to improve the energy efficiency of the entire energy system. There is enormous potential for improving the efficiency of energy use in every sector:

housing, industry, transportation. The general public must work towards new ways of managing water resources, in particular measures to store water. This could include creating dams, recharging groundwater resources, and water recycling and reuse. Developed countries have to take more actions; otherwise developing countries will not follow. The realization is growing that developing countries cannot pursue the same path as the one established by industrialized countries. If the industrialized nations change this path themselves, it will restore the credibility they have lost in the eyes of developing countries. The European and US approaches to climate change show a difference in philosophies. Actually, we need a combination of both approaches: a technology based response and regulations. For example, a carbon tax would be a strong signal to the automobile sector, which would respond with new fuels and new designs. A very large part of economic activity is driven and managed by industrial sector. It is important for governments to treat industries as partners. And current energy resources are going to be depleted and the markets linked to low carbon technologies are going to develop. In the interest of industry itself, it has to look at these new markets in order to maintain a leading role in bringing about new solutions to preserve natural resources and reduce carbon emissions.[40]

### Environmental Laws in India

The Government of India has formulated comprehensive legislations to enable the institutions like pollution control boards to effectively protect the environment. A list of laws is given below.[41]

1. The Water (Prevention and Control of Pollution) Act, 1974, as amended up to 1988
2. The Water (Prevention and Control of Pollution) Rules, 1975
3. The Water (Prevention and Control of Pollution) (Procedure for Transaction of Business) Rules, 1975
4. The Water (Prevention and Control of Pollution) Cess Act, 1977, as amended by Amendment Act, 1991
5. The Water (Prevention and Control of Pollution) Cess Rules, 1978

6. The Air (Prevention and Control of Pollution) Act, 1981, as amended by Amendment Act, 1987
7. The Air (Prevention and Control of Pollution) Rules,1982
8. The Air (Prevention and Control of Pollution) (Union Territories) Rules, 1983
9. The Environment (Protection) Act, 1986
10. The Environment (Protection) Rules, 1986
11. Environmental Impact Assessment of Development Projects
12. Hazardous Wastes (Management and Handling) Rules, 1989
13. Manufacture, Storage and Import of Hazardous Chemical Rules, 1989
14. Manufacture, Use, Import, Export and Storage of Hazardous Micro-Organisms Genetically Engineered Organisms or Cells Rules, 1989
15. Scheme of Labelling of Environment Friendly Products (ECO-MARKS)
16. Restricting Certain Activities Range in Special Specified Area of Aravalli
17. Bio-Medical Waste (Management and Handling) Rules, 1998
18. The National Environment Tribunal Act, 1995
19. The National Environmental Appellate Authority Act, 1997
20. The Environment (Protection) (Second Amendment) Rules, 1999—Emission Standards for New Generator Sets
21. The Public Liability Insurance Act, 1991
22. The Public Liability Insurance Rules, 1991
23. National Forest Policy, 1988
24. Forest (Conservation) Act, 1980
25. Forest (Conservation) Rules, 1981
26. The Eco Sensitive Zone—Pachmarhi, Notification, 1998
27. Re-cycled Plastics Manufacture and Usage Rules, 1999
28. 2-T Oil (Regulation of Supply and Distribution) Order, 1998
29. Coastal Regulation Zone—Notifications
30. Environment (Siting for Industrial Projects) Rules, 1999—Notification
31. Taj Trapezium Zone Pollution (Prevention and Control) Authority—Order
32. Dumping and Disposal of Flyash - Notification
33. Noise Pollution (Regulation and Control) Rules, 2000

34. Municipal Solid Wastes (Management & Handling) Rules, 1999—Notification
35. Ozone Depleting Substances (Regulation) Rules, 2000—Draft Notification

**Purpose of the Book**

Since independence, the Government of India has been formulating many plans and developing strategies for rapid overall development of the country and liberating the country from the shackles of poverty. For this, various plans have been made and modified from time to time. Emphasis has been given to raise the productivity, to remove poverty, to avoid unemployment problems, etc. Not only this, economic reforms had taken place in 1991, in which the motto of privatization, liberalization and globalization was fixed, but no consideration has been given to protect the environment so that economic development can be achieved at a faster rate without exploiting the environmental resources.

In the pace of rapid economic development, we have exploited our natural resources at a rapid rate. It has disturbed the ecological balance and the environment has become human unfriendly. With the process of development, the quality of environment is deteriorating. If such a process will continue, then in near future, we will not get good quality of environment, which is very essential for welfare of the people. This will adversely influence the process of economic growth as well as socio-economic life.

This book, *Political Economy of Development and Environmental Degradation in India,* tries to interlink the political issues of economic development with environmental degradation. In this work the *deforestation* across the country and the *Air and Water Pollution* in various cities in India are considered to be the indicators of environmental degradation. Many indicators such as *Electricity Consumption, Net State Domestic Products (Agricultural Production Index), Population Growth, Urbanization, etc.* are considered as the development indicators in the country. In addition to this, the book also examines factors of economic development such as *natural factors, social factors* or *economic activities* which are playing vital role in degrading the environment in terms of deforestation, air pollution and water pollution. Further, the present book has economic and social implications. There have been several major research efforts on the rate and causes of deforestation and the impact of economic development on it in recent years. Though there is much associated literature at global level, there is still very little consensus in the research community on these issues especially in India. My book tries to focus the areas of uncertainty and confusion, and proposes questions that must be answered to get a better grasp of the subject.

This book attempts to highlight the important facts and issues involved in the field of development issues and environmental degradation in India. It is hoped that this book would provide, insight for future research work in this field. The results and suggestions of this book will help economists draw some hypotheses and principles, required for the environment protection authorities and economists to frame the policies in order to protect our natural resources and bring an accelerated economic development.

## NOTES

1. The social science that deals with political science and economics as a unified subject and the study of the inter-relationships between political and economic processes is known as Political Economy. According to *Peter Burnham*, political economy is that branch of the art of government concerned with the systematic inquiry into the nature and causes of the wealth of nations, although it is now often used loosely to describe political aspects of economic policy-making. Since the seventeenth century the meaning of the term has fluctuated widely. It is possible nevertheless to identify three broad traditions of political economy which currently influence political science. These are, first, the tradition of classical political economy; secondly, the Marxian tradition; and finally, the tradition of political economics which uses statistical and modelling techniques to test hypotheses about the relationship between government and the economy. *Source*: Political Dictionary, http://www.answers.com/topic/political-economy
2. Maps of India.com's India Business Directory, "Political Economy of India", for more details please see http://business.mapsofindia.com/india-economy/political.html
3. I.G. Patel advocates that strategy implies essentially a deliberate choice – a choice of the point and timing and manner of attack on the problems at hand.
4. *Development and Environment Inter-relationship in MP, from Environmental Issues of Development*, The Associated Publisher, Amabala Cantt, 2006.

5. For details please refer Arvind Panagariya, "India in the 1980s and 1990s: A Triumph of Reforms".http://ideas.repec.org/p/wpa/wuwpit/0403005.html.
6. Brouzes, Raymond J.P., "Impact of Environmental Concerns on the Bauxite Industry and its Economic Significance", from "Bauxite, Economic Outlook" http://www.onemine.org, 1984.
7. The Club of Rome was founded in April 1968 by Aurelio Peccei, an Italian industrialist, and Alexander King, a Scottish scientist. It was formed when a small international group of people from the fields of academia, civil society, diplomacy, and industry met at a villa in Rome, Italy, hence the name.
8. *Limits to Growth* was discussed in hundreds of seminars, round tables, newspaper articles, radio and television programmes. Quite wrongly, the Report tended to be perceived as presenting an inescapable scenario for the future, and the Club was assumed to be in favour of zero economic growth. In fact the projection of trends and the analysis of their cross impacts were intended to highlight the risks of a blind pursuit of growth in the industrialised countries, and to induce changes in prevailing attitudes and policies so that the projected consequences should not materialise.
9. The Architecture of Modern Political Power; http://www.clubofrome.org
10. Club of Rome - Wikipedia, the free encyclopedia.mht
11. The Brundtland Commission, formally the World Commission on Environment and Development (WCED), known by the name of its Chair Gro Harlem Brundtland, was convened by the United Nations in 1983. The Commission was created to address growing concern "about the accelerating deterioration of the human environment and natural resources and the consequences of that deterioration for economic and social development." In establishing the commission, the UN General Assembly recognized that environmental problems were global in nature and determined that it was in the common interest of all nations to establish policies for sustainable development.
12. United Nations, 1987. "Report of the World Commission on Environment and Development", General Assembly Resolution 42/187, 11 December 1987. Retrieved: 2007-4-12
13. The supportable population of an organism, given the food, habitat, water and other necessities available within an environment is known as the environment's carrying capacity for that organism. For the human population, more complex variables such as sanitation and medical care are sometimes considered as part of the necessary infrastructure. As population density increases, birth rate often increases and death rate typically decreases. The difference between the birth rate and the death rate is the "natural increase". The carrying capacity could support a positive natural increase, or could require a negative natural increase. Carrying capacity is thus the number of individuals an environment can support without significant negative impacts to the given organism and its environment. A factor that keeps population size at equilibrium is known

as a regulating factor. The origins of the term lie in its use in the shipping industry to describe freight capacity, and a recent review finds the first use of the term in an 1845 report by the US Secretary of State to the Senate (Sayre, 2007).

14. Stivers, R. 1976. *The Sustainable Society: Ethics and Economic Growth.* Philadelphia: Westminster Press.
15. Meadows, D., Meadows, D.L., Randers, J., & Behrens, W. 1971. *The Limits to Growth.* New York: Universe Books.
16. Daly, H. E. 1973. *Towards a Steady State Economy.* San Francisco: Freeman. Daly, H. E. 1991. *Steady-State Economics* (2nd ed.). Washington, D.C.: Island Press.
17. IUCN. 2006. *The Future of Sustainability: Re-thinking Environment and Development in the Twenty-first Century.* Report of the IUCN Renowned Thinkers Meeting, 29-31 January, 2006 http://cmsdata.iucn.org/downloads/iucn_future_of_sustanability.pdf
18. The 2005 World Summit, 14–16 September 2005, was a follow-up summit meeting to the United Nations' 2000 Millennium Summit, which led to the Millennium Declaration of the Millennium Development Goals (MDGs). Representatives (including many leaders) of the 191 (now 192) member states met in New York City for what the United Nations described as "a once-in-a-generation opportunity to take bold decisions in the areas of development, security, human rights and reform of the United Nations."
19. 2005 World Summit Outcome Document, World Health Organization, 15 September 2005.
20. Agenda 21 is a programme run by the United Nations (UN) related to sustainable development. It is a comprehensive blueprint of action to be taken globally, nationally and locally by organizations of the UN, governments, and major groups in every area in which humans impact on the environment. The number *21* refers to the 21st century.
21. Will Allen. 2007."Learning for Sustainability: Sustainable Development."
22. Hasna, A.M. (2007). "Dimensions of sustainability". *Journal of Engineering for Sustainable Development: Energy, Environment, and Health,*, 2 (1): 47-57.
23. Report of the United Nations Conference on the Human Environment, Stockholm, 5-16 June 1972 (United Nations publication, Sales No. E.73.II.A.14 and corrigendum), chap. I.
24. The Kyoto Protocol is a protocol to the United Nations Framework Convention on Climate Change (UNFCCC or FCCC), an international environmental treaty produced at the United Nations Conference on Environment and Development (UNCED), informally known as the Earth Summit, held in Rio de Janeiro, Brazil, from 3 to 14 June 1992.
25. "Article 2". *The United Nations Framework Convention on Climate Change.*
26. "Kyoto Protocol: Status of Ratification" (PDF). United Nations Framework Convention on Climate Change. 2008-10-16. http://unfccc.int/files/kyoto_protocol/status_of_ratification/application/pdf/kp_ratification.pdf.

Retrieved on 2008-07-01.

27. United Nations Environment Programme (1997-12-11). *Industrialized countries to cut greenhouse gas emissions by 5.2%.* Press release. http://unfccc.int/cop3/fccc/info/indust.htm. Retrieved on 2007-08-06.
28. *The Hindu* daily. New Delhi, Online edition of India's National Newspaper. Thursday, February 17, 2005.
29. http://en.wikipedia.org/wiki/United_Nations_Environment_Programme
30. http://www.unep.org/
31. Global surface temperature is defined in the IPCC Fourth Assessment Report as the average of near-surface air temperature over land and sea surface temperature.
32. 'Summary for Policymakers', *Climate Change 2007: The Physical Science Basis. Contribution of Working Group I to the Fourth Assessment Report of the Inter-Governmental Panel on Climate Change.* Intergovernmental_Panel_on_Climate_Change. 2007-02-05. http://ipcc-wg1.ucar.edu/wg1/Report/AR4WG1_Print_SPM.pdf. Retrieved on 2 February 2007.
33. Hegerl, Gabriele C. *et al.* (2007-05-07). "Understanding and Attributing Climate Change". *Climate Change 2007: The Physical Science Basis. Contribution of Working Group I to the Fourth Assessment Report of the Inter-Governmental Panel on Climate Change.* Inter-Governmental Panel on Climate Change. 690. http://ipcc-wg1.ucar.edu/wg1/Report/AR4WG1_Print_Ch09.pdf. Retrieved on 20 May 2007. "Recent estimates (Figure 9.9) indicate a relatively small combined effect of natural forcings on the global mean temperature evolution of the second half of the twentieth century, with a small net cooling from the combined effects of solar and volcanic forcings."
34. The 2001 joint statement was signed by the scientific academies of Australia, Belgium, Brazil, Canada, the Caribbean, China, France, Germany, India, Indonesia, Ireland, Italy, Malaysia, New Zealand, Sweden, and the UK. The 2005 statement added Japan, Russia, and the U.S. The 2007 statement added Mexico and South Africa. Professional societies include American Meteorological Society, American Geophysical Union, American Institute of Physics, American Astronomical Society, American Association for the Advancement of Science, Stratigraphy Commission of the Geological Society of London, Geological Society of America, American Chemical Society, and Engineers Australia.
35. "Don't fight, adapt". National Post. December 2007. http://www.nationalpost.com/news/story.html?id=164002. Retrieved on 18 November 2007.
36. Archer, David (2005). "Fate of fossil fuel $CO_2$ in geologic time" (PDF). *Journal of Geophysical Research* 110 (C9): C09S05.1–C09S05.6. doi:10.1029/2004JC002625. http://geosci.uchicago.edu/~archer/reprints/archer.2005.fate_co2.pdf.

Retrieved on 27 July 2007.

37. Lu, Jian, Gabriel A. Vecchi, Thomas Reichler (2007). "Expansion of the Hadley cell under global warming". *Geophysical Research Letters* 34: L06805. doi:10.1029/2006GL028443. http://www.atmos.berkeley.edu/~jchiang/Class/Spr07/Geog257/Week10/Lu_Hadley06.pdf. Retrieved on 12/06/2008.
38. Dr. Rajendra Kumar Pachauri (born August 20, 1940, Nainital, India) is an economist who has served as the chair of the Inter-Governmental Panel on Climate Change (IPCC) since 2002. Pachauri is also the Director General of the The Energy and Resources Institute in New Delhi, an institution devoted to researching and promoting sustainable development and the chancellor of TERI University. To honour his contribution to the environment, he was awarded the Padma Bhushan, India's third highest civilian award, in January 2001. On December 10, 2007, Dr. Pachauri accepted the Nobel Peace Prize on behalf of the IPCC, along with co-recipient Al Gore.
39. Democracy now! The war and peace report, Chair of UN Climate Panel Says Nobel Peace Prize Signals a "Clarion Call for the Protection of the Earth", December 11, 2007. http://www.democracynow.org/
40. Veolia Environment, Annual Reprt, 2006. http://www.sustainable-development.veolia.com/en/Articles/20080108, rajendra-pachauri.aspx
41. Central Pollution Control Board, Annual Report 2004-05.

# 2

# Political Economy of Development and Environmental Degradation

The objective of this chapter is to critically review, synthesize and interpret the literature on the inter-relationship between economic growth and environmental issues. Will the world be able to sustain economic growth indefinitely without running into resource constraints or destroying the environment beyond repair? What is the relationship between steadily increasing economic activities and environmental quality? This analysis scrutinizes the relationship between economic growth and environmental quality.

## ENVIRONMENTAL ISSUES

This section of the chapter attempts to highlight some of the environmental issues and concerns that have an effect on all of us — from what we do, to what we don't do. There are many environmental issues, which are seen in this modern economic era. Some of them are climate change, conservation, dams, energy, genetic engineering, intensive faming, land degradation, soil, nanotechnology, nuclear issues, over population, ozone depletion, air pollution, water pollution, resource depletion, consumerism, fishing, logging, mining, toxins, urban sprawl, waste, etc. Now-a-days all these issues are highly burning so as to make ourselves more concerned to protect our environment to live a peaceful and healthy life.

*Climate Change:* It reflects abnormal variations to the expected climate within the Earth's atmosphere and subsequent effects on other parts of the Earth, such as in the ice caps over durations ranging from decades to millions of years. The causes of climate change are global warming, fossil fuels burning, sea level rise, greenhouse effect, glaciations, hysteresis, plate tectonics, solar variation, volcanism, aerosols, cement productions, extensive land use and livestock.

*Conservation:* It may refer to energy conservation, the reduction of non-renewable energy consumption, habitat conservation, water conservation, marine conservation, soil conservation, etc. The earth is facing so many threats such as habitat destruction, habitat fragmentation, species extinction, pollinator decline, coral bleaching, whaling, holocene extinction event, invasive species, etc.

*Dams:* Dams generally serve the primary purpose of retaining water, while other structures such as floodgates, levees, and dikes are used to manage or prevent water flow into specific land regions. Recently, however, the negative impacts of dams have come increasingly into focus. The damming of a river has dramatic consequences on the nature of the environment both upstream and downstream of the dam. The magnitudes of these effects are usually directly related to the size of the dam.

*Genetic Pollution:* It is undesirable gene flow into wild population. The term is usually associated with the gene flow from a genetically engineered (GE) organism (or genetically modified organism—GMO) to a non-GE organism.[1] However, conservation biologists and conservationists are using it to describe gene flow from a domestic, feral, non-native or invasive species to a wild indigenous population. A 2004 study performed near a Oregon field trial for a genetically modified variety of creeping bent-grass (*Agrostis stolonifera*) revealed that the trans-gene and its associate trait (resistance to the glyphosate herbicide) could be transmitted by wind pollination to resident plants of different Agrostis species, up to 14 km from the test field.[2] In 2007, the Scotts Company, producer of the genetically modified bent-grass, agreed to pay a civil penalty of $500,000 to the United States Department of Agriculture (USDA). The USDA alleged that Scotts "failed to conduct a 2003 Oregon field trial in a manner which ensured that neither glyphosate-tolerant creeping bent-grass nor its offspring would persist in the environment.[3]

*Intensive Farming:* It affects the environment negatively in many ways such as it limits the natural habitat of some wild creatures and can lead to soil erosion. The use of fertilizers can alter the biology of rivers and lakes. Some environmentalists attribute the hypoxic zone in the Gulf of Mexico as being encouraged by nitrogen fertilization of the algae bloom. Pesticides can kill useful insects as well as those that destroy crops. Use of chemicals on fields creates run-off, excess runs off into rivers and lakes causing pollution.

*Land Degradation:* It is a concept in which the value of the biophysical environment is affected by one or more combination of human-induced processes acting upon the land.[4] Natural hazards are excluded as a cause; however, human activities can indirectly affect phenomena such as floods and bushfires. It is estimated that up to 40 per cent of the world's agricultural land is seriously degraded.[5]

*Pollution:* It is the introduction of contaminants into an environment that causes instability, disorder, harm or discomfort to the ecosystem, i.e. physical systems or living organisms. Pollution can take the form of chemical substances, or energy, such as noise, heat, or light energy. Pollutants, the elements of pollution, can be foreign substances or energies, or naturally occurring; when naturally occurring, they are considered contaminants when they exceed natural levels. The world is facing a heavy pressure of air pollution, water pollution, noise pollution and water crisis.

*Exploitation of Natural Resources:* Some exploitation of natural resources is an essential condition of the human existence. This refers primarily to food production and necessities. However, the exploitation of nature is often done in an unsustainable way, which is causing increasing concern, as the depletion of natural resources from economic growth and population growth ultimately threatens human existence.

*Solid Waste Management:* Waste is an unwanted or undesired material or substance. It is also referred to as rubbish, trash, garbage, or junk depending upon the type of material and the regional terminology. In living organisms, waste relates to unwanted substances or toxins that are expelled from them. Waste management is the human control of the collection, treatment and disposal of different wastes. This is in order to reduce the negative impact waste has on environment and society. Waste is directly linked to human development, both technologically and socially. The composition of different wastes have varied over time and location, with industrial development and innovation being directly linked to waste materials. Examples of this include plastics and nuclear technology. Some components of waste have economical value and can be recycled once correctly recovered.

*Overpopulation:* It is a condition where an organism's numbers exceed the carrying capacity of its habitat. In common parlance, the term usually refers to the relationship between the human population and its environment, the Earth. There are indirect economic consequences of this environmental degradation in the form of ecosystem services attrition. Due to overpopulation the world is facing a lot of problems such as inadequate fresh water, depletion of natural resources, deforestation and loss of ecosystems, changes in atmospheric composition and consequent global warming, mass species extinctions, high infant and child mortality, starvation, malnutrition, low life expectancy, unhygienic living conditions, elevated crime rate, etc.

*Stress on Bio-diversity:* Some of the most significant and insidious threats to bio-diversity and ecosystem processes include climate change, mass agriculture, deforestation, overgrazing, slash-and-burn agriculture, urban development, light pollution and pesticide use.[6] Habitat fragmentation poses one of the more difficult challenges, because the global network of protected areas only covers 11.5 per cent of the Earth's surface.[7] A significant consequence of fragmentation and lack of linked protected areas is the reduction of animal migration on a global scale. Considering that billions of tonnes of biomass are responsible for nutrient cycling across the Earth, the reduction of migration is a serious matter for conservation biology.[8] These figures do not imply, however, that human activities must necessarily cause irreparable harm to the biosphere. With conservation management and planning for bio-diversity at all levels, from genes to ecosystems, there are examples where humans mutually coexist in a sustainable way with nature.[9] However, it may be too late for human intervention to reverse the current mass extinction.[10]

## Political Economy of Development in India

Independence provided the political preconditions for undertaking planning of economic development. The directive principles of state policy set forth in the constitution are source for the objective and social premises of planning in India.[11] Before independence, there were National Planning Committee, Bombay Plan, Gandhian Plan and People's Plan in India. All these plans were only paper plans. In March 1950, the Government of India appointed Planning Commission under the chairmanship of Late Pundit Jawaharlal Nehru, the then Prime Minister of India to prepare the plans for the most effective and balanced utilization of the country's resources. Since

1951 till date, ten five-year plans and three annual plans have been formulated in India. These plans encompass various objectives of economic development such as economic growth, raising investment income ratio, reduction of inequalities in income and wealth, expansion of employment opportunities, removal of poverty, concentration of economic power, self-reliance, creation of the values and attitudes of a free and equal society and modernization. Including all these, it also focused on the elevation of bottlenecks of overall development such as agricultural production, industrial production and balance of payment in India.

In order to achieve the objectives of planning, Indian planners formulated a strategy of planned economic development. The strategy in economic development means the utilization of the available resources to win the war against poverty. I.G. Patel advocates that strategy implies essentially a deliberate choice—a choice of the point and timing and manner of attack on the problems at hand.[12] Thus, the major elements in development strategy are the size of the Plan, the pattern of investment envisaged in the Plan, i.e. the allocation of investment among the different sectors, the techniques or resource mobilization, the policy mix, i.e. fiscal policy, monetary policy, policy regarding controls and licensing, reliance on foreign aid, etc. Our development strategy has emphasized the coordination of all these elements with some variations in emphasis from plan to plan.

India is one of those countries where the strategy of planning is based on specific growth models. During the various five-year plans, India has used different growth models, for example the First Five-year Plan was based on the *Harrod-Domar* growth model,[13] the Second Five-Year Plan on four sector *Mahalanobis* model[14] and all other plans on more sophisticated models. However, these models did not get an official status and were used simply for fixing the targets. It was for the first time that the models prepared for the Fifth and Sixth Plans enjoyed an official status and have been continued in the rest of the five-year plans.

India's economic development strategy immediately after Independence was based primarily on the Mahalanobis model, which gave preference to the investment goods industries sector, with secondary importance accorded to the services and household goods sector (Nayar, 2001). For example, the Mahalanobis model placed strong emphasis on mining and manufacturing capital goods and infrastructural development including electricity generation and transportation. The model downplayed the role of the factory goods sector because it was more capital intensive and therefore, would not address the problem of high unemployment in India. Any increase in planned investments in India required a higher level of savings than existed in the country. Because of the low average incomes in India, the needed higher levels of savings had to be generated mainly by restrictions on the growth of consumption expenditures. Therefore, the Indian government implemented a progressive tax system not only to generate the higher levels of savings,[15] but also to restrict increases in income and wealth inequalities.[16]

Among other things, this strategy involved canalization of resources into their most productive uses. Investments were carried out both by the government and the private sector, with the government investing in strategic sectors and also those sectors in which private capital would not be forthcoming because of lags or the size of investment required. The private sector was required to contribute to India's economic growth in ways envisaged by the government planners. Not only did the government determine where businesses could invest in terms of location, but it also identified what businesses could produce, what they could sell, and what prices they could charge (Anil K. Lal and W. Clement Ronald, 2005). Using the plan models, the strategies adopted by the Indian planners are explained as follows.[17]

*Comprehensive Planning:* A policy of mixed economy is followed in the country. In a mixed economy, the public sector enterprises (government-owned) exist alongside the private sector to achieve a socialist pattern of society in a welfare state. In March 1950, Government of India constituted a statutory body with the Prime Minister of India as its Chairman called the Planning Commission. Pt. Jawaharlal Nehru was the first Chairman of the Planning Commission. It includes experts representing a cross-section of the Indian economy. Chief Ministers of the states, together with the members of the Planning Commission, constitute the National Development Council. The Prime Minister of India presides over the Council. The development plans are drawn by the Planning Commission to establish India's economy on a socialistic pattern in successive phases of five-year periods called the Five-Year Plans. The organisation was set up to formulate basic economic policies, draft plans and watch its progress and implementation. The plans include policies and programmes for economic development as well as for institutional change and cultural progress. These are the programmes for agriculture, industry, energy and transport as well as housing, civic amenities, education, health, family planning, uplift of backward classes and social welfare. All these aspects of plans are covered in India's planning process.

*Mixed Economy:* India is regarded as the best example of mixed economy in the world. Under a mixed economy, the entire economic system in a country is split up into three parts. Those are: (a) Sectors in which both production and distribution are entirely managed and controlled by the state to the complete exclusion of private enterprise; (b) Sectors in which the state and private enterprise jointly participate in production as well as in distribution; and (c) Sectors to which the private enterprise has complete access subject only to general control and regulation of the state. The mixed economy cleverly incorporates the salient features of capitalism and socialism. In the private sector of a mixed economy, a controlled capitalism operates. On the other hand the public sector industries are managed and operated on the basis of the welfare of the community. From Second Five-Year Plan, the Planning Commission adopted the concept of mixed economy with a deliberate expansion of the public sector.

*Priority Development of the Public Sector:* The public sector was seen as the *'Engine of Growth'* and was required to take up investment in the basic and heavy industries. Such areas, it was felt, required lumpy investment and had a long gestation period. Consequently, the government decided the overall pattern of the mixed economy, a *Big Push* to the economy should be given *via* the public sector. Actual practice has been somewhat different from the professed strategy. Since the Second Five-Year Plan, the successive plans have allocated a larger share of projected investment to the public sector, but all through, the private sector has undertaken the larger proportion of investment.

*Accelerated Growth:* Besides a more equal distribution of income, a much higher level of national income is necessary for the realization of the various plan's objectives. The plans have, therefore, sought to raise the rate of growth. The plans have emphasized the need to step up the rate of capital formation, which would be financed largely from domestic savings, and to which net inflow of capital from the rest of the world would contribute a very limited amount.

*Balanced Growth:* The planners have given equal importance to all sectors of the economy. Industrialization has not involved a lop-sided growth of the economy. Other sectors have also received due emphasis in the economy. It adopted a "differential development strategy" to equate national targets into balanced regional development as there is vast difference in the potentials and constraints of each state.

*Emphasis on Employment:* Policies and measures in the plans in India for the promotion of employment have included increase in investment activities; fuller utilization of available production capacities; avoidance of capital intensive techniques where labour incentive techniques would be as well; promotion of labour intensive activities such as agriculture, small industries, handicrafts etc.; credit and other assistance to small and marginal cultivators and other small producers; assistance to eligible persons without resources to set up their own business units; special employment programmes in areas with a high incidence of unemployment and underemployment; and education and training to improve the employability of young persons.

*Accelerated Development of Backward Regions:* Public policy has sought to tackle the problem of regional imbalances in development from several directions. (a) The Finance Commission has been transferring large amount to the states by way of their share of taxes and grants. The criteria, as also the procedures adopted by the Planning Commission, have tended to favour the backward states. (b) In the allocation of Central assistance to the states for plan purposes, population has been adopted as a major criterion. This has generally favoured the less developed states. In addition, backwardness by itself has been given especial weightage. (c) The policy of the public sector with regard to location of projects has favoured the backward regions. (d) The private entrepreneurs have been given special concessions if they locate their projects in backward and remote regions. (e) Special development plans have been mooted for particular categories of backward areas.

*Uplift of Backward Classes:* The plans included special programmes for the uplift of the backward classes, particularly the Schedule Caste and Schedule Tribes. In the First Five-Year Plan programmes were undertaken for meeting the special needs of these four sections of the population. Of the total provision in the plan of about Rs. 39 crore, Rs. 20 crore were allocated in the plans of States and the balance was provided at the Centre. About Rs. 25 crore were earmarked for the development of Scheduled Tribes and scheduled areas, Rs. 7 crore for Scheduled Castes, Rs. 3.5 crore for former criminal tribes and Rs. 3.5 crore for other backward classes.[18]

*Social Welfare:* There have been special plan programmes for the benefit of vulnerable and disadvantaged sections, such as grants-in-aid to voluntary agencies engaged in social welfare; family and child welfare projects, maintenance of National Institutes for blind, the deaf, the physically handicapped and mentally retarded persons; special employment exchanges for the placement of handicapped persons in employment; nutrition programmes for children and pregnant and nursing mothers belonging to vulnerable groups; hostel facilities for working women; research in technical aids for the poor; and programmes for the care; education, training and rehabilitation of delinquent and neglected children.

*Industrial Growth and Liberalization:* During the regime of late Rajiv Gandhi, a number of steps were taken to reform the overall industrial policy in such a way that it could become more conducive to the promotion of competition, modernization and cost efficiency. The reform measures had three basic objectives, namely to facilitate capacity creation, to facilitate output expansion, and to remove procedural impediments. Support for these policy reforms is also reflected in the underlying development strategy of the Seventh Five-Year Plan (1985-90). Some of the major industrial policy changes that resulted from the New Industrial Policy Initiatives were: delicensing of a wide range of industries, expansion of asset ceiling of the big monopoly houses and the MRTP companies, liberalization of depreciation provisions, reduction of both corporate and personal tax rates, drastic import liberalization, extension of *broad-banding* to a larger number of industries, elimination of many of the existing government controls, etc. The main objective of the industrial policy under the Government was thus to encourage economic growth led by the private sector, with the public sector playing more and more of a subordinate role. In fact, the modernization programme through technological rationalisation and managerial competence had been, since the independence, a very drastic one without any social cost consideration. As the Government had complete faith in the 'trickle down' approach of economic development, the direct programmes for poverty eradication of the previous Plan were no longer an important preoccupation of Mr. Gandhi's regime.

*Trade Reform:* The Rao Government, with the initiatives taken by the then Finance Minister, Dr. Manmohan Singh, was able to hastily introduce the New Economic Policy (NEP) in early July 1991. The NEP can be divided into two parts: the *stabilisation programmes* and the *structural adjustment and reform programmes.*[19] While the former of part basically aims at reducing macroeconomic imbalances (such as fiscal and current account deficits) by restraining aggregate demand, the latter essentially aims at increasing growth, by eliminating supply bottlenecks that hinder competitiveness, efficiency and dynamism to the economic system.

During first half of 1990s, almost all areas of the economy have been gradually opened to both domestic and foreign private investment, import licensing restrictions on intermediates and capital goods have been virtually eliminated, tariffs have been significantly reduced, and full convertibility of foreign exchange earnings has been established for current account transactions. Financial markets have been liberalized to a greater extent, international standards of regulation have been introduced in the financial sector and decontrol of the banking system continued during 1996-97.

One significant policy adopted in June 1997 by the government of I.K. Gujral was that of the liberalisation of outward investment flow, which was in keeping with the government's intention to move towards capital account convertibility. Accordingly, the Indian corporates were permitted to invest in an overseas joint venture up to 50 per cent of their resources raised through equity issues abroad.

Shri Atal Behari Vajpayee's government had taken some major steps which include delicensing of sugar, coal, mineral oils, etc.[20] shifting of 340 items of import from the restricted Open General List (OGL) to the special import licence list; passage of two Bills in December 1999—an industry friendly Foreign Exchange Management Act (FEMA) to replace Foreign Exchange Regulation Act (FERA), and the Insurance Regulatory and Development Authority Act (IRDA) to open the Indian insurance sector to both foreign and private domestic players; and widening of foreign direct investment (FDI) automatic route in February 2000; etc. The EXIM Policy announced in March 2001 has completed the process of removal of Quantitative Restrictions (QRs) on Balance of Payment (BOP) grounds by dismantling restrictions on the remaining 715 items.[21] It is to be noted that this policy has, however, put in place necessary mechanisms to provide a level playing field to domestic players *vis-a-vis* imports.[22]

## Rights and Environment

*Cultural Rights for Environmental Protection:* Cultural rights, as guaranteed in Article 27 of the International Covenant on Civil and Political Rights (ICCPR),[23] are crucial for the maintenance of social identities, and are invoked primarily when governments take steps that threaten to undermine the way of life of whole groups. Although some analysts have proposed that the right to culture involves nothing more than non-interference, the Human Rights Committee, the United Nations treaty body that enforces the ICCPR, has explicitly stated that cultural rights are 'positive' and not 'negative', meaning that governments must take affirmative steps to ensure their protection.[24] Often, the cultural argument reinforces the demand for environmental protection, for an example indigenous people have challenged the desecration of sacred sites, arguing that harm to the environment will also undermine the way of life of a people. In the Yanomami case (1985),[25] the Inter-American Commission on Human Rights held that failure of the Brazilian government to prevent development that destroyed the Yanomami way of life constituted "ethnicide." In cases such as this, environmental rights and cultural rights coincide, revealing a confluence of rights claims.

A new phase of environmental policy is based on a concept of "pristine nature" which does not allow human contacts and nation-states become more ecosystem-concerned. On the other hand, along with a rise of human rights issues, advocacy groups for the unorganized fourth world and aboriginal communities have been struggling to protect indigenous people's cultural rights. However, the more protected areas are assigned, the more indigenous peoples' lands are claimed as nature reserves. It makes local aborigines give up their cultural practices, such as hunting animals and gathering wild plants. Further, they are forcefully relocated from their traditional territories to remote sites, not to disturb endangered species. Consequently, there are conflicts between environmentalism and indigenous cultural rights in practice, and Botswana, too, has undergone the same problem and was trying to find a middle ground between two globalised guidelines. In the country, the San, indigenous foragers, were forced to leave their homelands which are now national parks, and their traditional activities were prohibited. However, the introduction of CBNRM (Community-Based Natural Resource

Management), devotes itself as a legitimized buffer zone, when both world polities conflict with each other.[26]

*Human Rights and the Environment:*[27] Every woman, man, youth and child has the human right to a safe and healthy environment, and to other fundamental human rights linked to and dependent upon a healthy environment. Human rights relating to the environment are set out in basic human rights treaties and include: The human right to a safe and healthy environment. It demands the highest attainable standard of health. It also stresses on ecologically sustainable development. It claims an adequate standard of living, including access to safe food and water. The human rights give more importance on the child to live in an environment appropriate for physical and mental development and to safe working conditions, including adequate safeguards for pregnant and lactating women. Human rights gives full and equal participation for all persons in environmental decision-making and development planning, and in shaping decisions and policies affecting one's community, at the local, national and international levels.

*Ethnic Community*[28] *and Environment Protection:* In 2004 the Department of Environment and Conservation, in partnership with the Sydney Catchment Authority and the Department of Energy, Utilities and Sustainability, conducted a new survey of the environmental knowledge, attitudes and behaviours of eight of New South Wales' largest ethnic communities. This research updated and expanded on landmark research with ethnic communities conducted by the Environment Protection Authority in 1996.[29] It was found that although there were significant differences between communities on many questions in the survey, overall:

1. People from the ethnic communities surveyed value the environment as an important part of their lives. Only family was rated as very or rather important by more participants. Significantly more people from non-English speaking backgrounds (NESB) rated environment as very important as in the DEC's 2003 community-wide survey, Who cares about the environment?
2. More than 80 per cent of people surveyed were concerned about environmental problems.
3. Issues related to water supply and conservation have increased markedly in importance since 1996 as an

environmental issue of concern for people, with the drought and water restrictions likely to be a key factor in this increase.

4. When combined with separately mentioned issues of water conservation, the environment is the third ranked issue for government attention after health and education.
5. People can discuss environmental issues in more detail than in 1996. The number of people who are 'unsure' or 'don't know' about environmental issues has decreased markedly.
6. More than two-thirds of those surveyed report 'often acting' to reduce their water and energy use and to avoid storm water pollution, and more than half also 'often' recycle paper and other materials and 'reuse' things instead of throwing them away.

**Development Strategy and Environmental Degradation**

Development activities carry with it the seeds of environmental damage, assisted and abetted by both needs and greed of man. Activities such as manufacturing, processing, transportation and consumption not only deplete the stock of natural resources but also add stress to the environmental system by accumulating the stock of wastes. The productivity of the economic system, however, depends on the supply and quality of natural and environmental resources. While water, soil, air, forest and fisheries resources are productive assets and the pollution of water, air, atmosphere and noise are the by-products of economic development, particularly industrialization and urbanization. "Greenhouse effects", "global warming" and "acid precipitation" are cases in points.

At the same time, because of growing population and high degree of mechanization, mindless and ruthless exploitation of natural resources, we have dragged our physical environment into decline. By physical environment we mean the whole complex of climate, soil, water and biotic factors on which we all subsist, and on which our entire agricultural and industrial development depends. Rapid economic development is actually turning India into vast wasteland.

However, various programmes were taken up in the Eighth and Ninth Plans to enhance the handling and management of hazardous substances and these are continued in the Tenth Plan (2002-07) as well. The Tenth Plan has asserted clearly that the sustainable use of bio-diversity is fundamental to ecologically sustainable development. India is identified as one of the 12 major bio-diversity countries of the world. However, since 1951, industrialization has put severe strain on the ecosystem, altering and even destroying it. The loss of bio-diversity arises from the destruction of the habitat, extension of agricultural, filling up of wetlands, conversation of rich bio-diversity areas for human settlement and industrial development, destruction of coastal areas and uncontrolled and unregulated commercial exploitation. A series of steps have been taken in recent years to protect and conserve bio-diversity.

## Knowledge and Environment

*Indigenous Knowledge and Environment:* Indigenous people and their lands, territories, resources and the environment are inextricably linked both spiritually and culturally. The environment is an essential part of their culture and spirituality. The environment brings together all the elements of indigenous peoples' cultural and spiritual references. Indigenous peoples have for centuries maintained a very unique relationship with their environment including the protection of the environment which is essential for their food sovereignty and food security.

Indigenous knowledge is the local knowledge that is unique to a given culture or society. It is the basis for agriculture, health care, food preparation, education, environmental conservation, and a host of other activities. Much of such knowledge is passed down from generation to generation, usually by word of mouth. Indigenous people have a wide knowledge of the ecosystem they live in and ways to ensure that natural resources are used sustainably. Therefore, indigenous knowledge which has been accumulated over centuries has potential value for sustainable development. It can also help other people learn how to live in harmony with nature and the environment in a sustainable fashion.[30]

Knowledge about the environment had been central to human survival throughout history. Survival was virtually impossible in hunting and gathering societies without a good knowledge about forest and wildlife—plant and animal species, their growth environments and habitats, growth cycles, behaviour of animals in relation to their environment, specific characteristics of plant and animal species and their uses. In the same way, the farming societies depended upon a keen understanding of the local natural environment and ecological processes leading to the regeneration of environmental resources, e.g. soil fertility and water. By interacting with their immediate environment over centuries, local people have gained an enormous volume of knowledge about their environment. Their knowledge involves not only environmental resources available within the locality but also how to manage these resources sustainably.[31]

*Traditional Knowledge and Environment:* It is practical common sense based on teachings and experiences passed on from generation to generation and a way of life using the heart and the head together. It covers knowledge of the environment such as snow, ice, weather, resources and the relationships between things. It is holistic and cannot be compartmentalized and separated from the people who hold it. Traditional knowledge is an authority system. It sets out the rules governing the use of resources respect, an obligation to share. It is dynamic, cumulative and stable. It comes from the spirit in order to survive and gives credibility to the people.

Traditional knowledge is deeply connected to the environment. It possess a wealth of knowledge about the environment that often precedes scientific data collection by many years and reaches at findings with the environmental effects of global warming, which may have untoward health effects for generations to come. It is associated with changing weather patterns, thinning ice, diseased and deformed wildlife, and changes in the look and taste of such subsistence foods as fish and meat. These early observations have been borne out by scientific research conducted in recent years that has found significant environmental damage to Arctic regions, such as accidental releases of radioactivity, elevated levels of persistent organic pollutants and heavy metals, and ozone depletion.[32] The environment and its resources provide more than just sustenance for people. Harvesting, processing, and consuming native foods is a common practice in traditional society and provides an opportunity to practice and teach humility and spirituality. Traditional foods are as important to social well-being as they are to physical health. For Native communities, degradation of the environment is a threat to culture at its core.[33]

*Cultural Capital and Environment:* Cultural capital[34] refers to factors that provide human societies with the means and adaptations to deal with the natural environment and to actively modify it. Cultural capital is based on factors such as social, political institutions, environmental ethics and traditional ecological knowledge in a society. The three types of capital are closely inter-related. Natural capital is the basis for cultural capital. Human made capital is generated by an interaction between natural and cultural capital. Cultural capital will determine how a society uses natural capital to create human made capital. Aspects of cultural capital, such as institutions involved in the governance of resource use and environmental worldview, are crucial for the potential of a society to develop sustainably in relation with the natural environment.[35]

The concept of cultural capital was developed by the French sociologist Pierre Bourdieu. In its valuing of the non-economic aspects of the socio-economic operations of society that result in economic gain, it has a direct relationship with other forms of capital.[36] Ecological economists have taken this concept and given it a crucial role by locating it at the interface between development and the environment; human capital and natural capital (Berkes and Folke, 1993,[37] 1994;[38] Constanza and Daly, 1992;[39] Daly, 1994.[40]) In this model of cultural capital, self-regulatory systems informed by traditions of resource management, worldview, and environmental philosophy enable social groups to mediate between economy and ecology (Berkes and Folke, 1994). Self-regulation is about the capacity of a region or community to build on the informal and formal stocks of knowledge held by locals as skills, practices, routines, rituals, conventions and seasonal activities (Bryden and Dawe, 1999).[41]

## Survey of Literature

According to some social and physical scientists such as Georgescu-Roegen (1971),[42] Meadows *et al.* (1972),[43] Ehrlich and Holdren (1971),[44] (1973),[45] and Cleveland (1984),[46] higher levels of economic activity (production and consumption) require larger inputs of energy and material, and generate larger quantities of waste byproducts. Increased extraction of natural resources, accumulation of waste and concentration of pollutants would overwhelm the carrying capacity of the biosphere and result in the degradation of environmental quality and decline in human welfare, despite rising incomes (Daly, 1977).[47] Furthermore, it is argued that degradation of the resource base would eventually put economic activity itself at risk (Jansson *et al.*, 1994).[48] To save the environment and even economic activity from itself, economic growth must cease and the world must make a transition to a steady-state economy.

At the other extreme, some economists argue that the fastest road to environmental improvement is along the path of economic growth. That means, with increase in incomes, there is increase in demand for goods and services, which are less material-intensive, and for improved environmental quality that leads to the adoption of environmental protection measures. As Beckerman (1992)[49] puts it, "The strong correlation between incomes, and the extent to which environmental protection measures are adopted, demonstrates that in the longer run, the surest way to improve your environment is to become rich" (quoted by Rothman, 1998, pp. 178).[50]

Yet, other economists like, Shafik and Bandyopadhyay (1977),[511] Panayotou (1993),[52] Grossman and Krueger (1993)[53] and Selden and Song (1994)[54] have hypothesised that the relationship between economic growth and environmental quality, whether positive or negative, is not fixed along a country's development path; indeed it may change sign from positive to negative as a country reaches a level of income at which people demand and afford more efficient infrastructure and a cleaner environment. The implied inverted-U relationship between environmental degradation and economic growth came to be known as the "Environmental Kuznets Curve," by analogy with the income-inequality relationship postulated by Kuznets (1965,[55] 1966.[56]) At low levels of development, both the quantity and the intensity of environmental degradation are limited to the impacts of subsistence economic activity on the resource base and to limited quantities of biodegradable wastes. As agriculture and resource extraction intensifies and industrialization takes off, both resource depletion and waste generation accelerate. At higher levels of development, structural change towards information-based industries and services, more efficient technologies, and increased demand for environmental quality result in levelling-off and a steady decline of environmental degradation (Panayotou, 1993).

The issue of whether environmental degradation increases monotonically, decreases monotonically, first increases and then declines along a country's development path, has critical implications for policy. A monotonic increase of environmental degradation with economic growth calls for strict environmental regulations and even limits on economic growth to ensure a sustainable scale of economic activity within the ecological life-support system (Arrow *et al.*

1995).[57] A monotonic decrease of environmental degradation along a country's development path suggests that policies that accelerate economic growth lead also to rapid environmental improvements and no explicit environmental policies are needed; indeed, they may be counterproductive if they slow down economic growth and thereby delay environmental improvement.

Finally, if the Environmental Kuznets Curve hypothesis is supported by evidence, development policies have the potential of being environmentally benign over the long run, (at high incomes), but they are also capable of significant environmental damage in the short-to-medium run (at low-to-medium-level incomes). In this case, several issues arise: (1) at what level of economic development is the turning point? (2) How much damage would have taken place by then and can it be reduced? (3) Would any ecological thresholds be violated and irreversible damages take place before environmental degradation turns down, and how can they be avoided? (4) Is environmental improvement at higher income levels automatic, or does it require conscious institutional and policy reforms? and (5) How to accelerate the development process so that poor countries can experience the same improved economic and environmental conditions enjoyed by developed countries?

Copeland and Taylor (1994),[58] in a simple, two-country static model of North-South trade, examine analytically the relationship between income, pollution, and international trade. The high-income country adopts more stringent environmental regulations, and specializes in the production of cleaner goods. Under these conditions (a) An income increase resulting from trade affects pollution differently than an income increase resulting from economic growth and (b) Economic growth effects pollution differently in the presence of trade than under autarchy. Income growth under autarchy can be made pollution-neutral through optimal environmental policy that induces a switch to cleaner technology, which exactly offsets the scale effect. Income growth resulting from trade creates composition effects (in the form of a cleaner product mix in the rich country, and a dirtier product mix in the poor country) that so dominate the scope and technology effects, as to increase aggregate world pollution. Furthermore, Copeland and Taylor found that, asymmetric growth that favours the wealthy North widens the gap in pre- and post-trade factor prices, resulting in composition effects that increase world pollution. In contrast, asymmetric growth that favours the poor South narrows the labour price gap, resulting in reduced world pollution levels.

Selden and Song (1994)[59] and Stern *et al.* (1996)[60] pointed out that because global income distribution is skewed (the median income per capita is less than the mean), total emissions of a pollutant can continue growing beyond the turning point at which per capita emissions peak and begin to decline. In other words, the turning point for total emissions may be attained at a significantly higher income level than average per capita emissions. Second, Ravallion *et al.* (1997[61]) examined the linkage between carbon emissions, economic growth and income distribution both between and within countries, and identified trade-offs between climate control and social equity. Third, Torras and Boyce (1998)[62] hypothesised that more equitable distribution of income and power (represented by literacy, political rights and civil liberties), contributes to larger improvements of air and water quality by increasing the influence on policy of those who are benefiting from polluting activities.

One of the channels through which income inequality may affect the income-environment relationship is through differential marginal propensities to pollute between the rich and the poor. If the marginal propensity to pollute is higher in poor than rich countries, higher inequality among countries would increase aggregate pollution levels for any given average world income level; and any effort to improve income distribution may come at the expense of environmental quality (Ravallion *et al.*, 1997). On the other hand, redistribution may interact with growth; the trade-off between equity and environmental quality may improve with growth; and the trade-off between growth and environmental quality may improve with redistribution. Another channel through which inequality may affect environmental outcomes, but in an opposite direction, is by strengthening the power of the rich to impose environmental cost on the poor (Boyce, 1994) and by reducing the ability of the society to reach co-operative solutions to environmental problems (Ostrom, 1990).[63]

Much of the income-environment literature assumes the relationship is homogeneous of degree one, i.e. population does not matter to emissions per capita independently of income per capita. This need not be the case. For example, Ravallion *et al.* (1997) argue that the demand for public goods, such as infrastructure and defence, may entail independent effects of population growth on emissions. The existence of public goods may result in both income per capita and total income having an effect on the demand of polluting goods; in other words, a higher population would result in higher emissions for given income per capita, and population growth would result in growth of emissions independently of the growth in per capita incomes.

Panayotou (1993) found that higher population density delays the turning point at which further income growth slows down deforestation, while Panayotou (1997) found that population density raises the height of the EKC for sulphur dioxide ($SO_2$) at every level of income. In the latter study, the relationship between population density and sulphur dioxide ($SO_2$) emissions was found to be highly non-linear, with higher impacts at low and high densities. Controlling for all other factors, "low population densities of under 50 persons per square kilometre are associated with high ambient sulphur dioxide ($SO_2$) level (70 kg/km$^3$) ... [because of] less pressure to control emissions; as population density rises to around 170 persons per square kilometre, sulphur dioxide ($SO_2$) level drops to their lowest level (45 kg/km$^3$) and begin to rise again as the household use of coal and informal fuels by a denser population overwhelms the population pressure for more pollution abatement" (Panayotou, 1997, p. 479).

Nguyen (1999)[64] hypotheses that fast growth of population damages natural resources and reduces the assimilative capacity of the environment, especially in countries that are highly dependent on natural resource exploitation. His hypothesis has two parts: (a) population is not neutral for the environment; and (b) it does affect the environment differently in different stages of economic development. He hypothesized that the higher the population density, the lower the turning point of the EKC and thus, the higher the environmental quality at any given level of income per capita. He tested these hypotheses for carbon dioxide ($CO_2$) emissions with data from three OECD countries (France, Japan, and the US) and three rapidly developing Asian countries (Korea, Thailand, and Vietnam). The results yield an EKC curve for carbon dioxide ($CO_2$) emissions reaching a turning point at $18,000 (1987 prices) per capita. At low-income levels (under $2,000 per capita) high population density affects the environment negatively; at $1,000 per capita, a 70 per cent increase in population density results in 12 per cent higher carbon dioxide ($CO_2$) emissions for the same level of income. At higher incomes, a more dense population has positive environmental impacts: at $10,000 per capita a 70 per cent increase in population density results in 22 per cent reduction of emissions, presumably reflecting increased pressures to control emissions as more people (at higher incomes) are being exposed to pollution.

The level of environmental problems of a country varies with the stages of development, current production technologies and the environmental policies implemented. Lack of economic development also contributes to environmental pollution in the form of inadequate sanitation and lack of availability of clean drinking water. Economic development without environmental considerations can cause serious environmental damage affecting the quality of life of the population of present and future. It is surprising that such type of research work in this direction has not been done in India. Therefore, it is very important to carry out research work to find out the trade-off between economic development and environmental degradation in India. It should at least ensure non-declining human welfare over time if not aiming at maximisation of the net benefits of economic development.

## NOTES

1. Gene flow from GM to non-GM population in the crop, forestry, animal and fishery sectors, Background document to Conference 7: May 31 - July 6, 2002.
2. L. Watrud *et al.* (2004), "Evidence for landscape-level, pollen-mediated gene flow from genetically modified creeping bentgrass with CP4 EPSPS as a marker", Proceedings of The National Academy of Sciences 101, p. 14533.
3. http://www.usda.gov/wps/portal usdahome? contentidonly=true & contentid=2007/11/0350.xml (United States Department of Agriculture).
4. Conacher, Arthur; Conacher, Jeanette (1995). *Rural Land Degradation in Australia.* South Melbourne, Victoria: Oxford University Press, Australia. p. 2.
5. "Land: Programmes and Activities". *United Nations Environment Programme.* http://www.unep.org/themes/land/index.asp?page=programmes. Retrieved on 19 July 2008.
6. Paul Ehrlich and Anne Ehrlich, *Extinction*, Random House, New York (1981)
7. Ana S. L. Rodrigues, Sandy J. Andelman, Mohamed I. Bakarr *et al.* 2004. Effectiveness of the global protected area network in representing species diversity. *Nature* 428, 640-643
8. Wilcove, D.S., Wikelski, M. (2008). Going, Going, Gone: Is Animal

Migration Disappearing. *PLoS Biol* 6(7): e188 doi:10.1371/journal.pbio.0060188

9. G. Schmidt. 2005. Ecology & Anthropology: A Field Without Future? *Ecological and Environmental Anthropology.* 1(1): 13-15.
10. D. B. Wake and V. T. Vredenburg. (2008). Are we in the midst of the sixth mass extinction? A view from the world of amphibians. *Proceedings of the National Academy of Sciences of the United States of America,* 105: 11466–11473.
11. The Commission recommends that the first and foremost step required by the Union and State Governments is to sensitise the people and to create a general awareness of the provisions of fundamental duties among the citizens on the lines recommended by the Justice Verma Committee 18 on the subject. Consideration should be given to the ways and means by which Fundamental Duties could be popularized and made effective; right to freedom of religion and other freedoms must be jealously guarded and rights of minorities and fellow citizens respected; reform of the whole process of education is an immediate but immense need, as is the need to free it from governmental or political control; it is only through education that will power to adhere to our Fundamental Duties as citizens can be inculcated; and duty to vote at elections, actively participate in the democratic process of governance and to pay taxes should be included in Article 51A. The Commission fully endorses the other recommendations of the Justice Verma Committee on operationalisation of Fundamental Duties of Citizens and strongly suggests their early implementation.
12. Chapter X in 'Right to Health' on Economic, Social and Cultural Rights by Ralpt Beddard, & Dilys' Hill, 1992; 'Towards an Improved Understanding of the International Human Right to Health by Brigit Toebes, Vol. 21, (1999).
13. The Harrod-Domar model is used in development economics to explain an economy's growth rate in terms of the level of saving and productivity of capital. It suggests that there is no natural reason for an economy to have balanced growth. The model was developed independently by Sir Roy F. Harrod in 1939 and Evsey Domar in 1946. The Harrod-Domar model was the precursor to the exogenous growth model.
14. The Mahalanobis model is a model of economic development, created by Indian statistician Prasanta Chandra Mahalanobis in 1953. Mahalanobis became essentially the key economist of India's Second Five-Year Plan, becoming subject to much of India's most dramatic economic debates.
15. The huge saving-investment gap could not be filled by the amount of foreign aid that was both sought and available. Further, additional foreign investments (both direct and portfolio) were never seriously considered as a way to close this saving-investment gap.
16. Higher levels of income and wealth were taxed at much higher rates relative to lower income and wealth.
17. The model was created as an analytical framework for India's Second Five-Year Plan in 1955 by appointment of Prime Minister Jawaharlal Nehru, as

India felt there was a need to introduce a formal plan model after the First Five-Year Plan (1951-1956). The First Five-Year Plan stressed investment for capital accumulation in the spirit of the one-sector Harrod-Domar model. It argued that production required capital and that capital can be accumulated through investment; the faster one accumulates, the higher the growth rate will be. The most fundamental criticisms came from Mahalanobis, who himself was working with a variant of it in 1951 and 1952. The criticisms were mostly around the model's inability to cope with the real constraints of the economy: its ignoring of the fundamental choice problems of planning over time; and the lack of connection between the model and the actual selection of projects for governmental expenditure. Subsequently, Mahalanobis introduced his celebrated two-sector model, which he later expanded into a four-sector version.

18. Second Five Year Plan, chapter no. 28, welfare of backward class.
19. A summary of the major reform measures adopted under the New Economic Policy is given in Dutta (1993).
20. In fact, Atal Behari Vajpayee's BJP government collapsed on 17 April 1999, but it continued as a caretaker government until Vajpayee's 23-party coalition government was voted back to power on 13 October 1999. Since its 1998-99 issue, Government of India's annual publication, *Economic Survey*, has been including in its first chapter a BOX 1.1 listing all the major economic reforms undertaken in the corresponding financial year.
21. Out of these 715 items, 342 are textile products, 147 are agricultural products including alcoholic bevearages and 226 are other manufactured products including automobiles (*Economic Survey:2001- 2002*, Section 1.99).
22. These mechanisms include shifting of imports of certain products under the state trading category, making imports subject to various existing domestic regulations on health and hygiene and environment, and need for bio-security and sanitary and phyto-sanitary permit for imports of primary products of plant and animal origin. The policy has also established a monitoring mechanism to monitor imports of 300 sensitive items on a regular basis (*Ibid.*).
23. Adopted and opened for signature, ratification and accession by General Assembly resolution 2200A (XXI) of 16 December 1966, but in accordance with Article 49, entry into force on 23 March 1976, Office of United Nations High Commissioner for Human Rights.
24. Alison Dundes Renteln, "Environmental Rights vs. Cultural Rights". *Human Rights Dialogue*: "Environmental Rights" (Spring 2004). http://www.cceia.org/resources/publications/dialogue/2_11/section_2/4453.html
25. Albert B., Yanomami, "Violence": Inclusive Fitness or Ethnographer's Representation? *Current Anthropology*, Vol. 30, No. 5 (December, 1989), pp. 637-640. The University of Chicago Press on behalf of Wenner-Gren Foundation for Anthropological Research.
26. "Conflicts between Environmentalism and Indigenous Cultural Rights and A Middle Ground: The CBNRM (Community-Based Natural Resource

Management) in Botswana", Paper presented at the annual meeting of the American Sociological Association, Montreal Convention Center, Montreal, Quebec, Canada Online <PDF>. 2009-02-04 from http://www.allacademic.com/meta/p103285_index.html

27. Universal declaration of human rights (Art. 1), adopted by General Assembly Resolution 217 a (iii) of 10 December 1948. *Source*: Fact Sheet No.2 (Rev.1), The International Bill of Human Rights. http://www.unhchr.ch/html/menu6/2/fs2.htm
28. An ethnic group is a group of human beings whose members identify with each other, usually on a presumed or real common heritage. Ethnic identity is further marked by the recognition from others of a group's distinctiveness and the recognition of common cultural, linguistic, religious, behavioural or biological traits, real or presumed, as indicators of contrast to other groups. http://en.wikipedia.org
29. A Report of Department of Environment and Climate Change, New South Wales Government.
http://www.environment.nsw.gov.au/community/ethniccom.htm
30. Warren, D.M., Brokensha, D. and Slikkenveer, L.J., eds. (1996), *Indigenous Knowledge and Sustainable Development,* Sri Lanka Centre for Indigenous Knowledge, University of Sri Jayewardenapura, 1996, pp. vii-viii.
31. Rohana Ulluwishewa, Adbul Aziz Kaloko and Dyhairuni Hj Mohammed Morican (1997) *Indigenous Knowledge and Environmental Education.* Paper presented at Environmental Education Workshop, University of Brunei, Darusalam, pp. 3-4.
32. Arctic Monitoring and Assessment Programme (AMAP) International Symposium on Environmental Pollution of the Arctic. Panel discussion highlights: are things getting better or worse? Available at: http://www.amap.no/
33. Arctic Monitoring and Assessment Programme (AMAP), Arctic pollution issues: a state of the Arctic environment report: peoples of the North. Available at: http://www.amap.no/
34. The term is a general anthropological sense of set of rules for a society, recognizing the existence of many distinct societies.
35. Jansson, A., Hammer, M., Folke, C., Costanza, R. "Investing in Natural capital: The Ecological Economics approach to Sustainability", Forwarded by Olof Johansson, Minister of the Environment, Sweden.
36. Patterson, C. "Cultural Capital and Development: The Dynamics of Change in a Small Coastal Community", Unpublished, School of Geography and Environmental Studies, University of Tasmania. (Ph.D. candidate).
37. Berkes, F. & Folke, C. 1993, 'A Systems Perspective on the Inter-relationship Between Natural, Human-made and Cultural Capital', *Ecological Economics*, Vol. 5, No. 1.
38. Berkes, F. and Folke, C. 1994, 'Investing in Cultural Capital for Sustainable Use of Natural Capital', in (eds) A. Jansson, M. Hammer, C. Folke & R.

Constanza, *Investing in Natural Capital*, Island Press, Washington DC, pp. 128-49.

39. Constanza, R. and Daly, H. 1992, 'Natural Capital and Sustainable Development', *Conservation Biology*, Vol. 6, No. 1, pp. 37-46.
40. Daly, H.E. 1994, 'Operationalising Sustainable Development by Investing in Natural Development', in (eds) A. Jansson, M. Hammer, C. Folke & R. Constanza, *Investing in Natural Capital*, Island Press, Washington DC, pp. 23-56.
41. Bryden J.M. and Dawe S.P. 1999, 'Development Strategies for Remote Rural Regions: what do we know so far?' *OECD*, pp. 1-23.
42. Georgescu-Roegen, N., *The Entropy Law and the Economic Process*, Cambridge, Harvard University Press (1971).
43. Meadows, D.H., Meadows, D.L., Randers, J. and Behrens, W.W., *The Limits to Growth, London*, Earth Island Limited (1972).
44. Ehrlich, P.R. and J.P. Holdren (eds), *Global Ecology: Readings Toward a Rational Strategy for Man*, New York, Harcourt Brace Jovanovich (1971).
45. *Human Ecology: Problems and Solutions*, San Francisco, W.H. Freeman (1973)
46. Cleveland, C.J., Costanza, R., Hall, C.A.S., and Kaufmann, R., Energy and the US Economy; a Biophysical Perspective, *Science* 225, 890-897 (1984)
47. Daly, H.E., *Steady-State Economics*, San Francisco, Freeman and Co.; 2nd edn, Washington, D.C., Island Press (1977).
48. Jansson, A.M., Hammer, M., Folke, C. and Costanza, R. (eds), *Investing in Natural Capital-The Ecological Economics Approach to Sustainability*, Covelo, CA, ISEE Press/Island Press, (1994).
49. Beckerman, W., Economic Growth and the Environment: Whose Growth? Whose Environment? *World Development,* 20, 481-496, (1992).
50. Rothman, S., Environmental Kuznets Curves - Real Progress or Passing the Buck? A Case for Consumption-based approaches, *Global Economics* (1988).
51. Shafik, N., and Bandyopadhyay, S., Economic Growth and Environmental Resources, *Journal of Environmental Economics and Management* 4, 1-24 (1977).
52. Panayotou, T., Empirical Tests and Policy Analysis of Environmental Degradation at Different Stages of Economic Development, Working Paper 238 Technology and Employment Programme, Geneva: International Labour Office (1993).
53. Grossman, G., and Krueger, A., Environmental Impacts of a North American Free Trade Agreement, *The U.S. Mexico Free Trade Agreement* (1993).
54. Selden, T.M., and Song, D., Environmental Quality and Development: Is there a Kuznets Curve for Air Pollution Emissions? *Journal of Environmental Economics and Management*, 27, 147-162 (1994).
55. Kuznets, S., *Economic Growth and Structural Change*, New York, Norton (1965).
56. *Modern Economic Growth*, New Haven, Yale University Press (1966).

57. Arrow, K., Bolin, B., Costanza, R., Dasgupta, P., Folke, C., Holling, C.S., Jansson, B.O., Levin, S., Mäler, K.G., Perings, C., and Pimental, D., Economic Growth, Carrying Capacity and the Environment, *Science* 268, 520-521 (1995).
58. Copeland, B.R., and Taylor, M.S., North-South Trade and the Environment, *Quarterly Journal of Economics*, 755-785 (1994)
59. Selden, T.M., and Song, D., Environmental Quality and Development: Is there a Kuznets Curve for Air Pollution Emissions? *Journal of Environmental Economics and Management* 27, 147-162 (1994).
60. Stern, D.I., Common, M.S., and Barbier, E.B., Economic Growth and Environmental Degradation: the Environmental Kuznets Curve and Sustainable Development, *World Development* 24 (7) 1151-1160 (1996).
61. Ravallion, M.H., and Jalan, J., *A Less Poor World, but a Hotter One? Carbon Emissions, Economic Growth and Income Inequality*, World Bank October 15 (1997).
62. Boyce, J.K., Inequality as a Cause of Environmental Degradation, *Ecological Economics*, 11, 169-178 (1994).
63. Ostrom, E., *Governing the Commons: The Evolution of Institutions for Collective Action,* Cambridge, Cambridge University Press (1990).
64. Tuan, Nguyen Anh, Evidences of Environmental Kuznets Curve from $CO_2$ Emissions in Six-Country Analysis, Working Paper, Institute d'Economie et de Polique de l'Energie (IEPE) BP 47, 38040 Grenoble Cedex 09 (1999).

# 3

# Models and Theoretical Framework

This study pertaining to environmental degradation is based on the secondary data collected from the Human Development Report 2001, the Annual Report of Planning Commission, the Eleventh Finance Commission Report 2000, and Central Statistical Organization, etc. We have used the cross-section data for all States in India. The period of investigation is 1990-91 to 2004-05. There are many indicators of economic development such as growth rate of national income, per capita income, and per capita consumption of electricity and so on. We have considered per capita income and electricity consumption as the indicators of economic development. They are better indicators of standard of living in the country. The primary objective of this book is to identify the links between economic growth and natural resources (environment) degradation in India with particular emphasis on deforestation in all major states and air and water pollution in the metropolitan cities of India. Hence, the study is based on the following proposed objectives:

## CONCEPTUAL FRAMEWORK

Environmental degradation is a complex issue. On the one hand, economic development creates pressure on the stock of natural resources and on the other it pollutes the quality of natural resources like air, water, soil, etc. The data on these indicators are not available yearly state-wise. We, therefore, have considered the rate of deforestation as the indicator of environmental degradation. It refers to the removal of forest covers from forest area to fulfil the demand of land in other uses. It can be measured as:

$$\text{Deforestation Rate} = \frac{\text{Forest Area in 1990-91} - \text{Forest area in 2000-01}}{\text{Forest Area in 1990-91}} \times 100$$

Economic development is the process by which countries raise the level of their per capita income and become industrialized. Development means modernization and transformation of the entire economy into advanced industrialized economy. Thus, it is a process whose impact can be observed on increase in per capita Income, GDP growth rate, per capita consumption of electricity, etc. We have considered level of Per Capita Income (PCI) and Per Capita Consumption of Electricity (PCCE) as indicators of economic development in the States of India.

The relationship between economic development and environment has now come to be known as the environmental transition hypothesis or the Environmental Kuznets Curve (EKC) hypothesis. The basic premise of the EKC hypothesis is that there exists 'inverted-U' shaped relationship between a variety of indicators of environmental degradation and economic development. For example, with increase in per capita income, environmental degradation initially increase, but then eventually decline once a threshold level of per capita income is reached.

Although agricultural land expansion is a major source of deforestation, cash and food crop prices, timber prices, agricultural input prices, agricultural wages and credit availability to farmers have been identified as immediate causes of deforestation in Cameroon that determine the profitability of farming and logging activities (Daniel Gbetnkom *et al.*, 2005). To be in a position to mitigate or halt the effects of forest clearing with relevant counter-policies, one needs to appreciate the extent to which the immediate factors propel deforestation agents to deforest.

The areas for action in the industrial sector as articulated in Agenda 21 emphasize the integration of environmental concerns in industrial planning, ensuring full participation in industrial activity, enhancing international trade and minimizing social costs. Four main issues can thus be identified for the industrial sector: environmental management, strengthening the role of the private sector, trade liberalization and environmental regulation and employment generation and labour welfare.

## Theoretical Approach for Growth and Environment

This section considers macroeconomic models of the interaction of environmental degradation on growth. These are divided into four major categories: optimal growth models, models in which the environment (rather than pollution) is a factor of production, endogenous growth models, and other macroeconomic models of growth and the environment.

(a) *Optimal growth models* build on a Ramsey (1928)[1] framework, as extended by Koopmans (1965)[2] and Cass (1965)[3]. These are dynamic optimization models, in which the utility-maximization problem of the infinitely lived consumer is solved using the techniques of optimal control theory. Either the stock, or the flow of pollution is an argument of both the production function and the utility function of the representative consumer. Most of these models support the Environmental Kuznets Curve that has been found empirically, and which has been discussed in detail in the previous section.

(b) *Models of the environment as a factor of production* include not only pollution as an argument of the production and utility function, but the environment itself (Arrow *et al.*, 1995). This may be interpreted as the stock of natural capital that the economy is endowed with, or as the aggregate level of environmental quality. In these models, property rights are decisive in determining whether environmental degradation eventually declines with growth.

(c) *Endogenous growth models* relax the neo-classical specification of the production function assumed in the optimal growth models. Building on the work of Romer (1986,[4] 1990[5]) in particular, production functions in these models are characterized by increasing returns to scale, and spillover effects. Tightening pollution standards with economic growth is optimal in these models.

(d) *Other macroeconomic models* include an overlapping generation model (Diamond, 1965)[6] and a two-country general equilibrium model of growth and the environment in the presence of trade. These models add support to the results of the optimal growth models and suggest that their results may be arrived at in other contexts as well.

## Empirical Models of Growth and Environment

The environment-economic growth debate in the empirical literature has centred on the following five questions. First, does the often-hypothesised inverted-U shaped relationship between income and environmental degradation, known as the Environmental Kuznets Curve actually exist, and how robust and general is it? Second, what is the role of other factors, such as population growth, income distribution, international trade and time and space dependent (rather than income-dependent) variables? Third, how relevant is a statistical relationship estimated from cross-country or panel data to an individual country's environmental trajectory and to the likely path of present day developing countries? Fourth, what are the implications of ecological thresholds and irreversible damages for the inverted-U shaped relationship between environmental degradation and economic growth? Can a static statistical relationship be interpreted in terms of carrying capacity, ecosystem resilience and sustainability? Finally, what is the role of environmental policy both in explaining the shape of the income-environment relationship, and in lowering the environmental price of economic growth and ensuring more sustainable outcomes?

Grossman and Krueger (1993, 1995) estimated EKCs for sulphur dioxide ($SO_2$), dark matter (smoke) and suspended particles using GEMS (Global Environmental Monitoring System) data for 52 cities in 32 countries during the period 1977-1988, and in per capita GDP data in Purchasing Power Parity (PPP) terms. For sulphur dioxide ($SO_2$) and dark matter, they found turning points at $4,000-$5,000 per capita; suspended particles continually declined at even low-income levels. However, at income levels over $10,000-$15,000 all three pollutants began to increase again, a finding which may be an artifact of the cubic equation used in the estimation and the limited number of observations at high-income levels.

Shafik and Bandyopadhyay (1977) estimated EKCs for ten different indicators for environmental degradation, including lack of clean water and sanitation, deforestation, municipal waste, and sulphur oxides and carbon emissions. Their sample includes observations for up to 149 countries during 1960-1990 and their functional specification log-linear, log-quadratic and logarithmic cubic polynomial functional forms. They found that lack of clean water and sanitation declined uniformly with increasing incomes and over time; water pollution, municipal waste and carbon emissions increase; and deforestation is independent of income levels. In contrast, air pollutants conform to the EKC hypothesis with turning points at income levels between $300 and $4,000.

Panayotou (1992, 1993, and 1995), using cross-section data and a translog specification found similar results for these pollutants, with turning points at income levels ranging from \$3,000 to \$5,000. (The lower figures are due to the use of official exchange rates rather than PPP rates).

Panayotou also found that deforestation also conforms to the EKC hypothesis, with a turning point around \$800 per capita; controlling for income, deforestation is significantly greater in tropical, and in densely populated countries. Cropper and Griffith on the other hand, using panel data for 64 countries over a 30-year period, obtained a turning point for deforestation in Africa and Latin America between \$4,700 and \$5,400 (in PPP terms). These turning points are a multiple of those found by Panayotou and by Shafik and Bandyopadhyay's studies, a possible consequence of Cropper and Griffith's use of panel data.

A study by Antle and Heidebrink (1999),[7] which used cross-section data, found turning points of \$1,200 (1985 prices) for national parks and \$2,000 for afforestation. On the other hand, Bhattarai and Hammig, who used panel data on deforestation for 21 countries in Latin America, found an EKC with a turning point of \$6,800. Furthermore, while earlier studies of deforestation were content to control for population density, more recent studies have controlled for institutional factors such as the quality of government institutions and macroeconomic factors, such as the level of indebtedness, and found them to have the expected signs, negative and positive respectively.

Returning to urban environmental quality, the mid-1990s have seen a large number on studies focusing on airborne pollutants. Selden and Song (1994)[8] estimated EKCs for $SO_2$, $NO_x$, and SPM and CO using longitudinal data on emissions in mostly developed countries. They found turning points of \$8,700 for $SO_2$, \$11,200 for $NO_x$, \$10,300 for SPM, and \$5,600 for CO. These are much higher levels than Grossman and Krueger's, a discrepancy that which the authors explain in terms of reduction of emissions lagging behind reductions in ambient concentrations. However, this reasoning does not explain the large difference of their results from those of Panayotou, who also uses emissions data; the use of longitudinal data *versus* cross-section may help explain part of the difference. Cole *et al.* (1997)[9] estimated income-environment relationship for many environmental indicators, including total energy use, transport emissions of $SO_2$, SPM and $NO_2$, nitrates in water, traffic volumes, CFC emissions and methane. They found inverted-U shaped curves only for local air pollutants and CFCs and concluded that "meaningful EKCs exist only for local air pollutants, while indicators with a more global, more indirect, environmental impact either increase with income or else have high turning points with large standard errors". This conclusion would lead one to expect that carbon dioxide ($CO_2$), the global pollutant *par excellance*, would increase monotonically with income, at least within any observable income range since the impacts of global warming are (totally) externalized to other countries and future generations. Indeed, earlier studies (e.g. Shafik and Bandyopadhyay, 1992) obtained such a result. Holtz-Eakin and Selden (1995) estimated EKCs for carbon dioxide ($CO_2$) using panel data, and found that carbon dioxide ($CO_2$) emissions per capita do not begin to decline until income per capita reaches $35,000, a result that confirms earlier findings by Shafik (1994).[10]

However, more recent studies, using better data and more sophisticated estimation techniques, have obtained turning points for Carbon Dioxide ($CO_2$) emissions, while higher than those of local pollutants, still within the range of observable income levels. Schmalensee *et al.* (1997),[10] using a spline regression with ten piece-wise segments and the Holtz-Eakin and Selden have obtained an inverted-U shaped relationship between carban dioxide ($CO_2$) emissions and income per capita in PPP$ (1985). They found negative carbon dioxide ($CO_2$) emission elasticities with respect to income per capita at the lowest and highest income splines, and a turning point in the range of $10,000 to $17,000 per capita. Galeotri and Lanza (1999 a, b)[11] have tested alternative functional specifications for the carbon dioxide ($CO_2$)—income relationship, including Gamma and Weibrill functions as well as quadratic and cubic functions. They found turning points between $15,000 and $22,000 depending on the specification and sample. Another recent study by Panayotou, Sachs, and Peterson (1999),[12] using a ten segment piece-wise spline function and panel data for 150 countries during 1960-92, have found results quite similar to those of Schmalensee *et al.* The income elasticity of emissions was low at the lowest income spline, and rose to a maximum at around $11,500 per capita (tuning point) and turned negative at incomes of about $17,500. Finding an inverted-U shaped relationship for an invisible pollutant with much delayed effects and ample scope for a free-riding behaviour is a bit puzzling but fully explainable by structural changes accompanying economic growth: from agriculture, to industry, to services, three sectors with different carbon emissions intensities.

The linkages between trade and the environment can be explained *via* the impact of economic growth on the environment. One approach is to look at the impact of economic growth on the environment in terms of what is called the 'Environmental Kuznets Curve.' Grossman and Krueger (1993) were the first economists to publish a study based on this concept which indicated environmental conditions deteriorate initially as per capita income rises, but then improve as per capita income increases beyond a certain turning point. Their study is the most widely cited of several studies that purport to provide empirical evidence of the inverted 'U' relationship–depicted as–which the well-known economist Simon Kuznets (1955, 1966) postulated existed between economic growth and inequality. The application of the Kuznets Curve to the relationship between economic development and environmental pollution postulates environmental conditions deteriorate in the early stages of development (especially with industrialization) and they improve as countries reach the middle-income level of development, and improve greatly as countries graduate into the higher income bracket of development. However, no country has yet reached the downward sloping part of the Environmental Kuznets Curve when it comes to spatially or temporally spread pollutants such as the greenhouse gas carbon dioxide.

## Model Specification

**(A)** For the estimation of compound annual growth rate the following semi log trend equation has been used.

$\text{Log } Y = \beta_1 + \beta_2 T + U$

Where Y = dependent variable

T = Time

$\beta_1$ and $\beta_2$ are regression coefficients and

U = the error term.

Trend compound growth rate can be estimated as

$\text{Growth rate} = (\text{Antilog } \beta_2 - 1)100$

The constancy of long-term growth rate of GDP, exports and imports of goods and services has been tested with help of following semi log quadratic equation:

$$\text{Log } y = \beta_1 + \beta_2 T + \beta_3 T^2 + U_t$$

where, βs are regression coefficients. The value of $\beta_3$ explains the nature of growth rate. Insignificant value of $\beta_3$ supports the hypothesis of constancy in growth over the period under consideration. Positive and significant value of $\beta_3$ indicates acceleration in growth rate while negative and significant value will reflect deceleration in the growth rate.

In case of acceleration in growth rate, there must be some point of shift in the growth rate. In order to find out the year of shift in GDP growth, exports and imports of goods and services, following equation with dummy variables has been used (Rao & Miller):

$$\text{Log } Y = \beta_1 + \beta_2 T + \beta_3 D + \beta_4 DT + U_t$$

Where βs are regression coefficients $\beta_3$ represents intercept of dummy variable and $\beta_4$ is the slope of dummy. D is the dummy variable representing the shift in the growth rate. It takes 0 for the period shift or break through and 1 otherwise. Thus the trend equation before and after shift will be as follows:

$\text{Log } Y = \beta_1 + \beta_2 T$ before shift (D = 0).
And $\text{Log } Y = (\beta_1 + \beta_3) + (\beta_2 + \beta_4) T$ after shift (D = 1).

Respective growth rate are estimated from the estimation for two periods.

**(B)** To examine the trade-off between economic development and environmental degradation, we have used following functional relationship on state level data.

1. $Y = \beta_1 + \beta_2 (PCI) + \beta_3 (PCI)^2 + Ut$
   Where $Y_1$ = Deforestation rate.
   βs = Regression Coefficients.
   PCI = Per capita NSDP.
   $PCI^2$ = Square of per capita NSDP.
   Ut is the error term.
2. $Y = \beta_1 + \beta_2 (PCCE) + \beta_3 (PCCE)^2 + Ut$
   βs = Regression Coefficients.
   PCCE = Per capita Consumption of Electricity.

$(PCCE)^2$ = Square of per capita Consumption of Electricity.
Ut is the Error term.

In the above regression equations the positive value of $\beta_2$ and negative value of $\beta_3$ with statistically significant, will confirm EKC hypothesis about environmental degradation and economic development in India.

3. $Y = \beta_0 + \beta_1 E_1 + \beta_2 E_3 + \beta_3 D + Ut$

Where $E_1$ is PCI, $E_3$ is $(PCI)^2$ and D is the dummy variable. In the above regression equations the positive value of $\beta_1$ and negative value of $\beta_3$ with statistically significant, will confirm EKC hypothesis about environmental degradation and economic development in India.

**(C)** In order to identify the factors explaining the deforestation rate in India, we have used following regression models with several combinations of the independent variables such as Per Capita Consumption of Electricity ($X_1$), Decadal Growth of Population ($X_2$), Population Density ($X_3$), Percentage of Population BPL ($X_4$), Urbanization Rate ($X_5$), Road Density ($X_6$), Percentage of Area under Forest ($X_7$), Female literacy ($X_8$), and per capita production of Milk ($X_9$).

Along with these variables we have also tried the impact of per capita income ($E_1$), percentage change in per capita income ($E_2$), square of per capita income ($E_3$), population growth rate ($E_4$), rural poverty ($E_5$), population density ($X_3$) and cropping intensity ($E_6$) on the deforestation rate (Y). Increase in population demands more land for fulfilling the basic needs—food, clothing and shelter. This decreases the forest cover. Hence a positive relationship is hypothesised between rate of deforestation and population growth rate ($dy/dx_1 > 0$).

**(D)** The trade-off between agricultural development and environmental Degradation is studied by the following log linear model for empirical analysis.

$$\text{Log FOR} = \alpha_0 + \alpha_1 \text{Log TPI} + \alpha_2 \text{Log JPI} + \alpha_3 \text{Log CPI} + \alpha_4 \text{Log SPI} + \alpha_5 \text{Log GSPI} + \alpha_6 \text{Log FGPI} + \alpha_7 \text{Log FPI} + \mu$$

Where $\alpha$ represents the respective coefficients of the independent variables, and $\mu$ is the error term associated to the regression of the equation. FOR stands for annual data on the forest area used to capture deforestation. TPI, JPI, CPI, SPI, GSPI, FGPI and FPI stand for Tea Price Index, Jute Price Index, Cotton Price Index, Sugar Khandsari and Gur Price Index, Groundnut Seed Price Index, Food Grain Price Index and Fertilizer Price Index respectively. These are the prices paid to the producers. We have also transformed the above primary model to make it free from the problem of autocorrelation and multicollinearity as follows:

$$\text{Log FOR} = \alpha_0 + \alpha_1 \text{ Log JPI} + \alpha_3 \text{ Log FGPI} + \mu$$
$$\text{Log FOR} = \alpha_0 + \alpha_1 \text{ Log TPI} + \alpha_2 \text{ Log CPI} + \alpha_3 \text{ Log FPI} + \mu$$

**(E)** Trade intensity or 'openness' is estimated as (IMPt + EXPt) / GDPt. Per cent Capital Inflow is estimated by taking the per cent of FDI to total capital formation in India. We theorise that the effects of capital accumulation on pollution depend on the techniques of production in place. We believe that total income gain due to trade may be disfigured by population figures that may not be reliable. Therefore, we measure the technique effect by the real gross national product (real GNP).

**(F)** To study interlink between trade strategy and environment, we have used regression model. The specification of the model is as follows:

$$POL_t = \alpha_0 + \alpha_1 [(EXP_t + IMP_t)/GDP_t] + \alpha_2 (Ft/TCF_t) + \alpha_3 RGNP_t + \mu_t$$

Where pollution POLt is the yearly quantity of carbon dioxide emission due to flaring and combustion processes in India only and environmental degradation $RGNP_t$ is real gross national product. We have also made proper transformation of the above primary model due to make it free from problem of autocorrelation and multicollinearity. To avoid the problem of multicollinearity, we have increased the number of observation and dropped Scale of Economic Activity from the model. We have used lag model to avoid the problems of autocorrelation.

**Definitions of Variables**

1. *Per Capita Consumption of Electricity ($X_I$)* – Higher per capita consumption of electricity increases the demand for

goods and services in the market. This can force the diversion of forest land to other use to fulfil the higher demand for goods and services. This can result in forest degradation. So, there should be a positive relationship between per capita income and deforestation rate ($dY/dX_1 > 0$).

2. *Decadal Growth of Population ($X_2$)* – Population growth is measured by the percentage change in population during the decade. With increase in population, more requirement of food arises. Hence more land is brought under cultivation. There should be a positive impact of this on percentage change in agricultural land. We thus can hypothesise that population growth will have positive impact on agricultural land extension ($dY/dX_2 > 0$).
3. *Population density ($X_3$)* - It is defined as number of persons living in per square kilometre of area. With the increase in population density the pressure on land increases. Hence to fulfil the local needs of the population, more land will be diverted from cultivation to other uses. We thus can hypothesise negative impact of $X_3$ on Y ($dY/dX_3 < 0$).
4. *Percentage of Population BPL ($X_4$)* – It is defined as number of people living below poverty line. With the increase in population BPL the pressure on forest increases. Hence to fulfil the local needs of poor people, forest area will be diverted from cultivation to other uses. We thus can hypothesise negative impact of $X_4$ on Y ($dY/dX_4 < 0$).
5. *Urbanization Rate ($X_5$)* – It is defined as ratio of urban population to the total population. With increase in urbanization rate, there may be much pressure on forest to fulfil the demand of the urban population such as fire wood, wooden furniture etc. We thus can hypothesise positive impact of $X_5$ on Y ($dY/dX_5 > 0$).
6. *Road Density ($X_6$)* – It is assumed that Road Density has positive relationship with deforestation. This is because of construction of roads by clearing the forest area. Therefore, we can hypothesise positive impact of $X_6$ on Y ($dY/dX_6 > 0$).
7. *Percentage of Area under Forest ($X_7$)* – It may be put in plain words that level forest area may be important cause of deforestation in the country. It is because, if there is more

forest area, people will be keenly involved in clearing the forests and *vice versa.* We thus can hypothesise positive impact of $X_7$ on Y ($dY/dX_7 > 0$).

8. *Female Literacy ($X_8$)* – It may be explained as ratio of female literates to the total number of adult female population. It is a positive indicator of economic development as it has a direct impact on health, nutrition, cleanliness, education and other quality of life indicators. Thus, the higher female literacy reflects better level of development in the country. Therefore, we can hypothesise positive impact of $X_8$ on Y ($dY/dX_8 > 0$).
9. *Per Capita Production of Milk ($X_9$)* – This is a demand side factor. It is assumed that higher the availability of per capita production of milk, lesser will be the forest degradation. We, thus, can hypothesise positive impact of $X_9$ on Y ($dY/dX_9 > 0$).
10. *Per Capita Income ($E_1$)* – It is measured by per capita net state domestic product. Higher per capita income increases the demand for goods and services in the market. This can force the diversion of forest land to other use to fulfil the higher demand for goods and services. This can result into forest degradation. So, there should be a positive relationship between per capita income and deforestation rate ($dY/dE_1 > 0$).
11. *Percentage Change in Per Capita Income ($E_2$)* – Sometimes it is not the level of development, but rate of growth that creates pressure on forest land. High economic growth rate generates more pollution and degrade natural resources. We, therefore, can hypothesise positive impact of $E_2$ on $Y_2$ ($dY/dE_2 > 0$).
12. *Square of Per Capita Income ($E_3$)* – The level of development cannot have uniform impact on deforestation. Higher level of development may generate more demand for better quality of environment. This shall increase the demand for aforestation and recycling of waste in the economy. Thus, after a certain level of development we can hypothesise less rate of deforestation as explained by EKC hypothesis ($dY/dE_3 < 0$).

13. *Population Growth ($E_4$)* – Population growth is measured by the percentage change in population during the decade. With increase in population, more requirement of food arises. Hence more land is brought under cultivation. There should be a positive impact of this on percentage change in agricultural land. We thus can hypothesise that population growth will have positive impact on agricultural land extension ($dY/dE_4 > 0$).
14. *Rural Poverty ($E_5$)* – Poor have fewer assets to fulfil their needs. They are thus dependent mainly on cheaply available resources and forest land for their livelihood. Limited economic opportunities of these households force them to go for short run optimization from these resources. This can thus increase deforestation and we, therefore, can hypothesise the positive impact of it on Y ($dY/dE_5 > 0$).
15. *Dummy Variable (D)* – We have pooled the two sets of cross section data for two different periods in order to see the change in the attitude towards deforestation over a period of time through dummy variable. We have assigned D = 0 for the period 1990-91 and D = 1 for the period 2000-01. Improvement in the standard of living and government intervention to protect forest assets should have negative impact on deforestation over a period of time. We, therefore, can assume negative coefficient of dummy variable in over all analysis ($dY/dD < 0$).
16. *Cropping Intensity ($E_6$)* – One of the methods of increasing the agricultural productivity is by increasing intensity of cultivation. It is defined as gross sown area divided by net sown area. The intensive use of land will increase agricultural output without going for extensive agriculture. Hence higher the cropping intensity less should be the land extension for agriculture. We thus can hypothesise negative impact of $E_6$ on Y ($dY/dE_6 < 0$).

## NOTES

1. Ramsey, F.P., A Mathematical Theory of Saving, *Economic Journal,* 38, 543-559 (1928).

2. Koopmans, T.C., On the Concept of Optimal Economic Growth, *The Economic Approach to Development Planning* (1965).
3. Cass, D., Optimum Growth in an Aggregate Model of Capital Accumulation, *Rev. Economic Studies*, 32, 233-240 (1965).
4. Romer, P.M., Increasing Returns and Long-run Growth, *Journal of Political Economy*, 94, 1002-1037 (1986).
5. National Debt in a Neoclassical Growth Model, *American Economic Review*, 55, 1126-1150 (1965).
6. Diamond, P., National Debt in a Neoclassical Growth Model, *American Economic Review*, 55, 1126-1150 (1965).
7. Antle, J.M., and Heidebrink, G., Environment and Development: Theory and International Evidence, in *Environmental Economics and Development* (1999).
8. Selden, T.M., and Song, D., Environmental Quality and Development: Is there a Kuznets Curve for Air Pollution Emissions? *Journal of Environmental Economics and Management*, 27, 147-162 (1994).
9. Cole, M.A., Rayner, A.J., and Bates, J.M., *The Environmental Kuznets Curve: An Empirical Analysis* (1997).
10. Shafik, N., and Bandyopadhyay, S., Economic Growth and Environmental Resources, *Journal of Environmental Economics and Management* 4, 1-24 (1977).
11. Schmalensee, R., Stoker, T.M., and Judson, R.A., *World Carbon Dioxide Emissions: 1950-2050* (1997).
12. Galeotti, M. and Lanze, A., Richer and Cleaner; A Study on Carbon Dioxide Emissions in Developing Countries, Rome, Proceedings from the 22nd IAEE Annual International Conference, June 9-12 (1999).
13. Panayotou, T., Sachs, J., Peterson, A., Developing Countries and the Control of Climate Change: A Theoretical Perspective and Policy Implications, *CAER II Discussion Paper No. 45. August* (1999).

# 4

# Economics of Development in India

The Indian economy exhibits the important features of typical underdeveloped economy such as widespread poverty, low per capita income, predominance of agricultural sector, rapid population growth, etc. India is considered a part of low level income countries with $ 450 per capita GNI for year 2000 (2002 WDI Database). On 21 June 1991, when Shri P.V. Narasimha Rao government took charge of the country, the economy was in deep crisis. The balance of payment situation was precarious, with reserves going down just enough to pay for 3-day import bill, the weakening of international confidence having resulted in a sharp decline in capital inflows through commercial borrowing and NRI deposits. Inflation reached double digits hurting the poor sections of our society. Economic growth had slowed down; also, before 1980s the economy remained stangant to 3.5 per cent growth rate. The origin of these problems is directly traceable to large and persistent macro economic imbalances most notably the large fiscal deficits, fragile balance of payment situation and low productivity of last investments. The crisis in Middle East had exacerbated the situation by contribution to a higher oil import bills in 1990-91 and the temporary loss of export markets and remittance earnings.

The Rao government took a series of corrective measures to bring the situation under control. These included short-term measures (stabilization reforms) aimed at crisis management as well as longer-term measures of structural reforms, aimed at improving efficiency and productivity and putting the economy back on track or path of sustainable growth. Stabilization policies work mainly on the demand side to reduce inflation and external deficits. Structural policies are concerned with the supply side; they address the efficiency of resource use, emphasising reforms in specific sectors like trade, finance, and industry. It is possible to postpone structural reforms during stabilization, but structural reforms are unlikely to succeed unless they are preceded or accompanied by stabilization. Similarly, stabilization is unlikely to be sustainable without structural reforms.

India received appreciation of its new economic policies from international observers and multilateral financial institutions. The IMF and the World Bank not only provided loans for immediate relief but liberally aided India's efforts at restructuring its economy during next five years along the lines negotiated and mutually agreed between both the sides. The net outflow of the Foreign Currency Non Resident Deposits stopped and got converted into net inflows. Foreign exchange reserves increased to their highest level, reversing not only the phase of extreme import compression to phased efficient import liberalization, but also supporting the cause of capital account convertibility. Further, the rise in the rate of inflation was arrested. Thus, government received more time for the country to concentrate on medium term economic reforms.

## FIVE-YEAR PLANS AND ECONOMIC DEVELOPMENT

Under a series of Five-Year Plans through 2000, the government became a participant in many industrial fields and increased its regulation of existing private commerce and industry. Long the owner-operator of most railway facilities, all radio broadcasting, post and telegraph facilities, arms and ammunition factories, and river development programmes, the government reserved for itself the right to nationalize any industries it deemed necessary. Yet the government's socialist approach was pragmatic, not doctrinaire; agriculture and large segments of trade, finance, and industry remained in private hands. Planning is supervised by an eight-member Planning Commission, established in 1950 and chaired by the Prime Minister.

India's first four Five-Year Plans entailed a total public sector outlay of Rs. 314.1 billion. The First Plan (1951–1956) accorded top priority to agriculture, especially irrigation and power projects. The Second Plan (1956–1961) was designed to implement the new industrial policy and to achieve a "socialist pattern of society". The plan stressed rapid industrialization, a 25 per cent increase in national income (in fact, the achieved increase was only 20%), and reduction of inequalities in wealth and income. The focus of the Third Plan (1961–1966) was industrialization, with 24.6 per cent spent on transportation and communications and 20.1 per cent on industry and minerals. Drought, inflation, and war with Pakistan made this plan a major disappointment; although considerable industrial diversification was achieved and national income rose, per capita income did not increase (because of population growth), and harvests were disastrously low. Because of the unsettled domestic situation, the Fourth Five-Year Plan did not take effect until 1969. The 1969–74 plan sought to control fluctuations in agricultural output and to promote equality and social justice. Agriculture and allied sectors received 16.9 per cent, more than in any previous plan, while industry and minerals received 18.5 per cent, transportation and communications 18.4 per cent, and power development 17.8 per cent, also more than in any previous plan.

The Fifth Plan (1974–1979) aimed at the removal of poverty and the attainment of self-reliance. A total outlay of Rs. 393.2 billion was allocated (26% less than originally envisaged), and actual expenditures totalled Rs. 394.2 billion. Once again, the emphasis was on industry, with mining and manufacturing taking 22.5, electric power 18.7, transportation and communications 17.2, and agriculture 12.1. The Fifth Plan was cut short a year early in 1978, and, with India enmeshed in recession and political turmoil, work began on the sixth development plan (1980–1985). Its goal, like that of the fifth, was the removal of poverty, although the planners recognized that this gigantic task could not be accomplished within five years. The plan aimed to strengthen the agricultural and industrial infrastructure in order to accelerate the growth of investments and exports. Projected outlays totaled Rs. 975 billion, of which electric power received 27.1 per cent, industry and mining 15.4 per cent, transportation and communications 12.7 per cent, and agriculture 12.2 per cent. The main target was a GDP growth rate of 5.2 per cent annually. The seventh development plan (1985–1990) projected 5 overall GDP growth (which was largely achieved and even exceeded) based on increases of 4 per cent and 8 per cent in agricultural and industrial output, respectively. Outlays were to total Rs.1,800 billion.

The eighth development plan (for 1992–1997), drafted in response to the country's looming debt crisis in 1990–91, laid the groundwork for long-term structural adjustment. The plan's overall thrust was to stimulate industrial growth by the private sector, and thereby free government resources for greater investment in basic infrastructure and human resources development. In addition to liberalized conditions for private and foreign investment, the foreign exchange system was reformed, the currency devalued, the maximum tariff reduced from 350 per cent to 85 per cent, import barriers generally loosened, and those for key intermediate goods removed altogether. Reform of the tax system, reduction of subsidies, and restructuring of public enterprises were also targeted. While the Eighth Plan generally supported expansion of private enterprise, unlike structural adjustment programmes in other developing countries, it did not stipulate a large-scale privatization of the public sector.

As the Eighth Plan came to an end in 1997 most analysts proclaimed it a success; economic growth averaged 6 per cent a year, employment rose, poverty was reduced, exports increased, and inflation declined. The ninth development plan (1997–2002) focused on the redistribution of wealth and alleviation of poverty, the further privatization of the economy and attraction of foreign investment, and the reduction of the deficit. Overall there were improvements in the reform era including an increase in the GDP growth rate from an average of about 5.7 per cent to about 6.1 per cent in the Eighth and Ninth Plan periods, a reduction of the per cent in poverty from a third of the population to a fourth, increased literacy from 52 per cent in 1991 to 65 per cent in 2001, and India's emergence as a competitor in state-of-the-art technologies of the new information age economy. However, persistent inefficiencies—unemployment and underemployment, and welfare deficiencies—remained. Moreover, since 1998 a series of domestic and international shocks have brought a disturbing deceleration to India's economic growth.

In the Tenth Five-Year Plan, 2002–2007, the government set the ambitious target of achieving an average 8 per cent growth, above the level achieved during the Ninth Plan and well ahead of the 5 to 5.5 per cent growth forecast for 2002-03. Other monitorable economic targets include a reduction of the poverty rate by 5 per cent by 2007, and by 15 per cent by 2012; providing gainful and high quality employment at least equal to the projected increases in the labour force; increase in forest and tree cover to 25 per cent, in 2007 and to 33 per cent by 2012; all villages with sustained access to potable water by 2007; and cleaning of all major polluted rivers by 2007. Agricultural development is viewed as the core element of the Tenth Plan with attention to sectors most likely to create employment opportunities. These include agriculture in its extended sense, construction, tourism, transport, small-scale industries (SSI), retailing, IT, and communications enabling services. Industrial policy includes continued emphasis on privatization and deregulation. The ambitious

8 per cent annual growth of the Tenth Plan is considered achievable because of the inefficiencies that have traditionally plagued Indian agriculture and industry. Because the scope for improvement is so wide, both in the public sector and in the private sector, strong growth can be expected from efficiency enhancing policies.

**India's Economy Since Independence**

A glance at Table 4.1 clarifies that economic growth in India accelerated noticeably around 1980. It is the case that the rate of growth of industrial production from 1980 onwards was not all that impressive, both by international standards, and in comparison to India's own record in the 1950s (Wallack, 2003).[1] Nevertheless, the growth in the 1950s was from a very low starting point and the performance since 1980 has been a significant improvement over the "decade of stagnation" that went before (Ahluwalia, 1985).[2] Moreover, Virmani (2004a and 2004b)[3] and Rodrik and Subramanian (2004)[4] have established via a variety of more formal tests that 1980 indeed represents a break from India's "Hindu growth rate". The overall rate of investment in the economy improved from 1980 onwards (the trend actually began in the second half of the 1970s) and, fluctuations notwithstanding, has remained in the range of 22-23 per cent per annum.

**Table 4.1:** Some Basic Growth Data, 1950-2004

| *Indicators (All figures in percentage per annum)* | *1950-1964* | *1965-1979* | *1980-1990* | *1991-2004* | *1980-2004* |
|---|---|---|---|---|---|
| GDP growth | 3.7 | 2.9 | 5.8 | 5.6 | 5.7 |
| Industrial growth | 7.4 | 3.8 | 6.5 | 5.8 | 6.1 |
| Agricultural growth | 3.1 | 2.3 | 3.9 | 3.0 | 3.4 |
| Gross investment/GDP | 13 | 18 | 22.8 | 22.3 | 22.5 |

*Source*: *EPW*, April 1, 2006, Government of India, *Economic Survey,* various issues

How India's economy has performed since the economic reforms, has remains a debatable. To illustrate, Arun Ghosh has argued that "the consequences of the NEP (new economic policy) are likely to be extremely adverse for the future of the Indian economy". He further asserts "in brief, in no sector or manner has the NEP succeeded" (Ghosh, 1997).[5] However, Kirti Parikh thinks: "the reforms have put the Indian economy on a higher growth path, which it should continue to ride even without a lot of additional new reform. With more sensible policies, we have an opportunity to accelerate our growth further and take-off into a high growth trajectory" (Parikh, 1997).[6] It is not surprising to find such unsupported statements in official government publications particularly of the finance ministry, but it is certainly dubious that in recent years well known economists have conveniently ignored the mixed outcome of the economic reform. By distorting the facts, these economists contend that the reforms instituted so far have been, by and large successful in achieving an accelerated growth in the new liberalized environment and thus help to reduce poverty.

Of the 16 major states listed in Table 4.2 and Fig. 4.1, notice that, when compared to the 1980s, economic growth rate in the post-reform period altered significantly in only half the states (i.e., increased or decreased by one percentage point or more (Fig. 4.2). Economic growth increased notably in Gujarat, Kerala and West Bengal; by contrast, following reforms, economic growth declined by more than a point in Bihar, Orissa, UP, Punjab and Rajasthan (Fig. 4.3). Those working with more specific state-level data on manufacturing in the registered sector have established that the decline in growth in select states was more statistically robust than the growth pickup. Somewhat broader data on growth rates in the secondary sector as a whole, however, are broadly consistent with the overall growth trends in Table 4.2, at least in terms of the eight states in which growth rates increased or decreased by a percentage point or more.

**Table 4.2:** Economic Growth in Major Indian States, 1980-2004

| *States* | *1980-1990* | *1990-2004* | *1980-2004* |
|---|---|---|---|
| Andhra Pradesh | 4.81 | 5.33 | 5.1 |
| Assam | 3.91 | 3.00 | 3.4 |
| Bihar | 5.20 | 4.2 | 4.6 |
| Gujarat | 5.71 | 8.11 | 7.1 |
| Haryana | 6.68 | 6.3 | 6.65 |
| Himachal Pradesh | 6.10 | 6.43 | 6.3 |
| Karnataka | 6.10 | 6.38 | 6.3 |
| Kerala | 4.50 | 5.69 | 5.2 |
| Madhya Pradesh | 5.18 | 4.74 | 4.9 |
| Maharastra | 5.98 | 5.92 | 5.95 |
| Orissa | 5.85 | 3.94 | 4.7 |
| Punjab | 5.14 | 4.14 | 4.6 |
| Rajasthan | 7.17 | 5.68 | 6.3 |
| Tamil Nadu | 6.35 | 5.70 | 5.97 |
| Uttar Pradesh | 5.88 | 3.76 | 4.64 |
| West Bengal | 5.20 | 7.12 | 6.32 |
| All India | 5.60 | 5.90 | 5.8 |

*Source*: Central Statistical Organisation (www.indiastat.com).

**Fig. 4.1:** Economic Growth in Major Indian States 1980-90

## Reforms and Economic Growth

The record of economic growth (annual rate of growth of real GNP) in independent India has been uneven. Until about 1980 growth rates were low and subject to considerable volatility. This record has improved since then. In Table 4.3 we depict salient characteristics of aggregate economic growth in India.

In aggregate terms growth appears to have picked up significantly since the 1980s. Further, the variability of this growth (as measured by the standard deviation) has come down significantly. Per capita GDP growth which was 1.2 per annum during 1972-82, accelerated to 3.0 during 1982-92 and further to 3.9 during 1992-2002. So the Indian economy has been enjoying high and relatively stable rates of growth for almost a quarter century now.[8]

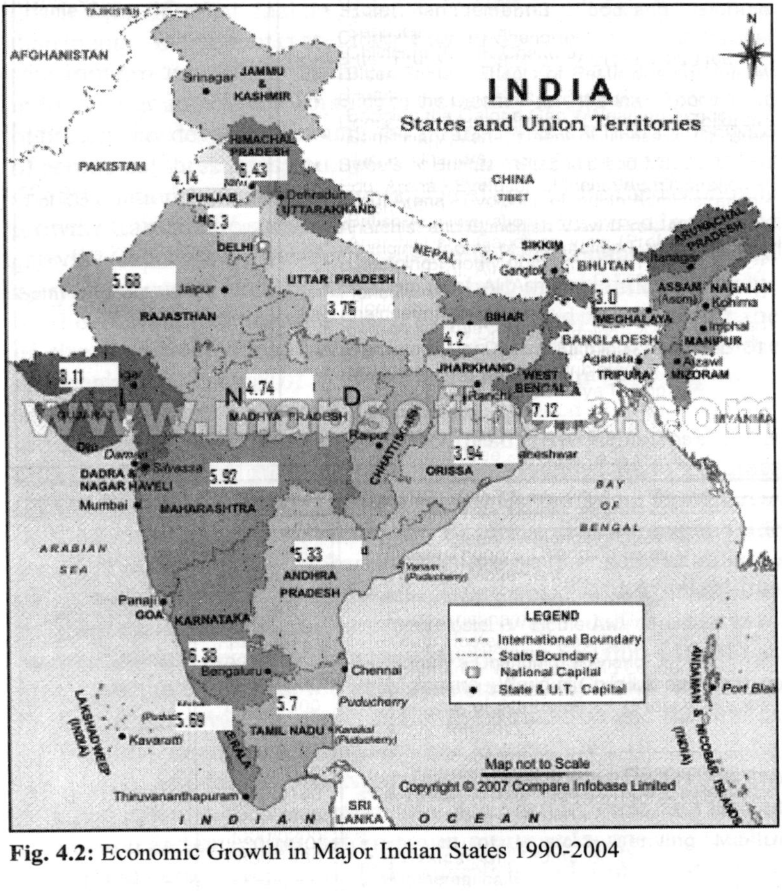


**Fig. 4.2:** Economic Growth in Major Indian States 1990-2004

Economic development is a long-term process. As a first step to understand the long-term trend in growth rate in pre- and post- reform era, we have filled the semi log equations to GDP at constant Price (Rs. crore) for the period 1980-81 to 1989-90 and 1990-91 to 2004-05. The estimated equations are shown in Table 4.4. The trend coefficients of semi log functions for the decade of 1980-81 to 1989-90 and 1990-91 to 2004-05 are positive and statistically significant.

Thus, it shows that there is a growth in the economy during these decades. The GDP growth rate during the 1980-90 is found to be 5.38 whereas, it is 6.003 during 1991-2005. It took a relatively small jump in the growth process. In order to test the acceleration in the growth of GDP, we tried alternative functional form. The coefficient of semi log quadratic function for the period of 1980-2005 is positive and significant. That means there is acceleration in the growth rate of GDP during this period.

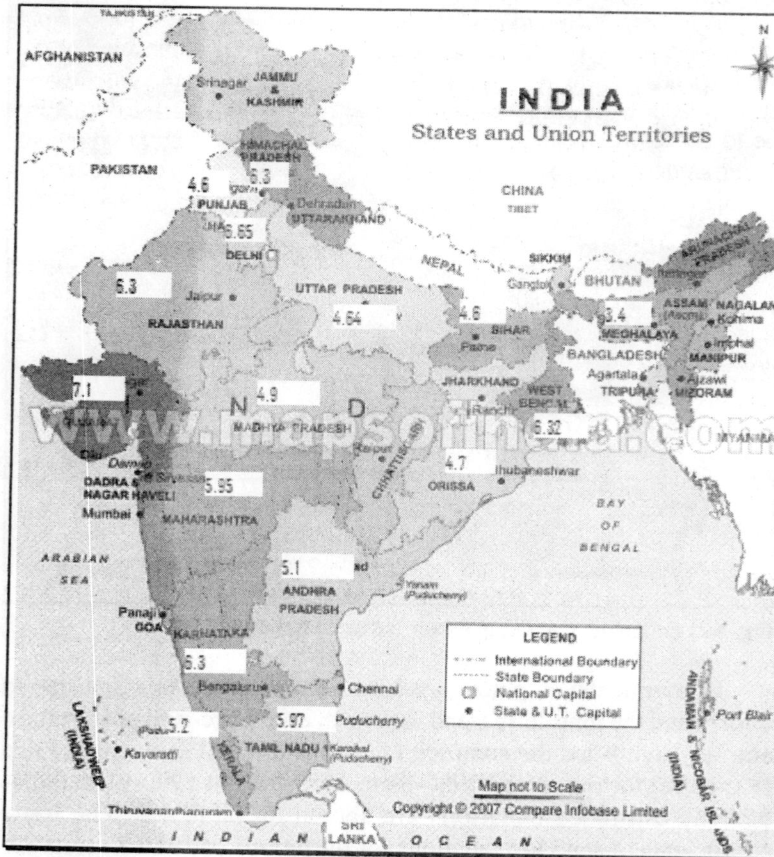


**Fig. 4.3:** Economic Growth in Major Indian States 1980-2004

**Table 4.3:** Some Basic Characteristics of Growth of Real GNP in India

| Period | Mean Annual Growth Rate (percentages) | Standard Deviation of Year to Year Growth Rate (percentages) |
|---|---|---|
| 1951-52 to 1959-60 | 3.58 | 2.62 |
| 1960-61 to 1969-70 | 3.91 | 3.64 |
| 1970-71 to 1979-80 | 3.05 | 4.16 |
| 1980-81 to 1989-90 | 5.65 | 2.27 |
| 1990-91 to 1999-2000 | 5.83 | 1.97 |
| 1992-93 to 1999-2000 | 6.46 | 1.16 |

*Source*: Author's calculation based on data from Reserve Bank of India, *Handbook of Statistics on the Indian Economy.*

In order to study the shift in the growth rate of GDP during reforms, we have used the semi-log function with dummy variable. The coefficient of this dummy variable is negative and statistically significant. That means there is substantial change in the growth rate due to Structural Adjustment Programmes (SAP). Therefore, it can be concluded that economic reforms in the country have brought positive effect on the growth of GDP.

**Table 4.4:** Growth of GDP at Constant Price

(*Rs. crore*)

| Year | Function | Intercept ($\beta_1$) | $\beta_2$ | $\beta_3$ | $\beta_4$ | $R^2$ | Growth Rate |
|---|---|---|---|---|---|---|---|
| 1980-90 | Log Linear | 5.5779* (0.0055) | 0.0227* (0.00089) | – | – | 0.9877 | 5.38% |
| 1991-2005 | Log Linear | 5.801* (0.00398) | 0.0253* (0.000437) | – | – | 0.9961 | 6.003% |
| 1980-2005 | Log Quadratic | 5.5802* (0.00484) | 0.0216* (0.00085) | 0.0001* (0.00003) | – | 0.9984 | – |
| 1980-2005 (1990-91) | Log linear with dummy | 5.5779* (0.00521) | 0.0227* (0.00084) | -0.03006* (0.198) | 0.00256* (0.00095) | 0.9983 | – |

*Note*: Value in parenthesis is standard error of the coefficient.
*Denotes significant at 5% level.
*Source*: Hand Book of Statistics, RBI 2006.

## Sector-wise Distribution of Economic Growth

Table 4.5 displays broad averages of sectoral growth rates as well as the significance of these sectors measured by their shares in GDP. Agricultural growth has continued to fluctuate considerably even as the share of agriculture in GDP has come down sharply.[9]

Manufacturing sector growth rates have not been particularly high and the share of industry in GDP has been stagnant at about 22 per cent. Manufacturing growth was high in the initial years of the post reforms period but fell sharply in 2001-02. The subsequent pick-up in 2002-03 was probably because of the lower base in 2001-02. Similar comments hold for mining. Growth in electricity production has been slow, perhaps reflecting the poor state of electricity generation, and particularly, transmission and distribution in India. The highest growth sector has been services. Growth in this sector has occurred across a broad range and has been the most stable of all sectoral growth rates. As a consequence, the share of services in GDP has gone up substantially.

**Table 4.5:** Growth Rates of Real GDP

*(per cent)*

| Sector | 2002-03 | 2001-02 | 1992-93 to 2001 |
|---|---|---|---|
| Agriculture and Allied Activities | -3.2 (22.1) | 5.7 (23.9) | 3.0 (27.9) |
| Industry, of which | 5.7 (21.8) | 3.2 (21.5) | 6.6 (22.0) |
| (i) Manufacturing | 6.1 | 3.4 | 7.2 |
| (ii) Mining and quarrying | 5.0 | 1.0 | 4.1 |
| (iii) Electricity, gas and water supply | 3.9 | 4.3 | 5.9 |
| Services, of which | 7.1 (56.1) | 6.5 (54.6) | 7.7 (50.1) |
| (i) Trade, hotels, restaurants, transport and communication | 7.8 | 8.7 | 8.3 |
| (ii) Financing, insurance, real estate and business services | 6.1 | 4.5 | 8.1 |
| (iii) Community, social and personal services | 6.8 | 5.6 | 7.3 |
| (iv) Construction | 7.2 | 3.7 | 5.5 |
| GDP at factor cost | 4.3 | 5.6 | 6.1 |

*Note:* Figures in brackets indicate share in GDP.
*Source:* Central Statistical Organization.

The evolution over time of the sectoral composition of Indian GDP is portrayed in Figure 4.4.

The current high rate of economic growth could well accelerate further as Kelkar (2004) has opined. Contributing to this acceleration is a broad series of reforms including financial sector reforms, increased globalization and widening and deepening of product and financial markets. The impact of such reforms gets reflected in key indicators such as market capitalization of the stock market, the technology and transparency of transactions, the sets of instruments traded, balance sheets of financial institutions and the degree of openness of the economy. At the same time a benign FDI policy framework has permitted greater tie-ups in high technology areas for production for domestic as well as external markets.

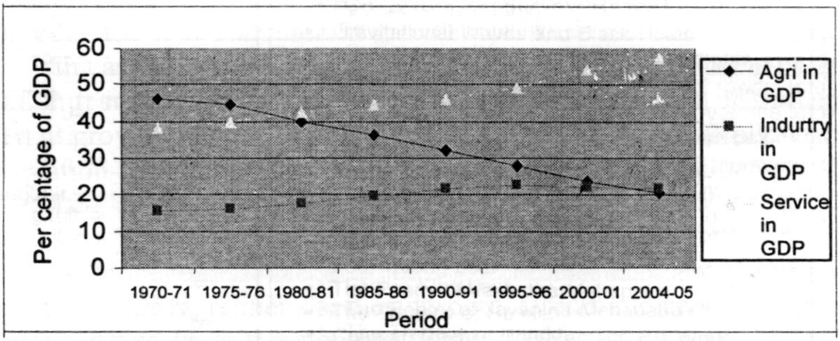


**Fig. 4.4:** Sector-wise Composition of India's GDP

*Source*: Based on data from *Handbook of Indian Statistics* (2001), Reserve Bank of India.

## Economic Reforms and Employment

The creation of employment opportunities has always been an important objective of various development programmes in India. The increasing population and labour force has led to increase in the volume of unemployment and under-employment from one plan period to another. In order to irradiate poverty and all forms of deprivation, the biggest challenge for the country would be to provide employment to a growing workforce. An effort to find out impact of new economic reforms on structure of employment has been made in Table 4.6.

Total employment increased from 302.75 million in 1983 to 397 million in 2000. The rate of employment growth fell from two per cent per annum during 1983-1994, to one per cent per during 1994-2000. The labour force participation rate fell across all age cohorts during 1994-2000, a trend reflected in the deceleration of labour force growth from 2.3 per cent per annum during 1988-1994, to one per cent during 1994-2000. In 2000, organized sector employment has accounted for about 7 per cent of total employment, which reduced from 8 per cent in 1988, largely because of the lack of public sector employment growth. In contrast, organized private sector employment growth accelerated from 0.45 per cent per annum to 1.87 per cent between 1983-94 and 1994-2000.

**Table 4.6:** Employment and Organized Sector Employment

| | *Employment (Million)* | | | | *Growth rate ( per cent per annum)* | |
|---|---|---|---|---|---|---|
| | *1983* | *1988* | *1994* | *1999/2000* | *1983-94* | *1994-2000* |
| Total population | 718.21 | 790.00 | 895.05 | 1004.10 | 2.12 | 1.93 |
| Total labour force | 308.64 | 333.49 | 381.94 | 406.05 | 2.05 | 1.03 |
| Total employment (a) | 302.75 | 324.29 | 374.45 | 397.00 (c) | 2.04 | 0.98 |
| Organized sector | | | | | | |
| Employment (b) | 24.01 | 25.71 | 27.37 | 28.11 | 1.20 | 0.53 |
| Public sector | 16.46 | 18.32 | 19.44 | 19.41 | 1.52 | –0.03 |
| Private sector | 7.55 | 7.39 | 7.93 | 8.70 | 0.45 | 1.87 |

(a) The total employment figures are on UPSS basis.

(b) The organized sector employment figures are as reported in the Employment Market Information System of the Ministry of Labour and pertain to 1st March 1983, 1988, 1994, 1999 and 2000.

(c) The rate of growth of total employment and organized sector employment are compounded rates of growth.

*Source*: 1. Ministry of Finance and Ministry of Labour, Government of India.
2. Economic Editors' Conference, October 17-19, 2001, Planning Commission, Government of India.
3. www.indiastat.com

## Capital Inflows

There had been a considerable rise in foreign capital after getting an opening in the Indian economy. Generally, capital inflows had seen a northward movement. But this rise had been under watch of certain economists. R. Nagraj asserts, "we suspect that a sizeable proportion of FDI represent a rise in, and acquiring of, managerial control in existing firms, effects of which on efficiency are debatable. Such transaction of existing assets by foreign control firm do not represent rise in the economy's output and investment demand. So, the effect of such investment on the real sector is likely to be limited" (Nagraj 1997). Jayati Shah has also noted that "limited foreign investment of the non-portfolio variety that has come into India during the past five years has been oriented to taking advantage of the domestic market rather than export promotion and has often implied simply replacing domestic investment or acquiring domestic assets through increase in shareholding, mergers and acquisition" (Shah, 1998).

As is clear from Table 4.7, foreign investment inflows were merely $ 133 million in 1991-92. These picked up considerably thereafter, as the government took several measures to encourage foreign investment. In 1993-94 itself total foreign investment inflows had exceeded 540 million of which the share of portfolio investment was as high as around $3,500 million. The largest amount of foreign investment inflows were registered in 1996-97 at $ 6,133 million. Total foreign investment inflows in 1997-98 were at $ 5,385 million. However, as can be seen from the table, foreign investment inflows fell drastically in 1998-99 to $ 390 million by foreign institutional investors in 1998-99. The overall outflow on portfolio investment in this year stood at $61 million. However, portfolio investment recovered strongly in 1999-2000 to post a total of $ 3,026 million. The bulk of this increase in portfolio investment was attributable to

**Table 4.7:** Foreign Investment Inflows by Different Category

| | *1991-92* | *1992-93* | *1993-94* | *1996-97* | *1997-98* | *1998-99* | *1999-2000* | *2000-01* |
|---|---|---|---|---|---|---|---|---|
| A. Direct Investment | 129 | 315 | 586 | 2821 | 3557 | 2462 | 2155 | 2339 |
| a. RBI automatic route | 0 | 42 | 89 | 135 | 202 | 179 | 171 | 454 |
| b. SIA/FIB route | 66 | 222 | 280 | 1922 | 2754 | 1821 | 1410 | 1456 |
| c. Non-Resident Indians | 63 | 51 | 217 | 639 | 241 | 62 | 84 | 67 |
| d. Acquisition of shares* | 0 | 0 | 0 | 125 | 360 | 400 | 490 | 362 |
| B. Portfolio Investment | 4 | 244 | 3567 | 3312 | 1828 | -61 | 3026 | 2760 |
| a. Foreign institutional investors** | 0 | 1 | 1665 | 1926 | 979 | -390 | 2135 | 1847 |
| b. Euro Equities and ADRs/GDRs+ | 0 | 240 | 1520 | 1366 | 645 | 270 | 768 | 831 |
| c. Offshore Funds and Others | 4 | 3 | 382 | 20 | 204 | 59 | 123 | 82 |
| TOTAL A + B | 133 | 559 | 4153 | 6133 | 5385 | 2401 | 5181 | 5099 |

* Relates to acquisition of shares of Indian companies by non-residents under Section 29 of FERA.

** Represents fresh inflow/outflow of funds by FIIs.

\+ Figures include Global Depository Receipts and American Depository Receipts amounts raised by the Indian corporate.

*Source*: Government of India, *Economic Survey*, 2001-02 (Delhi, 2002) Table 6.10, p. 154.

higher FII inflows. From a net outflow of $ 390 million in 1998-99. FII investment shot up to mote than $ 2 billion in 1999-2000. As a result although Foreign Direct Investment (FDI) fell from $ 2,462 million in 1998-99 to $ 2,155 million in 1999-2000, the total foreign investment inflows increased considerably from $ 2,401 million in 1998-99 to $ 5,181 million in 1999-2000. The total foreign investment inflows in 2000-01 amounted to $ 5,099 million of which the share of FDI was $ 2,339 million and the share of portfolio investment was $ 2,760 million.

## India's Trade Balance

When we glimpse over the data of India's foreign trade, we find that India's imports are always greater than the exports. Table 4.8 depicts that gap between exports and imports. The gap is rising tremendously over the period.

### *Reforms and Growth of Exports of Goods and Services*

To study the growth rate of exports of goods and services, exports of goods and services at constant price (Rs. crore) is taken. It should be examined over a long period of time in the economy particularly when the growth rate is studied. We have filled the semi log equations to exports of goods and services at constant price over the period 1980-1990 and 1991-2005. The estimated equations are shown in Table 4.9. The trend coefficient of semi log functions for the decade of 1981-90 and 1991-2005 are positive and statistically significant. Thus, it shows that there is a growth in the exports of goods and services during these decades.

The growth rate of exports of goods and services during the period 1980-1990 is found to be 14.92 per cent whereas, it is 17.16 per cent during 1991-2005. It looks like a jump in the growth process. In order to test the acceleration in the growth of exports we tried alternative functional form. The estimates are shown in Table 4.9. The coefficient of semi log quadratic function for the period of 1980-2005 is negative and statistically insignificant. That means there is no acceleration in the growth rate of export of goods and services.

**Table 4.8:** India's Foreign Trade

(Rs. crore)

| Year | Exports | | | Imports | | | Trade balance | | |
|---|---|---|---|---|---|---|---|---|---|
| | Oil | Non-oil | Total | Oil | Non-oil | Total | Oil | Non-oil | Total |
| 1 | 2 | 3 | 4 | 5 | 6 | 7 | 8 | 9 | 10 |
| 1970-71 | 8.56 | 1526.69 | 1535.25 | 135.89 | 1498.31 | 1634.20 | -127.33 | 28.38 | -98.95 |
| 1975-76 | 18.88 | 4017.38 | 4036.26 | 1225.70 | 4039.08 | 5264.78 | -1206.82 | -21.70 | -1228.52 |
| 1980-81 | 24.91 | 6685.80 | 6710.71 | 5263.47 | 7285.68 | 12549.15 | -5238.56 | -599.88 | -5838.44 |
| 1985-86 | 644.72 | 10249.87 | 10894.59 | 4989.39 | 14668.30 | 19657.69 | -4344.67 | -4418.43 | -8763. 10 |
| 1990-91 | 937.80 | 31619.83 | 32557.63 | 10816.11 | 32376.75 | 43192.86 | -9878.31 | -756.92 | -10635.23 |
| 1995-96 | 1517.75 | 104835.59 | 106353.34 | 25173.60 | 97504.54 | 122678.14 | -23655.85 | 7331.05 | -16324.80 |
| 2000-01 | 8541.67 | 195029.34 | 203571.01 | 71496.52 | 159376.24 | 230872.76 | -62954.85 | 35653.10 | -27301.75 |
| 2004-05 | 31404.15 | 343935.38 | 375339.53 | 134094.00 | 366970.54 | 501064.54 | -102689.85 | -23035.16 | -125725.01 |
| 2005-06 | 50979.05 | 403820.92 | 454799.97 | 194640.00 | 435886.77 | 630526.77 | -143660.95 | -32065.85 | -175726.80 |

*Source*: Directorate General of Commercial Intelligence and Statistics.

**Table 4.9:** Growth of Exports of Goods and Services

(*Rs. crore*)

| *Sl. No* | *Year* | *Function* | *Intercept* | $\beta_2$ | $\beta_3$ | $\beta_4$ | $R^2$ | *Growth Rate (%)* |
|---|---|---|---|---|---|---|---|---|
| 1. | 1980-1990 | Log linear | 3.747* (0.0359) | 0.0604* (0.00579) | — | — | 0.9314 | 14.92 |
| 2. | 1991-2005 | Log linear | 4.5356* (0.0244) | 0.06879* (0.00268) | — | — | 0.9805 | 17.16 |
| 3. | 1980-2005 | Log quadratic | 3.6602* (0.04359) | 0.08253* (0.007725) | -0.00022 (0.00028) | — | 0.98728 | — |
| 4. | 1980-2005 (1990-91) | Log linear with dummy | 3.7476* (0.03279) | 0.0604* (0.00528) | 0.10001 (0.0624) | 0.00838 (0.00601) | 0.9937 | — |

*Note*: Value in parenthesis is standard error of the coefficient.
*denotes significant at 5% level.

Source: Directorate General of Commercial Intelligence and Statistics.

In order to study the shift in the growth rate of exports due to presence of globalization, we use the semilog function with dummy variable. The intercept ($\beta_3$) of dummy variable is positive and statistically insignificant. That indicates there is no shift in the growth rate of exports of goods and services with the presence of globalization. But the $\beta_4$ is positive and statistically insignificant. That clearly shows that the trends of growth rate of export of good and services are not changing due to economic reforms.

## *Reforms and Growth of Imports of Goods and Services*

To study the growth rate of imports of goods and services, exports of goods and services at constant price (Rs. crore) is taken. It should be examined over a long period of time in the economy particularly when the growth rate is studied. We have filled the semi log equations to exports of goods and services at constant price (Rs. crore) over the period 1980-1990 and 1991-2005. The estimated equations are shown in Table 4.10. The trend coefficient of semi log functions for the decade of 1980-90 and 1991-2005 are positive and statistically significant. Thus, it shows that there is a growth in the imports of goods and services during these decades.

The growth rate of imports of goods and services during the period 1981-90 is found to be 11.18 per cent whereas, it is 17.86 per cent during 1991-2005. It looks like a relatively high jump in the growth process. In order to test the acceleration in the growth of imports we tried alternative functional form. The estimates are shown in Table 4.10. The coefficient of semi log quadratic function for the period of 1980-2005 is positive and significant at 5 level of significance. That means there is acceleration in the growth rate of imports of goods and services.

**Table 4.10:** Growth of Imports of Goods and Services

(*Rs. crore*)

| Sl. No. | Year | Function | Intercept | $\beta_2$ | $\beta_3$ | $\beta_4$ | $R^2$ | Growth Rate (%) |
|---|---|---|---|---|---|---|---|---|
| 1. | 1980-1990 | Log linear | 4.0232* (0.0239) | 0.04603* (0.003857) | — | — | 0.9468 | 11.18 |
| 2. | 1991-2005 | Log linear | 4.5903* (0.02208) | 0.071378* (0.002429) | — | — | 0.9851 | 17.86 |
| 3. | 1981-2005 | Log quadratic | 3.97039* (0.03482) | 0.05499* (0.00617) | 0.00055* (0.00023) | — | 0.9900 | — |
| 4. | 1981-2005 (1990-91) | Log linear with dummy | 4.0231* (0.02637) | 0.04603* (0.00425) | -0.146* (0.0501) | 0.0253* (0.0048) | 0.9950 | — |

*Note*: Value in parenthesis is standard error of the coefficient.
*denotes significant at 5% level.

*Source*: Directorate General of Commercial Intelligence and Statistics.

In order to study the shift in the growth rate of imports due to presence of globalization, we use the semilog function with dummy variable. The intercept ($\beta_3$) of dummy variable is negative and statistically significant. That indicates there is shift in the growth rate of imports of goods and services with the presence of globalization. And the $\beta_4$ is positive and statistically significant. That clearly shows that the trends of growth rate of imports of good and services are changing due to economic reforms.

## India at a Glance

Indian economy has significantly grown in the recent years. Both social and economic indicators have explained the march for the development of the economy. The important development, social and environmental indicators of India and leading States are shown in Table 4.11. In the economic sector, the growth rate of Gross Domestic Product (GDP) in India is 6.3 for the period 1991-2001, which was 5.8 during 1980-1990. The Per Capita Income is Rs. 10,574 in India in the year 2001 where as it was Rs. 8,187 in the year 1991.

The 2001 census of India shows that the population in India is 102.7 crore. The decadal growth of population (1991-2001) in the country is 21.34 per cent. As far as population density is concerned, the country has 324 persons/ km$^2$, whereas it was 258 persons/ km$^2$ in the year 1991. The literacy rate of India is 65.38 per cent in 2001. But, the decadal (1991-2001) change in literacy rate is only 13.75 per cent point for India as whole. The infant mortality rate is 71 per 1000 births in India during the same. As per 2001 census data, the infant mortality rate in India is 71 per 1000 births. The overall death rate is 8.4 per 1000 persons in the country. As far as birth rate is concerned, it is 25.4 per 1000 persons. This shows that the country has failed to improve its health status.

**Table 4.11:** India at a Glance

| *Indicators* | *1991* | *2001* |
|---|---|---|
| GDP Growth Rate % | 5.8 (1980-90) | 6.3 (1991-01) |
| Per Capita Income | Rs. 8187 | Rs. 10754 |
| Population | 846302000 | 1027015247 |
| Population Growth | 23.67% | 21.34 %(1991-2001) |
| Population Density per sq. km | 254 | 324 |
| Geographical Area (sq. km) | 3287263 | 3287263 |
| Forest Area (sq. km) | 639364 | 765253 (23.28%) GA |
| Degraded Land ('000 Hectares) | — | 172175 |
| Literacy Rate (%) | 52.20 | 65.38 |
| Change in Literacy Rate (% Pt.) | 8.63 | 13.75 |
| Sex Ratio per one thousand | 927 | 933 |
| Infant Mortality Rate | 77 | 71 |
| Birth Rate | 28.9 | 25.4 |
| Death Rate | 8.7 | 8.4 |
| BPL | 35.97 | 26.1 |
| Urbanization Rate | 25.7 | 27.78 |
| HDI | 0.381 | 0.472 |
| Per Capita Consumption of Electricity | 236 (KWH) | 354.75 (KWH) |
| Cropping Intensity | 129.8 | 132.5 |
| % Net Irrigated Area to Net Cultivated Area | 28.0 | 38.8 |
| Fertilizer Use per Hectare in kg. | 75.2 | 102.2 |
| Yield of Food Grain (kg/ Hectare) | 1380 | 1734 |
| Percapita Availability of Food grains kg/yr. | 186.2 | 151.9 |

*Sources*: Computed from madhyapradeshstat.com

The country has introduced many rural development programmes for the eradication of poverty. But, their results are not very encouraging and problem of poverty is still a challenging issue in the country. Around 26.1 population of the country is under the poverty line in 2001. It was 35.97 in the year 1991, which has the worst poverty affected State of the country like Orissa (45.15 %) and Bihar (42.6 %). Almost same is the story in most of the indicators of agricultural development in the country. All these explain the poorness of the country in the socio economic development and have rightly included the category of BIMARU States in it. The food-grain productivity in the country is average of 1734 kgs in 2001, whereas it was 1380 kgs during 1990-91. The overall Human Development Index of India was 0.381 in the year 1991. But it has increased to 0.472 in 2001. The percapita consumption is also increasing day by day. There is also improvement in the percapita availability of food grains in India. Therefore from the above analysis, we can conclude that India's socio-economic performance is improving over the decade.

After two decades of economic reforms the Indian economy is at a crossroads. The reforms programme has yielded considerable returns in the form of higher and more stable growth as well as considerable modernization of the economy. After more than two decades of impressive economic growth and some important reforms as well as deregulation, the Indian economy is at the threshold of even higher growth. However, unforeseen and stubborn challenges have been thrown up especially in the areas of the high fiscal deficit and financial sector weakness, increasing regional and personal inequality, and low elasticity of employment with respect to growth and inadequate infrastructure. Several of these, e.g., inadequate decline in poverty are such that they can be addressed best by high and sustained economic growth. However, these might act as short-term constraints on economic reforms, especially when they play themselves out through the democratic process. This is an important challenge for policymaking in India. The Indian economy is currently showing considerable promise in terms of growth performance. However, success in attaining high and sustained rates of economic growth is not automatically guaranteed.

## NOTES

1. Wallack, Jessica Seddon (2003): 'Structural Breaks in Indian Macro-economic Data', *Economic and Political Weekly*, October 11, pp. 4312-15.
2. Ahluwalia, Isher Judge (1985): *Industrial Growth in India: Stagnation since the Mid-Sixties*, Oxford University Press, Delhi.
3. Virmani, Arvind (2004a): 'India's Economic Growth: From Socialist Rate of Growth to Bharataya Rate of Growth', Working Paper No 122, Indian Council for Research on International Economic Relations, New Delhi, India.

   Virmani, A. (2004b): 'Sources of India's Economic Growth: Trends in Total Factor Productivity', Working Paper No 131, Indian Council for Research on International Economic Relations, New Delhi, India.
4. Rodrik, Dani and Arvind Subramanian (2004): 'From 'Hindu Growth' to Productivity Surge: The Mystery of the Indian Growth Transition', unpublished manuscript, March.
5. Ghosh, Arun "Budget 1997-98 : Underlining NEP," *Economic and Political Weekly,* May 17-23/24-30, 1997, p. 1139.
6. Parikh, Kirit "India's Economy; Raised for take-off," *Economic and Political Weekly,* May 17-23/24-30, 1997, p. 1151.
7. The figures for Bihar, Madhya Pradesh and Uttar Pradesh are not strictly comparable across years because, following 1994-1995, they do not include the regions that have come to constitute the states of Jharkhand, Chhattisgarh and Uttarkhand respectively.
8. Latest available data (RBI 2004) indicates that there has been a further sharp acceleration in the growth rate of real GDP in the second quarter of 2003-04. In the third quarter this reached double-digit levels. All sectors grew sharply. Agriculture recovered smartly from a downturn in 2002-03 on the back of two successive good harvests. The manufacturing and services sector continued their rapid growth. It remains to be seen whether this sharp rise is a temporary blip in the growth trend.
9. The share of agriculture in employment is, however, much higher. One of the current important anomalies in the Indian economy is that a sector that produces 25 per cent of GDP employs 65 per cent of the labour force.

# 5

# Contextualizing Environmental Degradation in India

The subsistence or the deficiency of favourable natural resources can make easy or slow down the process of economic development. According to Professor W.A. Lewis, "the extent of a country's resources is quite obviously a limit on the amount and type of development which it can undergo".[1] J.I. Fisher says, "Underdeveloped countries, embarking on programmes of economic development, usually have to begin with and concentrate on the development of locally available natural resources as an initial condition for lifting local levels of living and purchasing power, for obtaining foreign exchange with which to purchase capital equipment, and for setting in motion the development process".[2] The rapidly growing population and economic development are leading to the environmental degradation in India through the uncontrolled growth of urbanization[3] and industrialization,[4] expansion and massive intensification of agriculture, and the destruction of forests. One of the primary causes of environmental degradation in the country could be attributed to rapid growth of population, which is adversely affecting the natural resources and environment. The uprising population and the environmental deterioration face the challenge of sustainable development.[5]

Another consideration regarding the nature of natural resources is that some resources, e.g. land, water, fisheries and forests, are renewable and there are others like minerals and mineral oils which are exhaustible and can be used only once. Consequently, careful use of the exhaustible resources and maintenance of the quality of renewable resources like land are the principles in the process of development.

## LAND RESOURCES

India faces the most acute pressure on its agricultural land. Today every million hectares of land supports about 7.27 million people. 43 per cent of the land is currently under cultivation; one of the highest in the world. A change in land use pattern implies variation in the proportion of area under different land uses at a point in two or more time periods. Over the past fifty years, while India's total population increased by about 3 times, the total area of land under cultivation increased by only 20.27 per cent from 118,750,000 hectares in 1951 to 142,820,000 hectares in 2001. Most of this expansion has taken place at the expense of forest and grazing land. Despite past expansion of the area under cultivation, less agricultural land is available to feed each and every person in India. Out of total geographical area of 329,000,000 hectares, only 306,000,000 hectares is the reporting area (the rest being unadministered). The land for non-agricultural uses like housing, industry and others is increased from 9,360,000 hectares in 1951 to 22,970,000 hectares in 2001. More than 19,400,000 hectares are snow bound and remote leaving only 237,000,000 hectares for agriculture, forestry, pasture and other biomass production. The area under cultivation had increased by about 30 per cent until 1981 and thereafter declined marginally. The net sown area increased from 119,000,000 hectares in 1950-51 to 140,000,000 hectares in 1970-71 mostly through reclamation of old fallow and culturable wastelands and diversion of groves. The net area sown has increased marginally only from 140,000,000 hectares in 1970-71 to 141,000,000 hectares in 2000-2001, which indicates that the private efforts have peaked.[6]

The extent of agricultural intensification is characterized by increase in cropping and irrigation intensity and higher usage of chemical fertilizers, pesticides and insecticides. Agricultural intensification and intensification is leading to land degradation, over exploitation of underground water resources, increased use of chemical fertilizers leading to eutrophication and water pollution. It has also resulted into water logging, salinization and alkalinization of croplands and eutrophication of water bodies and ill health of oceans and thus reductions in bio-diversity. Appendices 1 and 2 describe the land utilization pattern in India for the period, 1950-51 to 2005-06. The total geographical area of India is about 329 million hectares, but statistical information regarding land classification is available for only about 306 million hectares; this information is based partly on village papers and partly on estimates.

*Barren Land:* The 42.5 million hectares or 13.8 per cent of the total reporting area in India is classified as: (a) Barren land, such as mountains, deserts, etc. which cannot be brought under cultivation, and (b) Area under non-agricultural uses, that is, lands occupied by buildings, roads and railways, rivers and canals, and other lands put to uses other than agricultural in 2005-06, which was 13 and 13.5 per cent in 1990-91 and 2000-01 respectively. In other words, 13.8 per cent of the total reporting area is not available for cultivation. With rapid increase in population and growing urbanization, this percentage would increase over the years. The remaining nearly 86 per cent of the land is put under three major uses, viz. forests, pastures and agriculture. The overall barren land is increasing with slight difference during the period 1950-2006. The area under barren and not available for agriculture is annually decreasing by 0.417 per cent every year from 1950-51 to 2005-06. It is explained in Appendix 3. However, when the rate of growth rate is measured, it is found that accelerating annually.[7]

*Area under Forests:* Appendices 1 and 2 show that 69 million hectares of land or 22.73 per cent of the total land area is under forests. Area under forests includes all land classified as forests by law or administered as forests, whether state owned or private, and whether wooded or maintained as potential forest land. It is increasing in nature. It was 40 million hectares in 1950-51 and increased to 63 million hectares in 1970-71. During 1990-91 it reached at 69 million hectares. Therefore, the forest area is increasing in India over the period of time.

*Pastures and Grazing Land:* Permanent pastures and other grazing lands include all grazing lands such as permanent pastures and meadows and village common land. Appendix 1 shows that 11 million hectares barely 3.5 per cent of the total land area is permanent pastures in 2000-01. It was 12 million hectare (4%) in 1990-91 and in it decreased into 3.4 per cent in 2005-06.

*Culturable Waste Lands:* The culturable waste lands, viz. lands available for cultivation but not cultivated during the previous five or more years. Appendix 1 also includes land under miscellaneous tree crops such as casuarina trees, thatching grasses, bamboo bushes and other groves for fuel, etc. These lands may either be fallow or covered with shrubs and jungles which are not put to any use. Such lands are called culturable waste lands; they account for 16.5 million hectares or 5.3 per cent of the total land area in 2005-06. The data predicts that the culturable waste land was 6.32 per cent in 1990-91 and it declined to 5.5 per cent in 2000-01. However, compound decreasing rate from 1950-51 to 2005-06 is -0.9323 per cent and the rate of decreasing rate is positive. This explains that it is accelerating through period of time (Appendix 3).

*Fallow Lands:* These are culturable and cultivated lands but remain uncultivated or remain fallow during a given year or for some period. Fallow lands are further classified into current fallows and other fallow lands. Current fallows represent cropped areas which are kept fallow during the current year, as, for example, the seeding area may not be cropped in the same year. Other fallow lands include all lands which are taken up for cultivation but are temporarily out of cultivation not less than one year not more than five years. The reasons for keeping such land fallow may be due to unremunerative nature of farming, poverty of the cultivators, inadequate supply of water, malarial conditions, silting of canals and rivers, etc. Land utilization figures (Appendices 1 and 2) show that fallow lands account for 25 million hectares in 2000-01 or constitute 8 per cent of the total reporting area in this country. It was 23 million hectares in 1990-91 (7.5 ) and 24 million hectares in 2005-06 (7.8 per cent).

*Agricultural Land:* Net area sown includes the total area sown with crops and orchards, counting area sown more than once in the same year, only once. Area sowed more than once represents the areas on which crops are cultivated more than once during the agricultural year. Total cropped area represents total area covered with crops and it is the sum total of all the land covered by all the individual crops; area sown with crops more than once during the year being counted as separate areas for each crop. Now, out of the total reported area of 306 million hectares, net area sown is only 140 million hectares or 45.75 per cent of the total land area. The total cropped area in India during 2000-06 was 190 million hectares. It was 185 million hectares in 1990-91 which is 60 per cent of total land area (Appendices 1 and 2).

*Problem of Increasing Cultivable Area:* At the time of Independence, with the partition of the country in 1947, India had the massive problem of achieving self-sufficiency in food. The various "Grow more food" programmes initially aimed at increasing the total cultivable area in the country. As a result, till the beginning of the

1960s, increase in agricultural production was more the result of expansion of cropped area. This was done by turning grazing lands and forest lands into cropped lands; bring cultivable waste lands under the plough, shifting the cropping pattern in such a way as to divert land under fodder crops to food crops and so on. However, as the National Commission on Agriculture (1976) estimated, the net area sown could increase only marginally, say up to 145 million hectares by the year 2001. Actually, the net sown area could be expected to decline, with the relentless growth of population and growing urbanization. Cultivated and cultivable land is in fact, fast disappearing under concrete buildings and tar roads and also good agricultural land is being destroyed to produce bricks for house construction.

The 2001 Census of India estimated India's population at a staggering 1,027 million as on March 1, 2001. Besides, India's population is rising at the rate of around 17 million per year. India has now to support 16.7 per cent of the global population with just 2.4 of the world surface. This necessitates the production of 240 to 250 million tonnes of food grains as against the present 200 million tonnes. Agricultural scientists have always been confident and optimistic that India can meet the challenge, as it has vast land, water and sunlight resources. Most of our land remains under-utilized: un-irrigated, single cropped and low yielding. The possibility of increasing the country's irrigated area is vast. Increased production is possible through multiple cropping. Between 1951 and 2000, area sown more than once had increased from 13 million hectares to 49 million hectares. There is, thus, vast scope for double cropping in India. But the biggest threat to increase agricultural is the growing mismanagement of our soils.

*Soil Degradation:* All India Soil and Land Use Survey under the Department of Agriculture and Co-operation initiated land degradation mapping during the Eighth Five Year Plan allowing for the development of district information system for degraded lands. It has so far covered 30 districts located in diversified agro-climatic zones. It has also developed soil information system. Department of Land Resources, Ministry of Rural Development, Government of India has identified different types of degraded wastelands (Table 5.12).

**Table 5.1:** Extent of Soil Degradation (Human Induced) under Different Degradation Types, 2002

(*in million hectare*)

| *Degradation type* | *Degree of Degradation* | | | | | *% to the geographical Area* |
|---|---|---|---|---|---|---|
| | *Slight* | *Moderate* | *Strong* | *Extreme* | *Total* | |
| *Water Erosion* | 27.3 | 111.6 | 5.4 | 4.6 | 148.9 | 45.3 |
| a. Loss of topsoil (wt) | 27.3 | 99.8 | 5.4 | — | 132.5 | 40.3 |
| b. Terrain (Wd) Deterioration | — | 11.8 | — | 4.6 | 16.4 | 5 |
| *Wind Erosion* | 0.3 | 10.1 | 3.1 | — | 13.5 | 4.1 |
| a. Loss of topsoil (wt) | 0.3 | 5.5 | 0.4 | — | 6.2 | 1.9 |
| b. Loss of topsoil /terrain deterioration (Et/Ed) | — | 4.6 | — | — | 4.6 | 1.4 |
| c. Terrain deformation/over blowing (Ed/Co) | — | — | 2.7 | — | 2.7 | 0.8 |
| *Chemical Deterioration* | 6.5 | 7.3 | — | — | 13.8 | 4.2 |
| a. Loss of nutrient (Cn) | 3.7 | — | — | — | 3.7 | 1.1 |
| b. Salinization (Cs) | 2.8 | 7.3 | — | — | 10.1 | 3.1 |
| Physical Deterioration | — | — | — | — | 16.6 | 3.5 |
| Waterlogging (w) | 6.4 | 5.2 | — | — | 11.6 | 3.5 |
| Total (affected area) | 36.8 | 137.9 | 8.5 | 4.6 | 187.8 | 57.1 |
| Land not fit for agriculture Stable Terrain | | | | | 18.2 | 5.5 |
| Under Natural Condition (Sn) | | | | | 31.2 | 9.8 |
| Total Geographical Area of India | | | | | 328.7 | 100 |

*Source*: Agricultural Research, Data Book 2002.

It is very clear from the above statistics that the land with or without scrub category, which is mainly land affected by soil erosion, records the highest percentage followed by degraded and underutilized forest land. The extent of soil degradation under different degradation types is very significant (Table 5.2). It is measured to 57 per cent of the total geographical area in India. Around 188 million hectares are affected by soil degradation. Out of which 149 million hectares are water erosion. Wind erosion and chemical deterioration are 13.5 per cent and 13.8 million hectares respectively. The physical deterioration is reporting to be 16.6 million hectares. The maximum medium of soil erosion is loss of top soil through water erosion. It is estimated to 132.5 million hectares, approximately 40 per cent of the total geographical area.

**Forest Resources**

Forests are an important natural resource of India. They help control floods and thus they protect the soil against erosion. They supply timber, fuel wood, fodder and a wide range of non-wood products. They are the natural habitat for bio-diversity and repository of genetic wealth. Forests, thus play an important role of environment and economic sustainability. Despite their potential to reduce poverty and contribute to economic growth of India and the significant contribution to local and global environment, forest resources were not given the importance due to them.

*Area under Forest:* Under land utilization pattern, the Government of India estimated the total area under forests as 69 million hectares or 23 per cent of the total geographical area (Appendix 1). Using remote sensing technology, the Forest Survey of India has been periodically assessing the forest cover of the country biennially since 1981. The assessments since 1950-51 show clearly that the forest cover in India had stabilized around 12.3 per cent of the total geographical area (i.e. around 40 million hectares). There is a growth of forest area in India. It was around 20 per cent of total geographical area in 1980-81. In 2005-06, the forest area is nearly 69 million hectare (21.22%), but it was 21.15 per cent of total geographical area in 2000-01.

The State of Forest Report 2003 published by the Forest Survey of India indicates a 2,795 $km^2$ increase in the forest cover in the country over the 2001 assessment. The area under dense forest cover in the 2003 assessment, however, is 26,245 $km^2$ less than in 2001, while mangroves are down by 21 $km^2$ (Table 5.2). But the open forests have increased by 29,040 $km^2$.

Change in any category of forests may be a result of improvement somewhere and degradation elsewhere. A change matrix gives a quantitative estimate of net change category-wise and also the flux of change among the categories. Three major reasons of flux in the change matrix are (i) Degradation of dense forest into open forest, scrub or non-forest, (ii) Improvement of open forest into dense forest

**Table 5.2:** Class-wise Change in Forest Covers (km²)

*(Sq. km)*

| Class | Assessment 1999 | Assessment 2001 | Change 1999-01 | Assessment 2003 | Change 2001-03 |
|---|---|---|---|---|---|
| Dense Forest* | 382229 | 416809 | +34580 | 390564 | -26245 |
| Open Forest | 255064 | 258729 | +3665 | 287769 | +29040 |
| Mangrove | 4871 | 4482 | -389 | 4461 | -21 |
| Total | 637293 | 675538 | +38245 | 678333 | +2774 |

*Including Mangroves.

*Source*: indiastat.com

at some places and its degradation to scrub or non-forest at other, and (iii) Improvement of scrub or non-forest generally into open forest and sparingly to dense forest. No effort to correlate the matrix of change with current policies, practices or programmes have been made. Thus, it is difficult to say how much forest has regenerated due to people's participation in joint forest management or regeneration due to afforestation by governments. The 1999 to 2003 assessments, however, are redeeming in the sense that the past trend of deforestation appears to have been halted.

*Present Status of Forest Resources:* India has a recorded forest area of 76.52 million hectares that is 23.28 per cent of its total geographical area (Appendix 5). The ownership of this forest area rests largely with the Government. It is estimated that 92.47 per cent of the recorded forest area is owned by the Forest Departments, 3.18 per cent by other Government Departments, 2.45 per cent by corporate bodies, and 1.91 per cent by others (Sagreiya, 1994). The total forest area has been classified into three categories, namely Reserved Forests (54.44%), Protected Forests (29.18%), and Unclassed Forests (16.38%). There are 87 National Parks and 485 Wildlife Sanctuaries created for *in situ* conservation of bio-diversity. These National Parks and Wildlife Sanctuaries covering 4.75 per cent (15.60 m ha) of the total geographical area are referred together as Protected Areas (Fig. 5.4).

The network of Protected Areas also include 23 Tiger Reserves spread over 3.30 million hectares overlapping with National Parks and Wildlife Sanctuaries. There are 11 Biosphere Reserves with an area of 4.76 million hectares part of which goes even beyond Protected

Areas (GOI, 2003). The post-independence experience has shown that both extent and quality of forest cover have deteriorated in India. It has been estimated that the actual forest cover of the country is only 19.39 of its total geographical area as against the recorded forest area as 23.28 of the total geographical area. In terms of the quality of the forest cover, only 59 per cent of the actual forest cover of the country is in the form of dense forests. The rest of the forest cover consists of open forests and mangroves. Over the years, a large area of forest land has been formally converted to non-forest use. The size of such converted land is reported as 5760.90 sq. km upto 31st October, 2002 (Appendix 6 for details). Further, a total of 13569.44 sq. km forest land is reported as encroached. It is also clearly shown in Fig. 5.2.

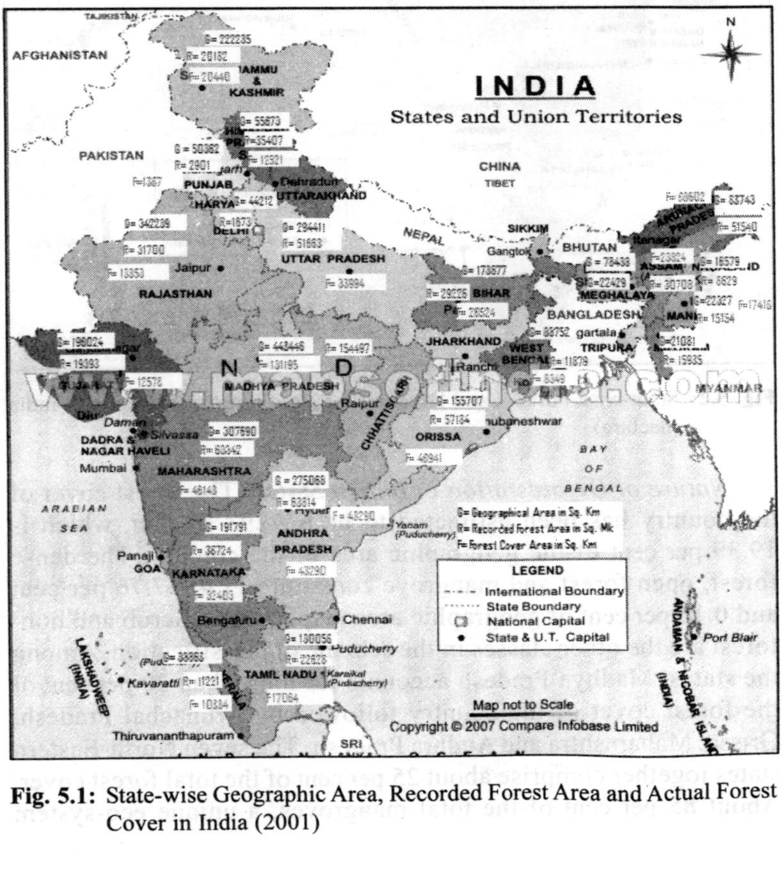


**Fig. 5.1:** State-wise Geographic Area, Recorded Forest Area and Actual Forest Cover in India (2001)

**Fig. 5.2:** State-wise Forest Land Diverted for Non-Forestry Purposes in India (hectare)

*Nature of Deforestation in Indian States:* The forest cover of the country has been estimated to be 637293 sq. km, which is 19.39 per cent of the geographic area of the country. The dense forest, open forest and mangrove constitute 11.48, 7.76 per cent and 0.15 per cent of geographic area respectively. Scrub and non-forest are the other classes in the scheme of classification. Among the states, Madhya Pradesh accounts for more than 20 per cent of the forest cover of the country followed by Arunachal Pradesh, Orissa, Maharashtra and Andhra Pradesh. The seven North-Eastern states together comprise about 25 per cent of the total forest cover. About 85 per cent of the total mangroves, a unique eco-system occurring in inter tidal regions are in West Bengal, Gujarat and Andaman and Nicobar Islands. Thus in India, the forest area presents a diversity in its composition. The overall forest cover has declined from 22 in 1990-91 to 19.4 per cent of total geographical area in 2000-01, declined at the rate of 0.26 per cent per annum (Table 5.3).

**Table 5.3:** Forest Area and Deforestation Rate in Indian States

| *Sl. No.* | *States* | *Forest Cover (%)* | *Deforestation Rate (%) (1991 to 2001)* |
|---|---|---|---|
| 1. | Andhra Pradesh | 16.23 | 23.51 |
| 2. | Assam | 35.33 | -39.7 |
| 3. | Arunachal Pradesh | 81.25 | -32.1 |
| 4. | Bihar | 6.07 | 2.98 |
| 5. | Gujarat | 7.73 | 19.49 |
| 6. | Haryana | 3.97 | -3.79 |
| 7. | Himachal Pradesh | 25.79 | -55. |
| 8. | Karnataka | 19.29 | -20.8 |
| 9. | Kerala | 40.04 | -43.9 |
| 10. | Madhya Pradesh | 25.07 | 4.51 |
| 11. | Maharashtra | 15.43 | 11.25 |
| 12. | Manipur | 75.81 | -181.0 |
| 13. | Meghalaya | 69.48 | -91.9 |
| 14. | Orissa | 31.36 | 12.38 |
| 15. | Punjab | 4.83 | -10.5 |
| 16. | Rajasthan | 4.78 | 27.19 |
| 17. | Tripura | 7.38 | -16.6 |
| 18. | Tamil Nadu | 16.52 | -2.74 |
| 19. | Uttar Pradesh | 5.71 | 26.58 |
| 20. | Jammu & Kashmir | 9.56 | 22.69 |
| 21. | West Bengal | 12.05 | 1.98 |

Note: As computed by Author.
*Source*: http://www.Indiastat.com

It is a matter of surprise that India is showing mixed experience of deforestation. When we glimpse over the trend of deforestation rate in different major states of India, we find during the period 1990-91 to 2000-01, some states like Rajasthan has shown highest rate of deforestation. Its forest area has declined by 27.19 during 1990-2001. In this period the other major states where greater deforestation rate is found are Uttar Pradesh (26.58%), Andhra Pradesh

(23.51%), Jammu & Kashmir (22.69%) and Gujarat (19.49% ). The states like Orissa and Maharashtra are also showing rate of deforestation as 12.25 per cent and 11.25 per cent respectively. Some states such as West Bengal (1.98%), Madhya Pradesh (4.51%) have shown very low degree of deforestation during the period of study. On the other hand the states like Manipur, Kerala, Assam, Arunachal Pradesh, Tamil Nadu, Meghalaya, Haryana, Himachal Pradesh, Karnataka etc. are showing afforestation. The rate of afforestation is highest in Manipur (181%) and lowest (27.4%) in Tamil Nadu during this period (Fig. 5.3). The positive figures show deforestation rate and negative figures show afforestation rate in the states of India.

**Fig. 5.3:** Deforested and Afforested Sates of India (%age)

*Water Resources of India:* Latest assessment in 1993 (MOWR 2002) indicates that out of total precipitation of approximately 4000 billion cubic metre (BCM) in the country, availability of water from surface and ground sources together account for 1869 BCM. About 60 of the available water, 690 BCM from surface water and 432 BCM from ground sources are usable. India is criss-crossed by network of numerous rivers broadly categorized as Himalayan, Peninsular, Coastal and Inland rivers. India faces an acute water stressed situation due to the tremendous growing pressure from various sectors ranging from agriculture to industry. Its water stressed economy is slowly becoming a water scarce economy. Ironically, we still use such a precious resource inefficiently. The maintenance of water quality is a Herculean task which beckons us. To meet these challenges, the country has taken up several positive steps through formulation of national policies and regulatory frameworks, its implementation along with establishment of monitoring networks, data analysis and dissemination of information.

However, the urban population is rising fast. Respectively, the waste water generation is also growing at an increasing trend. The waste water generation was 7007 mld in 1977 and per capita waste water generation was 116 litre per day which increased to 12145 mld in 1989-90 (119 Litres/Capita/Day) (Table 5.5). In 1994-95 it became 16662 mld which is 130 Litres/Capita/Day. It is assumed that it will reach at 59048 mld in 2021 and at 132253 mld (i.e. 121 Litres/Capita/ Day) in 2051.

**Table 5.5:** Projected Population and Respectively Wastewater Generation in India

| *Year* | *Urban Population* | *Litres/Capita/Day (lpcd)* | *Gross Wastewater Generation (mld)* |
|---|---|---|---|
| 1977-78 | 60 | 116 | 7007 |
| 1989-90 | 102 | 119 | 12145 |
| 1994-95 | 128 | 130 | 16662 |
| 2001 | 285 | — | — |
| 2011 | 373 | — | — |
| 2021 | 488 | 121 (Assumed) | 59048 (Projected) |
| 2031 | 638 | 121 (Assumed) | 77198 (Projected) |
| 2041 | 835 | 121 (Assumed) | 101035 (Projected) |
| 2051 | 1093 | 121 (Assumed) | 132253 (Projected) |

*Source*: Ministry of Environment & Forests, Government of India.

*Water Use in India:* In India, the use of water is generally categorized as abstractive and instream use. The abstractive uses include domestic water supply, irrigation and industrial use. It has been reported (CPCB, 2003) that during 1990, nearly 25 BCM of water was used for domestic purposes (Table 5.6). However, 85 per cent of population depends upon groundwater as a source of domestic water (Fig. 5.4). For irrigation, a total of 460 BCM per annum is used and about 10 BCM per year is used in industry sector as process water and 30 BCM per year as cooling water. It has been estimated that the water demand will shoot up to 770, 52 and 120 BCM for irrigation, domestic supply and industrial process water respectively during the year 2025.

Among instream uses, hydropower, fisheries, navigation, community bathing and washing, etc. are some of the common uses. Nearly140 BCM of groundwater is abstracted annually for use in irrigation. Industrial demand for groundwater is also high due to close proximity and low cost. Overall 85 per cent of India's population is dependent on groundwater for their daily requirements.

**Table 5.6:** Water use in India (Year 2000)

| *Sector* | *Water use in BCM* | *Per cent* |
|---|---|---|
| Irrigation | 541 | 85.33 |
| Domestic | 42 | 6.62 |
| Industry | 8 | 1.26 |
| Energy | 2 | 0.32 |
| Other | 41 | 6.47 |
| Total | 634 | 100.00 |

*Source*: www. Indiastat.com

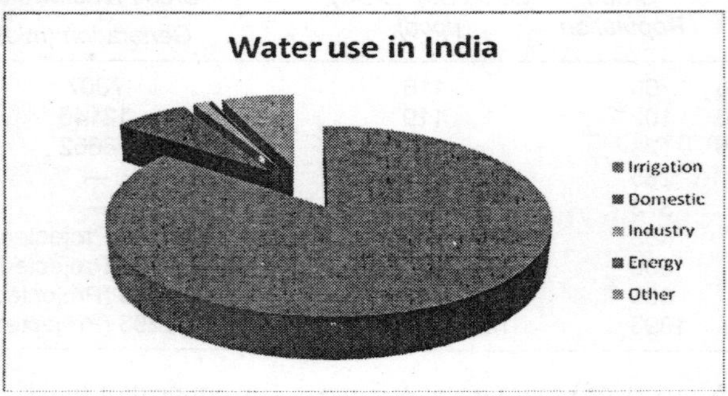


**Fig. 5.4:** Sector-wise water use in India

In 1990, the 53 million hectare metres were used for all sectors of the economy, out of which 46, 2.5, 1.5 and 3 million hectare metres were used in agriculture, domestic and live stock, industry and thermal power sector (see Table 5.7). In 2000, it increased to 75 million hectare metres, out of which agriculture sector consumed 63 million hectare metres. It is expected that 112 million hectare metres will be consumed in 2050 as population may increase to 1700 million in India.

**Table 5.7:** Sector-wise Present Water-use and Future Requirement (During 1990-2050)

| *Year* | *Population (million)* | *Sector-wise Water Use and Future Requirements (million hectare-metres)* | | | | |
|---|---|---|---|---|---|---|
| | | *Irrigation* | *Domestic and Livestock* | *Industry* | *Thermal Power* | *Total* |
| 1990 | 800 | 46 | 2.5 | 1.5 | 3 | 53 |
| 2000 | 1000 | 63 | 3.4 | 3.6 | 5 | 75 |
| 2025 | 1400 | 77 | 5 | 12 | 16 | 110 |
| 2050 | 1700 | 70 | 6 | 20 | 16 | 112 |

*Note*: Figures on population, past water use and future water requirements are approximate.

*Source*: Urban Statistics, Hand Book 2000, National Institute of Urban Affairs.

India is one of the wettest countries in the world, with average annual rainfall of 1100 millimetre. There is, however, no accurate information about India's water resources. Narottam Shah of the Bombay-based Centre for Monitoring Indian Economy, stated: "Unbelievable as it may seem, till now we have no arrangements in this country to compile and publish on an annual basis, comprehensive data regarding various aspects of water which are important for policy analysis and programme formulation for monitoring the efficiency of use of our scarce water resources." B.S. Nag and G.N. Kathpalia made an estimate of water resources of India for the National Commission on Agriculture. Their estimate is summarized in Table 5.8.

The total rainfall for 1974 and 2025 is estimated at 400 million hectare metres and this is distributed in three important ways: 70 million hectare meters evaporates immediately; 215 million hectare metres percolate into the soil and help soil moisture and recharge groundwater; and finally, 115 million hectare metres runoff into surface water bodies like rivers. Water actually utilized was 38 million

**Table 5.8:** Annual Water Resources of India, 1974 and 2025

| | Year (million hectare metres) | |
|---|---|---|
| | *1974* | *2025* |
| Total precipitation | 400 | 400 |
| a. Immediate Evaporation | 70 | 70 |
| b. Run-off to surface water bodies | 115 | 115 |
| c. Percolation into the soil water utilization | 215 | 215 |
| Water utilization | 38 | 105 |
| Of which, groundwater contributes | 13 | 35 |
| Surface flows | 25 | 70 |

*Source*: The State of India's Environment (1984-85), The Second Citizen's Report, Centre for Science and Environment.

hectare metres in 1974, which is expected to rise to 105 million hectare metres by the year 2025. It has been estimated that irrigation accounts for 92 per cent of the water utilization and domestic and industrial uses account for the balance 8 per cent. With the growth of population and the increase in demand for products of agriculture and industries, the demand for water will continually rise.

Scientists have attempted to estimate the maximum degree of exploitation of the annual precipitation. These estimates range from 86 million hectare metres to 105 million hectare metres. Even the maximum use of water supply of 105 million hectare metres by the year 2025 will be inadequate to meet the water demand of the country. Some authorities like Professor Chaturvedi of the Indian Institute of Management, New Delhi, predicted a state of nationwide inadequacy of water even by the year 1995. Acute water shortages are being experienced year after year by most parts of Tamil Nadu including the city of Chennai, Rajasthan, Gujarat, Orissa, etc. The problem of water scarcity is assuming crisis proportions with growth of cities and increasing urban population and rising demand for water for irrigation.

Water is one of the most abundant compounds found on the earth. However, water is a scarce and precious commodity. Although, India receive on an average 1050 mm of rainfall, but the rainfall is unevenly distributed with time and space. Thus, many areas in the country face water scarcity. Due to increasing demand for water, our water resources are over-exploited resulting in lowering of water table and rendered many rivers dry in non-monsoon season. This has a serious impact on water quality. To reduce the over exploitation of water,

water conservation is very important for our country. Several measures can be adopted to reduce the water consumption in agriculture, industries and in domestic use.

## Air Pollution

Air pollution is considered into the atmosphere of chemicals, particulate matter, or biological materials that cause harm or discomfort to humans or other living organisms, or damages the environment. Air pollution is often identified with major stationary sources, but the greatest source of emissions is mobile sources, mainly automobiles. Gases such as carbon dioxide, which contribute to global warming, have recently gained recognition as pollutants by climate scientists, while they also recognize that carbon dioxide is essential for plant life through photosynthesis. The atmosphere is a complex, dynamic natural gaseous system that is essential to support life on planet Earth. Stratospheric ozone depletion due to air pollution has long been recognized as a threat to human health as well as to the Earth's ecosystems.

Air pollution in India has been aggravated over the years by developments that typically occur as economies become industrialized; growing cities, increasing traffic, rapid economic development and industrialization, and higher levels of energy consumption. In India, air pollution is restricted mostly to urban areas, where automobiles are the major contributors, and to a few other areas with a concentration of industries and thermal power plants. The major sources of air pollution in the country are industries (toxic gases), thermal power plants (fly ash and sulphur dioxide), and motor vehicles (carbon monoxide, particulate matter, hydrocarbons and oxides of nitrogen). Major polluting industries and automobiles emit tonnes of pollutants everyday, putting citizens at great health risk. The incidence of respiratory diseases in most of the major cities in India has also increased considerably over the years. In a study of 2031 children and adults in five major cities of India, of the 1852 children tested, 51.4 had levels of lead in their blood above 10 μg/dl. The percentage of children having 10 μg/dl or higher lead levels ranged from 39.9 per cent in Bangalore to 61.8 per cent in Mumbai. Among the adults, 40.2 per cent had lead levels of about 10 μg/dl (George Foundation, 1999,[8] cited in CPCB, 2000a.[9]).

It is an issue of prime concern since these emissions are from ground level sources and thus have the greatest impact on the health of the population exposed to it. The increase in the number of vehicles contributes significantly to the total air pollution load in many urban areas. The number of motor vehicles in India has increased from 0.3 million in 1951 to 40.94 million in 1998 (MoST, 2000).[10] CO (Carbon monoxide) and HC (hydrocarbons) respectively account for 64 per cent and 23 of the total emission load due to vehicles in all cities considered together (CPCB, 1995).[11] Apart from the concentration of vehicles in urban areas, other reasons for increasing vehicular pollution include the types of engines used, age of vehicles, poor road conditions, outdated automotive technologies, poor fuel quality and traffic congestion resulting from clumsy traffic management systems.

*Increase in Urban Population:* Between 1951 and 1991, the urban population has tripled, from 62.4 million to 217.6 million, and its proportion has increased from 17.3 per cent to 25.7 per cent. Nearly two-third of the urban population is concentrated in 317 class I cities (population of over 100,000), half of which lives in 23 metropolitan areas with population exceeding 1 million.[12] The number of urban agglomerations/cities with population of over one million has increased from 5 per cent in 1951 to 9 per cent in 1971 and 23 per cent in 1991 (Pachauri and Sridharan, 1998).[13] This rapid increase in urban population has resulted in unplanned urban development, increase in consumption patterns and higher demands for transport, energy, other infrastructure, thereby leading to pollution problems.

*Increase in Number of Vehicles:* The number of motor vehicles has increased from 0.3 million in 1951 to 21.1 million in 2003 (indiastat.com).[14] Out of these, 32 per cent are concentrated in 23 metropolitan cities. Delhi itself accounts for about 20 per cent of the total registered vehicles and has more registered vehicles than those in the other three metros (Mumbai, Calcutta, and Chennai) taken together (Appendix 4). At the all-India level, the percentage of two-wheeled vehicles in the total number of motor vehicles increased from 9 per cent in 1951 to 70 per cent in 2003. This clearly points to a tremendous increase in the share of personal transport vehicles.

*Increase in Industrial Activity:* India has made rapid strides in industrialisation, and it is one of the ten most industrialised nations of the world. But this status, has brought with it unwanted and unanticipated consequences such as unplanned urbanisation, pollution and the risk of accidents. The CPCB (Central Pollution Control Board) has identified seventeen categories of industries (large and medium scale) as significantly polluting and the list includes highly air polluting industries such as integrated iron and steel, thermal power plants, copper/zinc/aluminium smelters, cement, oil refineries, petrochemicals, pesticides and fertiliser units. The state-wise distribution of these pre-1991 industries indicates that the states of Maharashtra, Uttar Pradesh, Gujarat, Andhra Pradesh and Tamil Nadu have a large number of industries in these sectors. The category-wise distribution of these units reveals that sugar sector has the maximum number of industries, followed by pharmaceuticals, distillery, cement and fertilizer. The status of pollution control as on 30 June, 2000 is as follows: out of 1,551 industries, 1,324 have so far been provided the necessary pollution control facilities, 165 industries have been closed down and the remaining 62 industries are defaulters (CPCB, 2000a). Small scale industries are a special feature of the Indian economy and play an important role in pollution. India has over 3 million small scale units accounting for over 40 per cent of the total industrial output in the country (CII and SII, 1996).[15] In general, Indian small scale industries lack pollution control mechanisms. While the larger industries are better organised to adopt pollution control measures, the small scale sector is poorly equipped (both financially and technically) to handle this problem. They have a very high aggregate pollution potential. Also, in many urban centres, industrial units are located in densely populated areas, thereby affecting a large number of people.

*Increase in Power Generation:* Since 1950-51, the electricity generation capacity in India has multiplied 55 times from a meagre 1.7 thousand MW to 93.3 thousand MW (MoF, 2000).[16] The generating capacity in India comprises a mix of hydro, thermal, and nuclear plants. Since the early seventies, the hydro-thermal capacity mix has changed significantly with the share of hydro in total capacity declining from 43 per cent in 1970-71 to 24 per cent in 1998-99. Thermal power constitutes about 74 per cent of the total installed power generation capacity. However, increasing reliance on this source of energy leads to many environmental problems. The increased dependence of the power sector on an inferior quality coal has been associated with emissions from power plants in the form of particulate matter, toxic elements, fly ash, oxides of nitrogen, sulphur and carbon besides ash, which required vast stretches of land for disposal.

The World Bank (1996) study shows that pollution is concentrated among a few industrial sub-sectors and that a sector's contribution to pollution is often disproportionate to its contribution to industrial output. For example, petroleum refineries, textiles, pulp and paper, and industrial chemicals produce 27 per cent of the industrial output but contribute 87 per cent of sulphur emissions and 70 per cent of nitrogen emissions from the industrial sector. Likewise, iron and steel, and non-metallic mineral products produce about 16 per cent of the industrial output but account for 55 per cent of the particulate emissions.

*Air Quality Profile:* In order to determine the air quality status and trends, assess health hazards, disseminate air quality data, and to control and regulate pollution, the CPCB (Central Pollution Control Board) initiated a nationwide framework of NAAQM (National Ambient Air Quality Monitoring) in 1984 with 28 stations at 7 cities. Presently, the network has 290 monitoring stations in 92 cities and towns throughout the country (CPCB, 1998). The pollutants being monitored are mainly SPM (suspended particulate matter), $SO_2$ (sulphur dioxide) and oxides of nitrogen. SPM is one of the most critical pollutants in terms of its impact on air quality and is also the most common pollutant across all sectors. The ranges of SPM concentration (annual average) in the major metropolitan cities in India are shown in Table 5.9.

**Table 5.9:** Range of Annual Averages of SPM in Major Indian Cities

| *Sl. No.* | *City* | *Area Land Use* | *Range of annual average of SPM (µg/m³) 1990-98* | | *Mean of annual average (µg/m³)* |
|---|---|---|---|---|---|
| | | | *Minimum* | *Maximum* | |
| 1. | Delhi | Residential | 300 | 409 | 355 |
| | | Industrial | 314 | 431 | 381 |
| 2. | Mumbai | Residential | 196 | 327 | 230 |
| | | Industrial | 150 | 276 | 224 |
| 3. | Kolkata | Residential | 205 | 491 | 327 |
| | | Industrial | 286 | 640 | 434 |
| 4. | Chennai | Residential | 72 | 118 | 99 |
| | | Industrial | 53 | 147 | 123 |
| 5. | Bangalore | Residential | 60 | 239 | 158 |
| | | Industrial | 99 | 153 | 125 |
| 6. | Ahmedabad | Residential | 198 | 316 | 261 |
| | | Industrial | 201 | 306 | 243 |
| 7. | Hyderabad | Residential | 135 | 184 | 158 |
| | | Industrial | 72 | 259 | 153 |

*Source*: CPCB 2000a

As against to the maximum permissible limits laid down by CPCB for annual average concentration of SPM in ambient air—70 $mg/m^3$ in sensitive areas, 140 $mg/m^3$ in residential areas and 360 $mg/m^3$ in industrial areas, it is clearly evident that the SPM levels are high in most of the metropolitan cities in India.

*Carbon Emissions:* In 2001, India, with 251 million metric tonnes of carbon equivalent emitted, ranked fifth in the world in carbon emission, behind the United States, China, Russia and Japan. Although India's carbon emission stood at only 80 per cent of Japan's (316 million metric tonnes of carbon equivalent) total and less than one-sixth of the United States' (1,565 million metric tonnes) carbon emission that same year, the rapid growth of India's carbon emissions—in combination with its exclusion from the Protocol—is the main point of controversy.[17] The rise in India's carbon emission has been exacerbated by the low energy efficiency of coal-fired power plants in the country. With the high capital cost associated with replacing existing coal-fired plants, a scarcity of capital, and the long lead time required to introduce advanced coal technologies, it stands to reason that many of India's highly-polluting coal-fired power plants will have to remain in operation for the next couple of decades.

According to Environmental Standards for Ambient Air, Automobiles, Fuels, Industries and Noise, Central Pollution Control Board, Ministry of Environment and Forests, the carbon emission in India is increasing very fast. The rising trend of carbon emission is lesser during 1990-91 to 2004-05 as compared to 1980-81 to 1989-90. The annual compound growth rate is 7.1 per cent during 1980-81 to 1989-90 (Table 5.10). During the same period it is accelerating as coefficient of time square is positive. But the growth rate is 4.7 per cent during 1990-91 to 2004-05. It is lesser than that of in previous decade. It is a positive sign that it is decelerating in this period.

As such, India's contribution to world carbon emission is expected to increase in coming years, with an estimated average annual growth rate between 2001 and 2025 of 3.0 per cent in the EIA International Energy Outlook 2003 reference case (compared to 3.4 per cent in China and 1.5 per cent in the United States). The absolute increase in emissions will partially be a function of the degree to which coal is relied upon as a major energy source. If coal consumption is substituted by oil and natural gas consumption, India's overall carbon emission would be reduced. India's per capita carbon emissions are relatively low at 0.25 metric tonnes of carbon per person in 2001;

India's per capita carbon emission was less than one-quarter of the world average and 22 times less than the United States. However, the country's per capita carbon emission is expected to increase in the coming years due to the rapid pace of urbanization, a conversion away from non-commercial towards commercial fuels, increased vehicular usage and the continued use of older and more inefficient coal-fired plants. In fact, due to fast-paced industrialization, per capita emission is expected to triple by 2020.[18]

**Table 5.10:** Compound Growth Rate of Carbon Emission from 1980-81 to 2004-05

| *Source* | *Function* | *Intercept ($\beta_1$)* | $\beta_2$ | $\beta_3$ | $R^2$ | *Grow Rate* |
|---|---|---|---|---|---|---|
| Carbon Emission from 1980-81 to1989-90 | Log Linear | 4.945905* | 0.029808* | | 0.997534 | 7.10 |
| | Log Quadratic | 4.951693* | 0.026914* | 0.000263* | 0.998031 | |
| Carbon Emission from 1990-91 to 2004-05 | Log Linear | 5.268089* | 0.020158* | | 0.9758 | 4.75 |
| | Log Quadratic | 5.234031* | 0.032179* | -0.00075* | 0.995838 | |

*Note*: *Denotes significant at 1% level.

*Source*: Environmental Standards for Ambient Air, Automobiles, Fuels, Industries and Noise, Central Pollution Control Board, Ministry of Environment and Forests.

*Solid Waste Generation:* There has been a significant increase in MSW (municipal solid waste) generation in India in the last few decades. This is largely because of rapid population growth and economic development in the country. Solid waste management has become a major environmental issue in India. The per capita of MSW generated daily in India ranges from about 100 g in small towns to 500 g in large towns.[19] Although, there is no National level data for MSW generation, collection and disposal, and increase in solid waste generation, over the years, it can be studied for a few urban centres. For example, the population of Mumbai grew from around 8.2 million in 1981 to 12.3 million in 1991, registering a growth of around 49 per cent. On the other hand, MSW generated in the city increased from 3200 tonnes per day to 5355 tonnes per day in the same period registering a growth of around 67 per cent (CPCB, 2000).[20] This clearly indicates that the growth in MSW in our urban centres has outpaced the population growth in recent years. This trend can be ascribed to our changing lifestyles, food habits, and change in living standards. MSW in cities is collected by respective municipalities and transported to designated disposal sites, which are normally low lying areas on the outskirts of the city.

Therefore, it may be concluded that India is facing a number of important challenges in terms of its environment. These include climate and atmospheric change, species loss, degradation of ecosystems and depletion of renewable natural resources. To a great extent, these challenges are driven by human activity in terms of consumption patterns, production processes and waste disposal.

## NOTES

1. Lewis, W.A., *The Theory of Economic Growth,* Allen and Unwin, p. 52.
2. J.I. Fisher, The Role of Natural Resources in *Economic Development: Principles and Patterns* (Eds.) H.F. Williamson and J.A. Buttrick, 1964. p. 32.
3. It is the physical growth of urban areas as a result of population in-migration to an existing urban area. Effects include change in density and administration services. While the exact definition and population size of urbanized areas varies among different countries, urbanization is attributed to growth of cities. *Urbanization and Global Change*. University of Michigan (2006-01-04).
4. It is a process of social and economic change whereby a human group is transformed from a pre-industrial society into an industrial one. It is a part of a wider modernisation process, where social change and economic development are closely related with technological innovation, particularly with the development of large-scale energy and metallurgy production. Industrialization also introduces a form of philosophical change, where people obtain a different attitude towards their perception of nature.
5. It is a pattern of resource use that aim to meet human needs while preserving the environment so that these needs can be met not only in the present, but in the indefinite future. The term was used by the Brundtland Commission which coined what has become the most often-quoted definition of sustainable development as development that "meets the needs of the present without compromising the ability of future generations to meet their own needs."
6. Department of Agriculture and Cooperation, Ministry of Agriculture, 2002
7. Linear and quadratic regression model is applied to find out this result. It is well explained in methodology part.
8. George Foundation (1999). 'Project Lead Free: A study of Lead poisoning in Major Indian cities'. International Conference on Lead Poisoning, Prevention and Treatment (Proceedings), 8-9 February, 1999, Bangalore.

9. CPCB (2000a). 'Polluting industries'. *Parivesh Newsletter* 2000, Delhi: Central Pollution Control Board.
10. MoST (2000). *Handbook on Transport Statistics in India (1999)*. New Delhi: Transport Research Wing, Ministry of Surface Transport.
11. CPCB (1995) 'Air pollution and its control'. *Parivesh Newsletter* 2(1), June 1995. Delhi: Central Pollution Control Board. 20 p.
12. India: State of Environment, (2001), published by United Nations Environment Programme, 2001.
13. Pachauri, R.K. and Sridharan, P.V. (1998) *Looking Back to Think Ahead: Growth with Resource Enhancement of Environment and Nature*. New Delhi: Tata Energy Research Institute. 346 p.
14. Ministry of Shipping, Road Transport and Highways, Govt. of India.
15. CII; SII. (1996) *India: an emerging environmental market—a handbook for trade and business opportunities*. New Delhi: Confederation of Indian Industry and Sanders International, Inc. 78pp.
16. MoF (2000). *Economic Survey (1999-2000)*. New Delhi: Economic Division, Ministry of Finance.
17. http://www.eia.doe.gov/emeu/cabs/indiaenv.html
18. *India: Environmental Issues*, 2001. http://www.eia.doe.gov/emeu/cabs/indiaenv.html
19. Shaleen Singhal and Sunil Pandey, *Solid Waste Management in India, Status and Future Directions*, TERI, Darbari Seth Block, Habitat Place, Lodhi Road, New Delhi.
20. CPCB (Central Pollution Control Board). (2000). *Management of Municipal Solid Waste*, Delhi Central Pollution Control Board.

# 6

# Trade-off between Economic Development and Environmental Degradation

The present chapter evaluates the trade-off between economic development and environmental degradation in India. The analysis is based on cross-state data on forest degradation and the level of economic development. It also examines the factors that affect environmental degradation. The study highlights that the rate of deforestation is not uniform in all Indian states since their response to the policy of forest appreciation varies. The trade-off between the level of electricity consumption and forest degradation in India supports the 'Environmental Kuznets Curve' (EKC) hypothesis. Neither social factors like literacy and growth of population, nor economic factors like urbanization and production of milk are responsible for forest degradation in India. To some extent the degree of deforestation can be explained by the consumption of electricity and forest cover. Economic development can thus overcome environmental degradation in India. An effective policy intervention by the government is essential to protect the environment in a liberalized economy.

The effect of economic development on environmental quality is much under dispute. It is interesting to note that poverty, population growth and environmental degradation are closely inter-related. That is, there is a mutual and spiralling relationship between poverty and environmental degradation. Environmental degradation and poverty reinforce each other: the poor are both agents and victims of environmental destruction. An increasing population leads to more intense use of land, shorter fallow periods and lower soil productivity. Further, it leads to more clearing of forest cover and hill sides. As a result, there are people who can no longer gain a secure livelihood in their homelands because of drought, soil erosion, desertification, deforestation and other environmental problems, together with associated problems of population pressures and profound poverty. Rapid economic growth is a necessary condition for eradication of environmental degradation problems. However, fast economic growth is often accompanied by adverse environmental consequences. While the linkage between economic growth and poverty reduction is generally obvious, the relationship between economic growth and improvement in the environment remains unclear. Thus, we can say that environmental regeneration is not about planting trees but about the deepening of democracy in societies. In recent times, the fast economic growth in many countries, including developing countries of the Asian and Pacific region, where two-third of the world's poor live, has often been accompanied by a range of adverse environmental impacts. Food, fuel, animal feed, building materials like timber and thatch, medicinal herbs and other such needs are largely met through locally available biomass resources or people survive within a biomass-based subsistence economy, that is, on products obtained from plants and animals. Apparently, there is a trade-off between economic growth and environmental improvement; achieving both of these goals simultaneously may not be easy, especially in the early stages of development.

Environmental degradation, therefore, has a serious impact on the lives of rural people. A large portion of the world's rural poor today live in highly degraded lands in China, South Asia, Africa and Latin America. For such people, improvements in the gross nature product are far more important than the gross national product. The poor do what is within their ability to conserve the environment and to make sustainable use of it. But they are caught in a daily struggle to survive and cannot invest in the rebuilding of the 'natural capital'. The 'economic globalisation' process is expected to leave a lot of these people untouched. The climate instability predicted for the twenty first century will make life even more difficult for the world's rural poor living in degraded lands.

Consequently, environmental degradation occurs when there is a decline in the quality of natural environment, in particular of air, water and land. The adverse impact of environmental degradation is increasingly being felt. The loss of forest cover, increase in water and air pollution influence the climate, which in turn results in the loss of bio-diversity. It is in this context that the policy for environmental degradation needs a paradigm change. It needs to be built on the mobilisation of local natural and human capital in which the poor are not the objects but the subjects of economic development. There is evidence that economic growth is generally associated with higher emission rates of carbon dioxide, the main anthropogenic greenhouse gas. This suggests that a trade-off might exist between raising average living standards and controlling global warming. In other words, the world is facing a trade-off between climate control and social equality.

Many recent studies have explored the relationship between economic development and environmental quality. Empirical evidence from different studies conducted by the World Bank (1992), Shafik (1994), Holtz-Eakin and Selden (1995) have shown cross-country comparisons and suggested that economic growth in poor countries entails worsening environmental outcomes. For most of the environmental indicators, the evidence also suggests that the direction of the relationship eventually reverses, so that with enough growth, the environmental outcomes start to improve, giving what has become known as the "Environmental Kuznets Curve (EKC)". This, however, does not appear to hold for carbon emission which (over the range of the data) rises monotonically as average income rises. Theoretical paper by Seldon and Song (1994) have derived transition paths for pollution, abatement effort and development under alternative assumptions about social welfare functions, pollution damage, the cost of abetment, and the productivity of capital. Empirical studies by Shafik (1994), Seldon and Song (1994) and Grossman and Krueger (1995) have searched for systematic environment and economic development relationships by using regression equations. They have regressed cross-country measures of ambient air and water quality on various polynomials specifications of per capita income popularly known as EKC hypothesis. The results have shown an inverted U-shaped EKC curve. Torras and Boyce (1998) tested the effects of the EKC hypothesis for various pollutants (not including carbon emission) and found that there is unequal distribution of income within the country. They found mixed evidence; higher inequality entailed higher levels of some pollutants but not others. The emphasis laid by Shafik and Bandhyopadhyay (1992), Shafik (1994), Seldon and Song (1994) and Grossman and Krueger (1995) on income growth and environmental quality have shown that some pollutants such as $SO_2$, SMP, nitrous oxides and river water pollutants follow an inverse U-shaped functional relationship with economic growth. As a result, Cole *et al.* (1997) find that meaningful EKCs only exist for local pollutants, while indicators with a more global or indirect environmental impact either increase monotonically with income or else have turning points at high per capita income levels with large standard errors—unless they have been subjected to a multilateral policy initiative. This encouraged Rothman (1998) to base his analysis on more consumption based measures such as $CO_2$ emission and municipal waste, for which impacts are relatively easy to externalise (to come in contact with other emissions) as well as costly to control – they show no tendency to decrease with higher per capita income. Another study conducted by Panayotou (1993) shows that as economic development accelerates with the intensification of agriculture and other resource extraction and the take-off of industrialisation, the rates of resource depletion begin to exceed the rates of resource regeneration, and waste generation increases in quantity and toxicity. At higher levels of development, structural change towards information—intensive industries and services, coupled with increased environmental awareness, enforcement of environmental regulations, better technology and higher environmental expenditures results in gradual decline of environmental degradation.

One of the primary causes of global environmental change is tropical deforestation, but the question of what factors drive deforestation remains largely unanswered. A variety of arguments have been produced by Williams (1994) and other prominent authors, but empirical evidence on the causes of deforestation continue to be largely based on cross-national statistical analyses. In some cases, these analyses are based on debatable data on rates of forest cover change. The two major mutually exclusive and still unsatisfactory explanations for tropical deforestation are, therefore, single factor causation and irreducible complexity. On the one hand, proponents of single factor causation suggest various primary causes such as shifting cultivation (Amelung and Diehl, 1992) and population growth (Allen and Barnes, 1985; Amelung and Diel, 1992). In contrast, correlations between deforestation and multiplicative causative factors are many and vary, revealing no distinct pattern.

From the analysis of the above review, a key issue of interest seems to be casualty as the degrading environment have impact not only on the lives of the poor but also on key environmental areas like environment and health, forest cover, soil degradation, water quantity and quality etc. Moreover, environmental concern is most important for the well-being of the people. In the present paper, therefore, an attempt has been made to examine the interdependence between economic development and environmental degradation. Deforestation has been considered as one of the indicators of environmental degradation. It also examines the factors, which affect forest degradation. This chapter is an investigation of a complex system of causes affecting tropical deforestation at the national level, considering all major states. It also examines the factors of economic development such as natural factors, social factors or economic activities which in turn are degrading the environment.

In India, the problem of environmental degradation is more severe due to the problems of unemployment and acute poverty. To achieve sustainable economic development various policy implications had to be made keeping in view various environmental tribulations. Further, the impact of environmental degradation has not been uniform, as the weaker sections of our society are most affected. This is because India is an agricultural based economy where majority of the population, which is poor, depends upon agricultural based activities. Degrading environment has an impact not only on their livelihood but also on key environmental areas like environment and health (including malaria, diarrhoea and respiratory problems, particularly arising from indoor air pollution), forest cover, soil degradation, water quantity and quality, fisheries and natural disasters (including floods, earthquakes, etc.). Moreover, environmental concern is most important in India as people's sustainable lives and well-being are at a stake. Environmentally, destructive economic development will impoverish the poor even further and destroy their base for livelihood.

## ECONOMIC DEVELOPMENT AND ENVIRONMENTAL DEGRADATION

The relationship between economic development and environment has now come to be known as the Environmental Transition Hypothesis or the Environmental Kuznets Curve (EKC) hypothesis. The basic premise of the EKC hypothesis is that there exists an 'inverted' U-shaped relationship between a variety of indicators of environmental degradation and economic development. An attempt is made to examine the impact of economic development [as measured by the level of Per Capita Income (PCI) and Per Capita Consumption of Electricity (PCCE)] in Indian states on the deforestation rate through regression analysis.

*Trade-off between Economic Development and Environmental Degradation:* The un-even rate of deforestation is the main concern in India. Some states have responded very well to the government policy of heavy plantation in forest cover area, and as a result, forest appreciation has occurred in these states. The EKC hypothesis about the trade-off between economic development and environmental degradation in terms of degree of deforestation with per capita income and per capita consumption of electricity has been examined. To find out this relationship, the quadratic regression model was used. The results are shown in Table 6.1.

**Table 6.1:** Trade-off between Economic Development and Environmental Degradation

| *Trade-off* | $\beta_1$ | $\beta_2$ | $\beta_3$ | $R^2$ |
|---|---|---|---|---|
| Per capita Income and Deforestation | 43.627<br>(102.018)<br>t = 0.42765 | -0.015808<br>(0.022367)<br>t = -0.7068 | 0.000000902<br>(-0.00000115)<br>t = 0.78726 | 0.0433 |
| Per capita Consumption of Electricity and Deforestation | -81.18061<br>(27.20583)<br>t = -2.9839 | 0.323225*<br>(0.143036)<br>t = 2.259 | -0.00026*<br>(0.00015)<br>t = -1.7709 | 0.275635 |

*Note*: The value in parenthesis is showing the standard error.
*Source*: indiastat.com
As computed by Author.

Moreover, here also, the trade-off between the coefficient of per capita income and deforestation and the coefficient of the square of per capita income and deforestation is found to be statistically insignificant. It, therefore, does not support the EKC hypothesis about environmental degradation and the level of economic development measured in terms of per capita income in India across different states.

Hence, it becomes essential to use some other indicator of economic development and thus we have chosen per capita consumption of electricity, which is one of the best indicators of economic activity. To establish the trade-off between the environmental degradation and per capita consumption of electricity we have used quadratic regression estimation. The results are shown in Table 6.1.

In this trade-off equation, there is improvement in the value of $R^2$. It is found that both coefficient of PCCE is positive and statistically significant, coefficient of $(PCCE)^2$ is negative and statistically significant. This result shows that at the first stage, as per capita consumption of electricity increases, environmental degradation initially increases, but then eventually declines, once a threshold level of economic development is reached. Therefore, it is supporting the EKC hypothesis of economic development and environmental degradation, providing the 'inverted-U' shape curve propounded by Simon Kuznets. Thus, the level of economic development is able to explain, to some extent the degree of environmental degradation in India.

## An Alternative Approach

To interlink economic development and environmental degradation, we have used a different regression model as follows. We have regressed deforestation rate on PCI, $PCI^2$ and dummy variable for trend (Table 6.2). In this exercise, we have considered only those states which have shown substantial decrease in forest area and we have pooled the data for two time period by using dummy variable technique. The positive impact of PCI followed by negative of $PCI^2$ on deforestation supports the Environmental Kuznet curve hypothesis on environmental degradation in India. This shows that the state can demand better quality of environment only after achieving certain level of growth. It is interesting to note that rural poverty is also responsible for forest degradation. The high dependency of rural poor on natural resources and absence of other economic resources and opportunity forces him to optimize returns in short run. This sometimes damages the quality of natural resources and hence degrades the environment.

**Table 6.2:** Trade-off between Economic Development and Environmental Degradation: An Alternative Approach

| *Variables* | *β's* | *Std. Error* | *t-value* |
|---|---|---|---|
| Intercept | -35.7191 | 12.64496 | -2.82477 |
| PCI ($E_1$) | 0.004272 | 0.001803 | 2.369097* |
| PCI sq. ($E_3$) | -2E-07 | 7.28E-08 | -2.7705* |
| D | 3.545872 | 0.909897 | 1.218556 |

Multiple R = 0.681704 R Square = 0.46472
Adjusted R = 0.0353972 Standard Error = 6.655444
* represents 5% level of significance
** represents 10% level of significance
*Source*: As computed

## Factors Affecting Deforestation

The above analysis has shown that the degree of deforestation is not uniform in different states of India during the study period. The level of standard of living, as measured by per capita consumption of electricity, is able to explain some variations in the level of deforestation. The states with low consumption of electricity are showing high degree of deforestation but when it increases to some critical level, it takes care to protect forest resources as a result, the level of forest degradation declines. Thus, enhancement of standard of living is the best way to control environmental degradation. But there are many other variables, which can also explain the tendency of deforestation. There is thus a need of some appropriate intervention by the society or government to check this environmental degradation especially in the early stage of development. This requires the identification of some factors, which affects the level of forest degradation. To identify these factors we have regressed degree of deforestation on many socio-economic and natural factors. The results are shown in Table 6.3.

In the preliminary stage we have considered the Per Capita Income (PCI) as an indicator of economic growth in the model, it is found that neither PCI nor $(PCI)^2$ are giving a statistically significant result. We therefore have replaced Per Capita Consumption of Electricity (PCCE) and $(PCCE)^2$ as indicators of economic well being in our study. We, thus, have Per Capita Consumption of Electricity along with many other variables to explain the degree of deforestation. The results are shown in Table 6.3. The overall explanatory power of this model is 39 per cent. It was found that the coefficient of per capita consumption of electricity is positive and square of per capita consumption of electricity is negative and statistically significant. Except these two variables, the coefficient of other variables such as decadal growth of population, population density and percentage of population below poverty line is positive but statistically insignificant. The coefficient of urbanization is negative but not giving statistically significant result. Therefore, from this estimation, we find that only per capita consumption of electricity is able to explain the degree of deforestation in the states of India.

**Table 6.3:** Factors Affecting Deforestation

| Eq. No. | Intercept ($\beta_0$) | Coefficients of Independent Variables | | | | | | | | | | $R^2$ |
|---|---|---|---|---|---|---|---|---|---|---|---|---|
| | | $X_1$ | $(X_1)^2$ | $X_2$ | $X_3$ | $X_4$ | $X_5$ | $X_6$ | $X_7$ | $X_8$ | $X_9$ | |
| 1. | -130.7674<br>(72.36641)<br>t = -1.807 | 0.41586<br>(0.1755)<br>t = 2.36 | -0.0003<br>(0.0001)<br>t = -1.90 | 0.47863<br>(1.7345)<br>t = 0.275 | 0.04918<br>(0.0400)<br>t = 1.227 | 0.80150<br>(0.9679)<br>t=0.828 | -0.80238<br>(1.43552)<br>t = -0.5589 | — | — | — | — | 0.393 |
| 2. | 39.19918<br>(80.8415)<br>t = 0.4848 | 0.03083<br>(0.0755)<br>t = 0.408 | — | — | — | 0.50530<br>(1.0882)<br>t=0.464 | -0.04071<br>(1.30179)<br>t = -0.0312 | 0.00519<br>(0.0135)<br>t = 0.383 | -1.51009<br>(0.43419)<br>t = -3.477 | -0.50102<br>(0.9781)<br>t = -0.5122 | -0.1386<br>(0.2277)<br>t = -0.608 | 0.59690 |
| 3. | 28.1742<br>(40.11716)<br>t = 0.70229 | 0.04946<br>(0.1455)<br>t = 0.339 | -0.000021<br>(0.000144)<br>t = -0.1473 | — | — | — | — | — | -1.49817<br>(0.45715)<br>t = -3.277 | — | -204.262<br>(178.964)<br>t = -1.141 | 0.567606 |
| 4. | 44.852<br>(37.9181)<br>t = 1.182 | 0.03346<br>(0.0755)<br>t = 0.442 | — | — | -0.0117<br>(0.0366)<br>t = -0.321 | — | -0.25059<br>(1.1993)<br>t = -0.208 | — | -1.60777<br>(0.4763)<br>t = -3.7546 | — | -220.098<br>(184.76)<br>t = -1.1912 | 0.5719 |

*Note*: Figure in parenthesis is showing the standard error.
As Computed by Author.

*Source*: indiastat.com

However, to identify other variables which are affecting the forest degradation, we have again estimated equation No. 2. The value of $R^2$ is improved to 59.69. It is very interesting to advocate that, this new model also fails to detect any factor, which is affecting the decay in forest cover. Per capita consumption of electricity, Percentage of total population of BPL, Urbanization Rate, Road Density, female literacy rate and per capita production of milk, all these variables are showing insignificant result on deforestation except percentage of area under forest cover. Its coefficient is negative and statistically significant. The negative coefficient of percentage of area under forest cover shows that the more is area under forest cover in the states; there is a lower rate of deforestation; rather afforestation is evolved. This indicates that the states, having more forest cover are more concerned with the protection of this natural stock. The states, having less forest cover, are more involved in decaying the forest cover. It is difficult to accept that neither demand side factor nor social side factors are able to explain the deforestation. This might be due to the presence of multicollinearity of dominance in the estimation of this equation. We have also tried an alternative regression equation (Eq. No. 3) to establish this relationship. In this equation we have emphasized on demand and supply side factors, which can explain the decay in the forest resources.

The estimates of equation No. 3 include the variable like per capita Consumption of Electricity and its square, per capita productions of milk and percentage of forest area. It explains around 56 variation in deforestation. Here again the coefficient of percentage forest area is negative and statistically significant. The coefficient of per capita milk production is negative but statistically insignificant. The demand side is thus not influencing the forest depletion. Only the supply factor, i.e. percentage of forest area is playing a key role in forest degradation.

We have also tried the equation No. 4. In this estimation we are getting the same result, i.e. the coefficient of percentage of area under forest cover is negative and statistically significant. We thus could not identify any other variable, which are responsible for the decay in forest area in India. We have also regressed deforestation rate on PCI, $PCI^2$, population growth, percentage of rural poverty, population density, cropping intensity and dummy variable for trend (Table 6.4).

**Table 6.4:** Impact of Forest degradation

| *Variables* | *β's* | *Std. Error* | *t-value* |
|---|---|---|---|
| Intercept | -16.7518 | 17.04681 | -0.98269 |
| $E_1$ | 0.003696 | 0.001826 | 2.024423* |
| $E_2$ | 0.149571 | 0.147552 | 1.013683 |
| $E_3$ | -1.8E-07 | 7.37E-08 | -2.44032* |
| $E_4$ | -0.02796 | 0.108267 | -0.25822 |
| $E_5$ | 0.301003 | 0.128947 | 2.33432* |
| $X_3$ | 0.001315 | 0.005533 | 0.237594 |
| $E_6$ | -0.09516 | 0.058764 | -1.61935** |
| D | 2.783705 | 2.931998 | 0.949423 |

Multiple $R^2$ = 0.716609 $R^2$ = 0.513528
Adjusted $R^2$ = 0.369388 Standard Error = 6.575558
N = 36
* represents 5 % level of significance
** Represents 10 % level of significance

*Source*: As computed by the Author.

In this exercise, we have considered only those states which have shown substantial decrease in forest area and we have pooled the data for two time period by using dummy variable technique. The PCI and rural poverty has positive and significant impact on deforestation whereas the impact of $PCI^2$ is negative and statistically significant. Growth in PCI has shown positive impact but statistically insignificant. The coefficient of cropping intensity is negative but significant only at 10 per cent level of significance. The states with high cropping intensity are showing low forest degradation. This indicates that these states are now going for more intensive cultivation in order to save their forest resources. The population growth and dummy for trend has negative coefficient but are statistically insignificant. It is, thus, clear from the analysis that level of PCI and rural poverty are important indicators to explain deforestation in the country. It is interesting to note that rural poverty is also responsible for forest degradation. The high dependency of rural poor on natural resources and absence of other economic resources and opportunity forces him to optimize returns in short run. This sometimes damages the quality of natural resources and hence degrades the environment.

Thus, our regression estimates could identify only Per capita Consumption of Electricity and the level of forest area as the factors explaining deforestation. All other variables mainly from demand side factors, like per capita milk production, urbanization, etc. failed to explain the variation in the level of deforestation. Only supply side factors like area under forest is able to explain the level of deforestation in the states. The states with more forest cover are mainly showing improvement in the forest area. The states with poor forest intensity are not able to control the decay in the forest resources. Their process of development is failed to protect the stock of this natural resources.

The usefulness and validity of results obtained in previous studies of cross-states regression analysis are questioned from econometric and methodological points of view. In our study, we have made an attempt to respond to some of these questions by establishing relationships between the rate of deforestation and its underlying/policy-oriented causes using data across 21 major states of India. States like Uttar Pradesh, Andhra Pradesh, Jammu & Kashmir, Gujarat, Orissa and Maharashtra with higher forest cover, have not been able to protect their forests rather keenly and are involved in the process of deforestation. But, states like Manipur, Assam, Arunachal Pradesh, Meghalaya, Haryana, Himachal Pradesh, Karnataka, Kerala and Tamil Nadu, are poor in forest cover, but still the process of reforestation/afforestation has begun in these states. From our analysis, it was found that neither social factors like literacy, decadal growth of population, etc., nor economic factors like per capita production of milk, urbanisation rate, etc. were causing the forest cover to diminish. Our regression analysis could identify only per capita consumption of electricity (PCCE), $(PCCE)^2$ and percentage of forest area as the factors affecting forest degradation. It is important to interpret that the interlink between economic development in terms of consumption of electricity and environment degradation in terms of deforestation in major Indian states supports the EKC hypothesis and provides an inverted U-shaped relationship between them. India's ongoing population explosion has placed a great strain on the country's environment. This rapidly growing population, along with a move towards urbanisation, has placed a significant pressure on India's infrastructure and its natural resources. Deforestation, soil erosion, water pollution and land degradation continue to worsen and hinder economic development in rural India, while rapid industrialisation and urbanisation in India's booming metropolises are straining the limits of municipal services and causing serious air pollution problems. The overall implication of the results in our present study implies that the underlying/policy-oriented causes leading to deforestation differ somewhat across the regions. Therefore, there is a need for specific policy recommendations for restraining the deforestation process of different regions.

# 7

# Agricultural Growth and Environmental Degradation

The significance of agriculture in India arises from the fact that the development in agriculture is an essential condition for the development of the national economy. Indian planners learnt a bitter lesson during the Second and Third Five-Year Plan periods and in recent years, during 2003-04, for example, when failure of the agricultural sector spelt disaster to the entire planning process. Thus, any change in the agricultural sector, positive or negative has a multiplier effect on the entire economy. The agricultural sector acts as a bulwark in maintaining food security and in the process, national security as well. To maintain the ecological balance, there is need for sustainable and balanced development of the agriculture and allied sectors. Recognizing the crucial role played by this sector in enabling the widest dispersal of economic benefits, the Tenth Plan has emphasized that agricultural development is central to rapid economic development of the country.

## AGRICULTURAL STRATEGY IN INDIAN ECONOMY

Importance of agriculture is indicated by many facts. For example, agriculture is the main support for India's transport system, since railways and roadways secure bulk of their business from the movement of agricultural goods. Internal trade is mostly in agricultural products. Further, goods crops implying large purchasing power with the farmers lead to greater demand for manufactures and, therefore, better prices, i.e. prosperity of industries. Likewise, bad crops lead to a depression in business. Generally, it is the failure in the agricultural sector that has led to failure of economic planning in particular periods. Agricultural growth has direct impact on poverty eradication.

It is also an important factor in containing inflation, raising agricultural wages and for employment generation.

It is clear, therefore, that agriculture is the backbone of the Indian economy and prosperity of agricultural sector can also largely stand for the prosperity of the Indian economy. At the same time, it is true that per capita productivity in agriculture is less than in industry. Naturally, most scholars of developing economies observe that this dominance of agriculture in India's economy is responsible for the low per capita income in the country. In their opinion, so long as the Indian economy is dominated by agricultural activity, per capita income will not rise to an extent which is necessary and desirable.

The Agricultural Development Strategy was revised in 1999, as the national strategy on Sustainable Agriculture and Rural Development (SARD). The strategy is essentially based on the policy on food security and alleviation of hunger. A regionally differentiated strategy, based on agro climatic regional planning which takes into account agronomic, climatic and environmental conditions, will be adopted to realize the potential of growth in every region of the country. The thrust will be on ecological, sustainable use of basic resources such as land, water, and vegetation, in such a way that it serves the objectives of accelerated growth, employment and alleviation of hunger.

In the accelerated growth scenario for the Ninth Five-Year Plan (1997-2002), an agricultural growth rate of 4.5 per annum is expected. Allied sectors such as horticulture including fruit and vegetables, fisheries, livestock, and dairy will continue to register greater growth during the Ninth Plan period. In the Ninth Plan, targets will be achieved through a regionally differentiated strategy based on agronomic, climatic, and environment-friendly conditions. At the macro level, the agriculture development strategy will be differentiated by broad regional characteristics of an agro-economic character. The north-western high productivity regions will promote diversification and high value crops, and strengthen linkages with agro-processing industries and exports. The Eastern region, with abundant water, will exploit this productivity potential through flood control, drainage management, improvement of irrigation facilities, and improved input delivery systems. The water scarce peninsular region, including Rajasthan, will focus on efficient water harvesting and conservation methods and technologies based on a watershed approach and appropriate farming systems. Ecologically fragile regions, including Himalayan and desert areas, will concentrate on eco-friendly agriculture.

The significance of agriculture in the national economy can be best explained by considering the role of agriculture under different heads. Figures provided by the Reserve Bank of India (Refer Table 7.1) reveal that between 1950-51 to 1960-61, the share of agriculture in GDP has been in the range of 55 to 49 per cent, though it was declining. It reached at 44 per cent in 1970-71. The process of declining is going on, attaining the range of 35-31 per cent during 1980-81 and 1990-91. Even as the process of industrialization and economic growth and LPG gathered momentum, the share of agriculture indicated a sharp decline and reached a level of 23 per cent in 2000-01. During 2006-07, the share of agriculture to the national income is 18 per cent.

**Table 7.1:** Share of Agricultural Sector in Total GDP at Factor Cost

*(At 1999-2000 prices) Rs. Crores*

| *Year* | *GDP at factor cost* | *Agriculture* | *2 as % of 1* |
|---|---|---|---|
| | *(1)* | *(2)* | *(3)* |
| 1950-51 | 224786 | 123884 | 55.112 |
| 1960-61 | 340060 | 166954 | 49.095 |
| 1970-71 | 474131 | 209843 | 44.258 |
| 1980-81 | 678033 | 243421 | 35.901 |
| 1990-91 | 1083572 | 339893 | 31.368 |
| 2000-01 | 1864773 | 445594 | 23.895 |
| 2006-07* | 2848157 | 525875 | 18.464 |

*Note*: Agriculture includes agriculture, forestry and fishing.
* Advance Estimates
*Source*: RBI Bulletin, Hand Book of Statistics, 2008.

## Agricultural Growth

According to J.P. Bhattacharjee, India's population rose by 38 per cent between 1901 and 1946, but the area of cultivated land rose only by 18 per cent, the average productivity of all crops rose by 13 per cent and of food crops by only 1 per cent.[1] With the introduction of economic planning in 1950-51 and with special emphasis on agricultural development, particularly after 1965; there was steady increase in area under cultivation, rise in average yield per hectare or rise in agricultural productivity; and as a result of the above two factors, production of all agricultural crops recorded a rising trend.

*Growth Rate in Agricultural Production:* Total production of any agricultural product reflects the combined effects of area and yield per hectare. During the first period (1994-95), after liberalization foodgrains production had increased at an impressive annual rate of 4.3 per cent. The major cereals, viz. rice and wheat recorded high rates of growth, i.e. 3.6 per annum, but coarse cereals and pulses recorded relatively lower growth rates. The output growth rate of non-foodgrains (7.32 per year) was also impressive (refer Appendix 7). This order of growth rate in agricultural production was due partly to area growth rate and partly to yield growth rate, in this period. In year 1999-2000, there was a declining rate in total foodgrain and non-foodgrain production. However, in 2006-07 it was better than past years. The foodgrains production had increased at an impressive annual rate of 3.6 per cent. The output growth rate of non-foodgrains (15.63 per year) was also impressive.

*Growth Rate in Cultivable Area:* Appendix 8 brings out the broad growth trends in area under cultivation, despite the fluctuations from year to year because of variation in monsoon and weather conditions. The average growth of cultivable area in the period 1994-95 to 2006-07 is 0.32 per cent. The area for foodgrain production has increased by 0.11 per cent per annum, in which total cereals production area increased by only 0.02 per cent and that of pulses by 0.6 per cent per annum. As far as non-foodgrain production area is concerned, it is increasing at 0.82 per cent per annum. Total oil seeds area is growing at 0.43 per cent annually during 1994-2007. During 1999-2000 and 2002-03, almost all categories of areas have declined from previous year.

*Growth Rate in Yield:* The year 1995-96 shows that yield of agricultural products have declined by 1 to 5 per cent. It has been repeated in the year 2000-01. However, the year 2003-04 has shown significant change in the yield of all crops in the economy (Appendix 9). The yield of total cereals, pulses, foodgrains, oilseeds and fibres have been increased by 13.02 per cent, 14.45 per cent, 13.05 per cent, 43.95 per cent and 52.62 per cent respectively. The oilseeds and fibres have shown a high jump in productivity. However, the average growth of all principal crops is 2.93 per cent during 1994-95 to 2006-07.

## Intensity of Factor Use

*Trends in Fertilizer Consumption in India:* After independence the use of fertilizers in India in the last 50 years has grown nearly 170 times. Fertilizer nutrient consumption trends in India from 1960 to 2001-02 are shown in Table 7.2. Fertilizer consumption in India has increased significantly in the last decades. Total NPK (N, $P_2O_5$ and $K_2O$) consumption increased nine-fold (from 2 million to 17.36 million tonnes) between 1970-71 and 2001-02. In 1960-61, use of fertilizer per hectare in India was 1.93 kg but by 2001-02 this figure has increased to around 90.12 kg per hectare. Green revolution during 1960s and subsequent increased intensification of agriculture were major causes behind this growth as seen in Fig. 7.1. Fertilizers and pesticides have become major cost of production in India along with the cost of other input like seeds, and labour cost.

**Table 7.2:** Fertilizer Consumption in India

| *Item* | *1960-61* | *1970-71* | *1980-81* | *1990-91* | *2001-02* |
|---|---|---|---|---|---|
| Consumption (000 t) | | | | | |
| Nitrogen (N) | 212 | 1,479 | 3,678 | 7,997 | 11,310 |
| Phosphorus ($P_2O_5$) | 53 | 514 | 1,214 | 3,221 | 4,382 |
| Potassium ($K_2O$) | 29 | 236 | 624 | 1,328 | 1,667 |
| Total | 294 | 2,256 | 5,516 | 12,546 | 17,360 |
| Consumption (kg/ha) | | | | | |
| N | 1.39 | 8.92 | 21.22 | 43.1 | 58.7 |
| $P_2O_5$ | 0.35 | 3.26 | 7.00 | 17.3 | 22.8 |
| $K_2O$ | 0.19 | 1.43 | 3.60 | 7.2 | 8.7 |
| Total | 1.93 | 13.61 | 31.82 | 67.6 | 90.12 |
| Ratio of $P_2O_5$ & $K_2O$ (N=1.0) | 0.37:0.16 | 0.37:0.16 | 0.33:0.17 | 0.40:0.17 | 0.39:0.14 |
| Highest consumption in a state (kg $N+P_2O_5+K_2O$) | 6.58 Kerala | 40.24 Punjab | 117.9 Punjab | 161.9 Punjab | 173.4 Punjab |

*Source*: Potash & Phosphate Institute (PPI), 655 Engineering Drive, Suite 110, Norcross, Georgia 30092-2837 USA

*Trends in Pesticides Consumption in India:* India is one of the world's largest agricultural economies. Demand for chemical pest control and resulting negative externalities have expanded greatly during the last four decades (Chand and Birthal, 1997)[2]. Three decades back, intensive and extensive cultivation of high yielding varieties of crops were introduced in India to increase foodgrain production. The new crop varieties and cropping sequences, especially monocropping, along with injudicious and indiscriminate use of pesticides created many problems. Several hitherto unimportant pest species began to cause economic losses. Others, especially

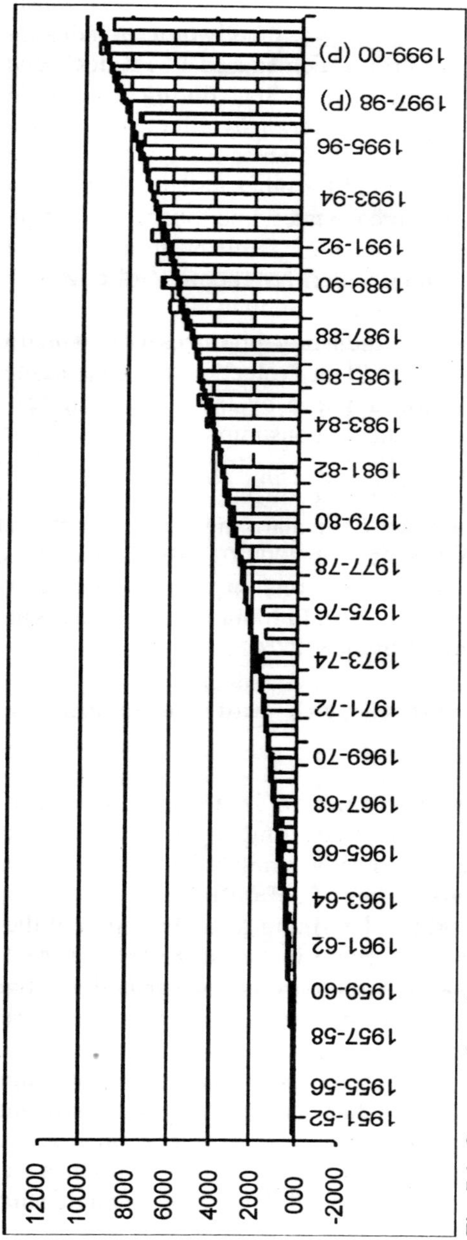


**Fig. 7.1:** Consumption of Total Plant Nutrient per hectare of Gross Cropped Area (1951-52 to 2000-01)

*Source:* Agricultural statistics at a glance. Adapted by author from the data at http://www.indiastat.com/

polyphagous insects, have precipitated national problems (Srinivasa, 1993).[3] One glaring example is the old world bollworm, *Helicoverpa armigera* (Noctuidae: Lepidoptera), which caused a 66 reduction in the yield of seed cotton in Andhra Pradesh State during the 1987-88 crop season. Previously, this pest only seriously affected rabi crops such as chickpea and was commonly known as the gram pod borer. Similar outbreaks have been reported for other insects: White fly in 1984-85 and 1985-86 in South Indian states, and tobacco caterpillar in 1977-78 and 1979-80 in the states of Tamil Nadu and Gujarat (Arunakumara, 1995) and more recently, coconut mite, *Aceria guererronis* (Eriophyidae: Acarinae).[4]

The agrochemical industry in India now produces 47,020 metric tonnes of pesticide (Directorate of Plant Protection and Quarantine, 2002). Growth in pesticide consumption by Indian agriculture is shown in Fig. 7.2. Although pesticide consumption in India is low (around 500 g per ha) compared to other countries like Japan (12 kg per cent ha) and Germany (3 kg per cent ha), problems in India resulting from unregulated use are quite alarming. The predominant classes of pesticides used in India (during 2000-01) were insecticides, accounting for 61 per cent of total consumption, followed by fungicides (19%) and herbicides (17%). In India, most pesticides are used on cotton (45%), followed by rice (22%)[5].

## Interlinking Agricultural Growth and Environmental Degradation

Although agricultural land expansion is a major source of deforestation, cash and food crop prices, timber prices, agricultural input prices, agricultural wages and credit availability to farmers have been identified as immediate causes of deforestation in Cameroon that determine the profitability of farming and logging activities (Daniel Gbetnkom *et al.* 2005).[6] To be in a position to mitigate or halt the effects of forest clearing with relevant counter-policies, one needs to appreciate the extent to which the immediate factors propel deforestation agents to deforest.

According to David Kalmomitz, Neil Byron and William Sunderlin, demand for tropical products is a function of the size and incomes of the consuming population, relative prices, quantitative trade restrictions, and consumer preferences. Policies that affect any of these variables can also affect demand. High prices and demand

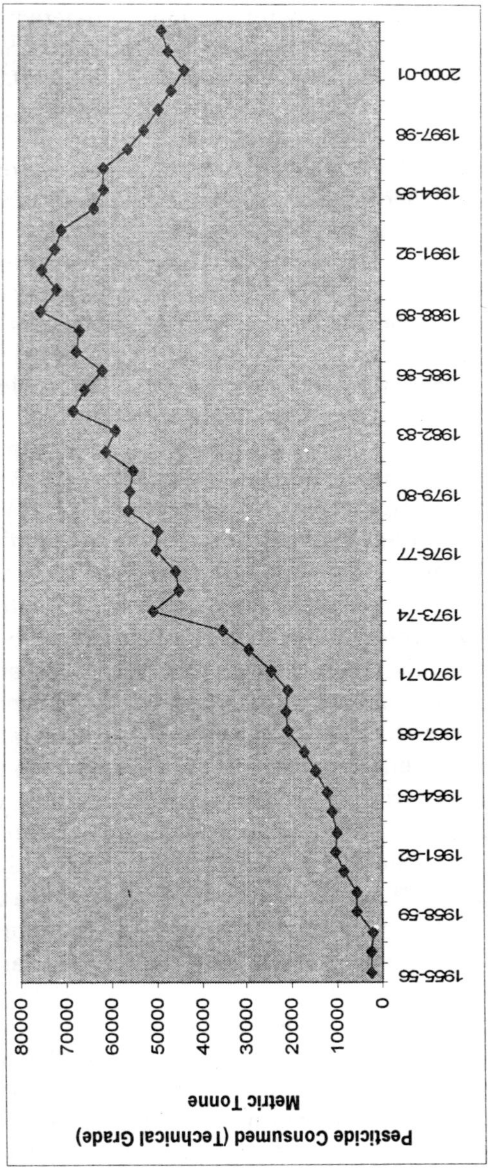


**Fig. 7.2:** Consumption of Pesticides in India

for tropical agricultural commodities can stimulate the clearing of forests to produce these commodities. Therefore, policies that reduce the demand for tropical agricultural products can limit the conversion of forests to croplands and pastures. This approach has certain advantages. The policies involved are mostly national in scope, and governments can implement some of them easily and cheaply (at least with regard to their direct costs). However, these policies rely entirely on the market to distinguish where and how supply should be reduced, and this is unlikely to meet environmental objectives efficiently. In addition, it is difficult to win political support for policies that restrict the demand for or production of tropical products, particularly export products, and which restrict the incomes of primary producers in tropical developing countries.[7]

Per capita income greatly influences the demand for tropical products. Some authors have speculated the existence of an "environmental Kuznets curve", whereby at lower levels of per capita income, economic growth leads to greater deforestation as a result of increased demand for tropical products, but after income levels reach a certain threshold, deforestation declines because the economies become less dependent on agricultural and forest products, primary production becomes more intensive, new employment opportunities arise, and demand for forest preservation grows (Capistrano, 1990).[8] The empirical evidence of this relationship is relatively weak and has been mostly based on the few economies of East Asia which may not reflect how the majority of tropical countries are likely to evolve in the future. Nevertheless, given existing levels of per capita income in most tropical countries, without a change in the pattern of development, economic growth is likely to lead to greater forest clearing in the medium term (Stern *et al.*, 1996).[9] This implies that one way to avoid a tradeoff between economic growth and deforestation is for countries to promote patterns of economic development that are less dependent on primary agricultural and forestry commodities.

*Agricultural Pricing and Deforestation:* Government actions that encourage intensive farming tend to reduce forest conversion, whereas interventions favouring extensive agriculture are likely to spur the destruction of forests. Intensive farming means increasing the amount of labour, capital, and information applied per hectare of land (Lutz *et al.* 1998).[10] Whether the expansion of market demands and higher product prices lead to more or less pressure on the forest-agriculture frontier will depend on the farmers' choice of technology (that is how much to intensify and how much to expand an area) in response to perceived opportunities.

Substantial increase in taxes and charges set by governments for the exploitation of natural forests might reduce logging in inappropriate areas and marginalize some of the least efficient operators from the industry, who may also be amongst the most destructive. Road construction also plays a crucial role in deforestation. The general idea is that new road construction presents the greatest threat to remaining forests by providing access to forested areas (Bryant *et al.*, 1997; Dudley *et al.*, 1995).[11] Roads are often essential both to market farm outputs and to deliver inputs to the farm and can greatly increase the profitability of agriculture and wood production in frontier areas. In many countries, one of the common forms of assistance requested by farmers is the extension and upgrading of road transport systems. However, the road construction and transport policy reforms that might be required to reduce deforestation activities do not necessarily involve less road building, but rather a change in the nature, type and location of roads built.

*Trade-off between Agricultural Pricing and Deforestation:* From the theoretical framework presented in the previous section, we have used log linear model for empirical analysis of the form: The model is well explained in the Chapter 3. The higher prices of agricultural products, the more the forest area diminish because of conversion of new forest portions into cultivable area. A negative relationship is, therefore, expected between these variables and FOR. Assuming complementarities between fertilizer and land area, increased fertilizer prices will reduce the area of cultivation. A positive relationship is expected between Fertilizer Price Index (FPI) and Forest Area (FOR). The regression results of the above explanation for India are explained in Table 7.3.

The regression analysis made to study the trade off between agricultural development and environmental degradation shows that the overall explanatory power of the used regression model is 97 per cent. The variables such as Tea Price Index, Groundnut Seed Price Index and Food Grain Price Index are showing positive and significant relationship with forest area. This clearly indicates that the higher these prices, the more the forest area diminish because of conversion of new forest portions into cultivable area. The coefficient of the variables such as Sugar Price Index and Fertilizer Price Index are negative and statistically significant. However, it is highly significant in case of Fertilizer Price Index. This means that assuming complementarities between fertilizer and land area, increased fertilizer prices will reduce the area of cultivation. Therefore, there is less pressure on forest area to convert into cultivable area.

**Table 7.3:** Trade-off between Agricultural Pricing and Environmental Degradation

| | | | |
|---|---|---|---|
| $R^2$ | = 0.97119 | | |
| Adjusted $R^2$ | = 0.9039 | | |
| Standard Error | = 0.001173 | | |
| Dependent variable: | FOR (Y) | | |
| Independent variables: | Coefficient | Standard Error | T Stat. |
| Intercept ($\alpha_0$) | 4.921292 | 0.03347 | 147.037 |
| TPI ($\alpha_1$) | 0.028259 | 0.006833 | 4.135443 |
| JPI ($\alpha_2$) | -0.00073 | 0.005877 | -0.12371 |
| CPI ($\alpha_3$) | 0.020887 | 0.016038 | 1.302349 |
| SPI ($\alpha_4$) | -0.05358 | 0.017999 | -2.97704 |
| GSPI ($\alpha_5$) | 0.038413 | 0.014403 | 2.666972 |
| FGPI ($\alpha_6$) | 0.060414 | 0.023462 | 2.574963 |
| FPI ($\alpha_7$) | -0.13412 | 0.02736 | -4.90202 |

*Source*: As computed by the author.

However, the above model is suffering from the problems of autocorrelation and multicollinearity as the $R^2$ is very high and the number of observation is also very less (11). Therefore, as explained in the methodology part, we have estimated the bivariate correlation among the variables. It is explained in the Appendix 10. Table 7.3 clearly indicates the multicollinearity among the variables included in the model by inspection method. So, we have broken down the model into two models and have excluded sugar price index and groundnut seed price index from our analysis. The model-1 depicts very interesting results. It is shown in Table 7.4.

The overall explanatory power of the model is 69 Per cent. We have tested for autocorrelation. The calculated value of d is greater than the table value of d (upper). Therefore, it is the sign of no autocorrelation in the model. The variables included in this model are seasonal crops. The use of fertilizer is also more in seasonal crops. The coefficient of food Price index is negative and highly statistically significant at 1 level of significance. The coefficient of jute price index is negative but statistically significant at 10 Per cent level of significance. The estimates show that there exist a negative relationship between the prices and forest area. In other words, the price index rise will give more return in cultivation. The farmer will prefer extensive cultivation due to the seasonal nature of the crops by clearing the forest area. This shows that the increase in prices of jute and food grains brings decay in forest area in India. That shows that the agricultural price has vital role in forest cleanings.

**Table 7.4:** Model-1—Agricultural Pricing and Forest Area

| | | | | |
|---|---|---|---|---|
| $R^2$ = | | | | 0.692 |
| Adjusted $R^2$ = | | | | 0.615 |
| Std. Error of the Estimate = | | | | 2.35E-03 |
| Durbin-Watson Test d = | | | | 1.855 |
| | Coefficients | Std. Error | t- value | Significance |
| (Constant) | 4.962 | .030 | 165.915 | .000 |
| Jute price index | -0.01293 | .008 | -1.676 | .132 |
| Food grain price index | -0.04565* | .013 | -3.439 | .009 |
| Dependent Variable: Forest Area | | | | |

The model-2 is explained in the Table 7.5, The explanatory power of this model is about 79 per cent. We have also tested the autocorrelation in this model. The d value clearly indicates that this model is free from autocorrelation.

**Table 7.5:** Model-2—Agricultural Pricing and Forest Area

| | | | | |
|---|---|---|---|---|
| *$R^2$* | | | = | *0.794* |
| *Adjusted $R^2$* | | | = | *0.706* |
| *Std. Error of the Estimate* | | | = | *2.05E-03* |
| *Durbin-Watson Test* | | | *d* = | *2.171* |
| | *Coefficients* | *Std. Error* | *t- value* | *Sig.* |
| (Constant) | 4.903 | .042 | 116.622 | .000 |
| Tea price index | 2.061E-02 | .008 | 2.593 | .036 |
| Cotton price index | 1.117E-02 | .019 | .600 | .568 |
| Fertilizer price index | -6.268E-02 | .012 | -5.027 | .002 |
| Dependent Variable: Forest Area | | | | |

However, the coefficients of tea price index is positive and statistically significant. This is not a seasonal crop. The increase in price index does not bring any decay in forest area because the farmer may be induced in intensive cultivation. However, the coefficient of fertilizer price index is negative and statistically significant. This explains that when there is increase in the price index of fertilizer, the farmer will prefer in extensive cultivation not utilizing the fertilizer more thereby clearing the forest area.

This chapter was aimed at addressing the relationship between agricultural strategy and environmental degradation. The strategy was used in agriculture to bring about increase in production and rural employment. The five-year plans use various programmes such as setting up of community development programmes and agricultural extension services throughout the country, expansion of irrigation facilities, fertilizers and pesticides, agricultural machineries, high yielding varieties of seeds, expansion of transportation, power, marketing and institutional credit. However, to reduce the pressure of population on land, the strategy used to set up agro-based industries and handicrafts in rural areas to promote rural transport and communication and to encourage the movement of people from agriculture to industries and service sector and reducing the disguised unemployment. But there is not any agricultural strategy to control environmental degradation. The trade-off between agricultural pricing and environmental degradation was well established. The planners should focus on this matter.

## NOTES

1. J.P. Bhattacharjee: *Studies in Indian Agricultural Economics.*
2. Chand, Ramesh and Birthal, P.S. (1997). Pesticide use in Indian agriculture in relation to growth in area and production and technological change. *Indian Journal of Agricultural Economics,* 52(3): 488-498.
3. Srinivasa, D.K. (1993). *Environment and human health, Environmental Problems and Prospects in India,* Oxford and IBH Publications, New Delhi.
4. Arunakumara, V.K. (1995). Externalities in the use of pesticides: An economic analysis in a Cole crop. M.Sc. Thesis (Unpublished), UAS, Bangalore.
5. A Report on Indian Pesticide Industry, published by Credit Analysis and Research Ltd, 4th Floor Godrej Coliseum, Off Eastern Express Highway, Somia Hospital Road, Mumbai, email/id=careresearch@careratings.com.
6. Gbetnkom, D., and Khan, S.A. (2002), *Determinants of Agricultural Exports: the case of Cameroon*, African Economic Research Consortium, Nairobi.
7. Public Policies to Reduce Inappropriate Tropical Deforestation by David Kalmowitz, Neil Byron and William Sunderlin; *Agriculture and the*

*environment, Perspective on Sustainable Rural Development,* A World Bank Symposium Edited by Ernst Lutz. Washington, 1999.

8. Capistrano, A.D. (1990). *Macro-Economic Influences on Tropical Forest Depletion :A cross country analysis*. University of Florida, Gainesville.
9. Stern, D.I, M.S. Common, and Edward B. Barbier (1996). Economic Growth and Environmental Kuznets Curve and sustainable development. *World Development* 24 (7): 1141-160.
10. Kaimowitz, D.N. Byron, and W. Sunderlin (1998). "Public policies to reduce inappropriate tropical deforestation." In Lutz, E. *et al.* (eds), *Agriculture and the Environment: Perspective on Sustainable Rural Development.* A World Bank Symposium, Washington, DC.
11. Bryant, D., D.Nielsen, and L.Tingley (1997). *The last frontier Forests: Ecosystems and economies on the Edge*. Washington D.C: World Resources Institute.

# 8

# Industrial Growth and Environmental Degradation

The path of industrialization adopted by India after Independence emphasized on building heavy industries, the role of the public sector and a high degree of protection. In 1991, economic reforms were introduced, the role of the public sector was reduced and measures for increasing efficiency and integration with international markets were taken. The last decade has also witnessed an increased awareness of the environmental impacts associated with economic and industrial activity, as reflected in the concerns voiced at the Earth Summit in 1992.

## INDUSTRIAL GROWTH

The Government of India has given major thrusts to industrial development for rapid economic growth since it gained independence in 1947. India is one of the ten most industrialized nations of the world. The industrial policy resolution of 1956 entrusted the public sector with a major role in India's economic development. Targets were fixed for industrial investments in Five-Year Plans which were the backbone of India's planned development. The contribution of industry to the GDP has increased from 22 per cent in 1970-71 to 30 per cent in 1996-97. The economic reforms initiated by the Government of India in 1991 have led to a critical phase of transition and restructuring of the Indian industry. The New Industrial Policy (NIP) was introduced in 1991 with an emphasis on deregulation. The basic objectives of the NIP were to promote growth, to increase efficiency and to enhance international competitiveness. Salient features of the NIP are given below.

- Substantial reduction in the scope of industrial licensing
- Simplification of procedures, rules and regulations
- Reforms in the MRTP (Monopolies and Restrictive Trade Practices) Act
- Reduction of areas reserved exclusively for the public sector
- Disinvestment of selected public sector enterprises
- Enhancing limits for foreign equity participation in domestic industrial undertakings
- Liberalization of trade and exchange rate policies
- Rationalization and reduction of customs and excise duties
- Extension of the scope of MODVAT (modified value-added tax), etc.

Industrial production grew at an average rate of 6.77 per cent per annum in the period 1994-95 to 2004-05. This growth was mainly on account of the manufacturing sector, while electricity and mining and quarrying sectors witnessed much lower growth rates in production. This relative picture is reflected in the trend in the Index of Industrial Production for these sectors (Fig. 8.1).

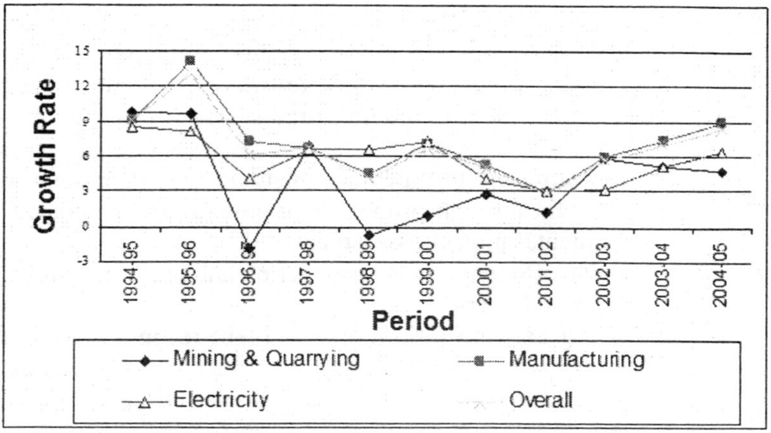


**Fig. 8.1:** Annual Growth Rate of Industrial Production in Major Sectors of Industry (Based on Index of Industrial Production Base: 1993-94 = 100)

*Source*: Central Statistical Organization.

The overall industrial growth path in the 1990s has been marked by cyclical fluctuations with the industrial growth rate increasing to a height of 13 Per cent in 1995-96 before falling to 4.1 per cent in 1998-99. There was a significant improvement in overall growth in industrial value added to 6.7 per cent in 1999-2000 due to acceleration in growth rate of the manufacturing and construction sectors, which declined to 5 per cent in 2000-01. However, it has again increased to 8.4 per cent in 2004-05. The targeted growth rate for the industrial sector in the Tenth Plan period is over 10 per cent, in line with a targeted GDP (Gross Domestic Product) growth rate of 8 per cent (Planning Commission, 2001a).[1]

*Industry and Agenda 21:* The areas for action in the industrial sector as articulated in Agenda 21 emphasize the integration of environmental concerns in industrial planning, ensuring full participation in industrial activity, enhancing international trade and minimizing social costs. Four main issues can thus be identified for the industrial sector: environmental management, strengthening the role of the private sector, trade liberalization and environmental regulation, and employment generation and labour welfare. These issues are discussed in the following sections.

*Environmental Management:* Governments were urged to promote policies or programmes, including administrative, social or economic measures to encourage industrial development in a manner that would minimize adverse environmental impacts. Six key mechanisms were visualized in Agenda 21 for improved environmental management in the industrial sector:

- Incorporating environmental considerations in industrial development through proper siting policies and mandatory environmental impact assessments.
- Increasing efficiency in the production and use of materials, resources and energy.
- Improving existing pollution abatement technologies and developing new clean technologies, products and processes.
- Developing and implementing emission and effluent controls and standards.
- Ratifying multilateral environment agreements (MEA) such as the Montreal Protocol and the Basel Convention on the Transboundary Movement of Hazardous Wastes and their Disposal.
- Corporate environmental responsibility: The role of business

in improving the efficiency of resource use, reducing risks and hazards, minimizing wastes and safeguarding the environment.

*Achievements of Environmental Management:* Over the past two decades, the government has developed and set standards for regulating emissions and effluents from polluting industries. Based on the information provided by SPCBs/UT-Administrations, a total of 2155 large and medium units have been identified in the country under the 17 highly polluting industrial sectors. The year-wise progresses of these polluting industries are given in Appendix 11. From the Figure 8.2, it is clear that the total number of industries which are declared polluted is not changing. It has increased to 2155 in the period 2002-03. During 1992 and 2002, the total number of identified polluting industries remained same (1551). The data implies that the environmental control regulator is making excellent progress to reduce the number of polluting industries by strong implementation of Pollution Control Programme. The number of defaulting industries

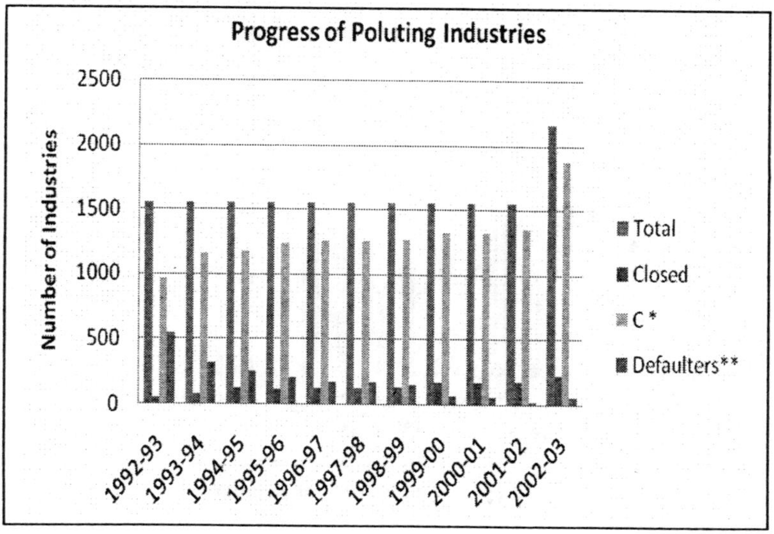


* Having adequate facilities to comply with the standards
** Not having adequate facilities to comply with the standards
*Source*: Ministry of Environment and Forests.

**Fig. 8.2:** Year-wise Progress of Polluting Industries in India

which do not have adequate facilities to comply with the standards are declining through the period. But the industries which are having adequate facilities to comply with the standards are increasing. However, it is very important to study the number of industries category-wise.

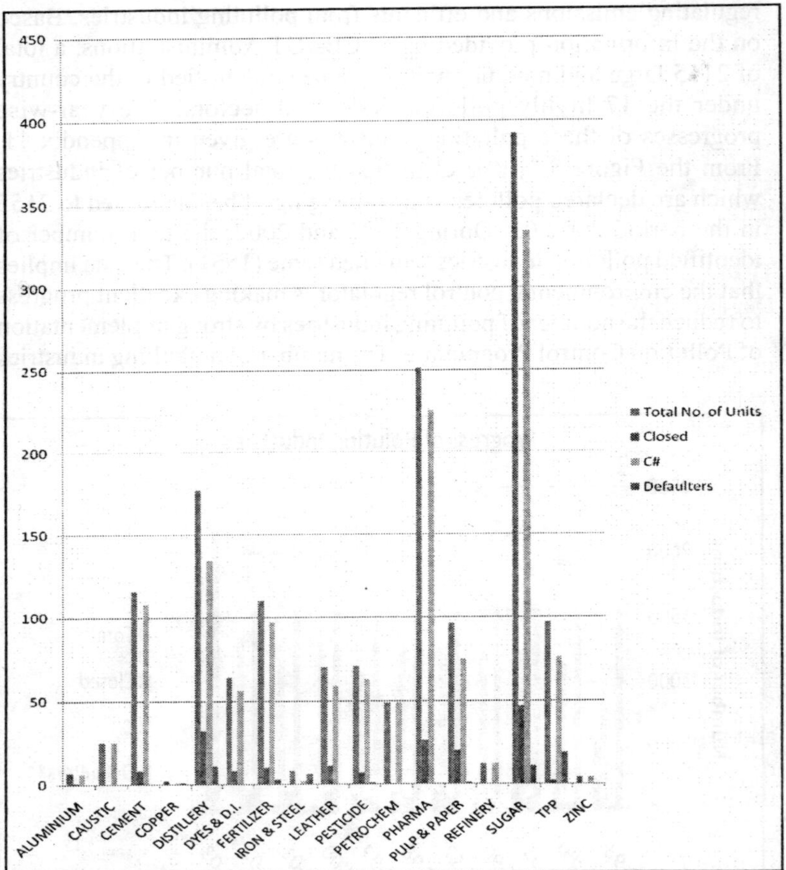


# Having adequate facilities to comply with the standards

*Source*: Ministry of Environment and Forests.

**Fig. 8.3:** Category-wise Distribution of Industries (as on 2001-02)

*Category-wise Distribution of Industries:* The category-wise distribution of these 1,551 units reveals that sugar sector has the maximum number of (i.e. 392) industries, followed by pharmaceuticals, distillery, cement and fertilizer. It has been distributed as 17 categories. It also indicates that agro-based and chemical industries have major shares of 47 per cent and 37 per cent of the total number of industries respectively. About 77 per cent and 15 per cent of the industries is predominantly water polluting and air polluting respectively, and 8 per cent of the industries are potentially both air and water polluting. It is explained in the Appendix 12. The most polluting categories of industries are sugar, pharmaceutical, distillery, fertilizer and paper and pulp. Out of 392 sugar industries, 47 units have been closed (Figure 8.3). The defaulter list depicts that TPP group has maximum number of defaulter units. Till now, 11 units of sugar industries are identified as defaulters.

## Trade-off between Industrial Development and Environmental Degradation

In the process of rapid industrial development, a huge amount of residuals has been generated, which have an undesirable impact on air, water and the land environment. Table 8.1 presents the contribution of industries to pollution by sub-sector.[2] For instance, the iron and steel sector in industrial growth rate can be attributed to the poor performance of the industry and non-metallic mineral products contribute 16 per cent of the total industrial output, but share 55 per cent of the particular matter load. Similarly, food products share 15 per cent of the total industrial output, but 38 per cent of the total industrial BOD. Industrial chemicals, food products and paper and pulp together account for about 25 per cent of the industrial output but are responsible for as much as 86 per cent of the water pollution load. Industrial chemicals and iron and steel contribute about 70 per cent of the toxic release (e.g. heavy metals, cyanides and pesticides) but produce only about 20 per cent of the industrial output.

Some of the highly air polluting industries as per the Central Pollution Control Board (CPCB) are integrated iron and steel, thermal power plants, copper/zinc/aluminum smelters, cement, oil refineries, petrochemicals, pesticides, and fertilisers. Many small-scale industries are also highly polluting to air and water and are located within or in close proximity of cities and towns. Major hazardous waste generating industries include petrochemicals, pharmaceuticals, pesticides, dyes, fertilisers, paints, petroleum, asbestos, tanneries and chlor-alkali.

Indian industries are undergoing through rapid changes including process changes, technological upgradation, organizational restructuring, business re-engineering and globalisation. Industries need to play a proactive role in bringing about these changes so as to ensure an environmentally sound development, which has positive impact on the environment and the society.[3]

**Table 8.1:** Industrial Contribution (%) to Pollution by Sub-sector

| *Sector* | *Share of Industrial Output* | *Share of Total Industrial Pollution (%)* | | | | |
|---|---|---|---|---|---|---|
| | | *Toxic* | *BOD* | *Particulate* | *Sulphur* | *Nitrogen* |
| Iron and steel | 12.5 | 23 | 0 | 23 | 2 | 5 |
| Industrial Chemicals | 7.5 | 44 | 29 | 8 | 11 | 15 |
| Non-Ferrous Metals | 2.1 | 6 | 10 | 3 | 1 | 0 |
| Other Chemicals | 6.8 | 6 | 1 | 1 | 0 | 1 |
| Food Products | 15.3 | 1 | 38 | 11 | 4 | 8 |
| Paper and Pulp | 2.0 | 2 | 19 | 4 | 15 | 11 |
| Non-metallic mineral products | 3.4 | 1 | 0 | 32 | 3 | 10 |
| Petroleum refineries | 6.8 | 6 | 2 | 6 | 31 | 21 |
| Textile | 11.1 | 3 | 1 | 6 | 30 | 23 |
| Total | 67.5 | 92 | 100 | 94 | 97 | 94 |

*Source*: World Bank, 1996.

To study the trade-off between quantum of pollution and industrial development in India, we have examined the EKC hypothesis. Industrial development is explained by the per capita industrial production and environmental degradation in terms of emition of Carbon Dioxide ($CO_2$). To find out this relationship, we have used quadratic regression model. The results of quadric regression equation are given in Table 8.2. In this trade-off equation, the value of $R^2$ is 0.9951. It is found that both coefficient of PCIP is positive and statistically significant; coefficient of $(PCIP)^2$ is negative and statistically significant. This result shows that at the first stage, as per capita industrial production increases, environmental degradation initially increases, but then eventually declines, once a threshold level of industrial development is reached. Therefore, it is supporting the EKC hypothesis of economic development and environmental degradation, providing the 'inverted-U' shape curve propounded by Simon Kuznets. Thus, the level of industrial development is able to explain, to some extent, the degree of environmental degradation in India.

**Table 8.2:** Inter-linkage of Industrial Development and Environmental Degradation

| *Variables* | *β's* | *Std. Error* | *t-value* |
|---|---|---|---|
| Intercept | -96161.94* | 10414.5541 | -9.233 |
| PCIP | 183.531* | 13.139 | 13.969 |
| $PCIP^2$ | -0.01014* | 0.003676 | -2.757 |

Dependant Variable = Carbon Dioxide ($CO_2$)
PCIP = Per Capita Industrial Production
$PCIP^2$ = Square of Per Capita Industrial Production
Adjusted R = 0.9948153
$R^2 = 0.9951$
Standard Error = 6916.198
* represents 1% level of significance

*Source*: As computed by the Author.

With the pace of development, India has made significant efforts in the field of environmental protection, developing environmental standards for both products and processes, requiring environmental impact statements in certain areas, and introducing environmental audits. India's strong support of air quality and alternative fuel initiatives has brought progress as well as growing pains to the country. However, in the absence of coordinated government efforts, including stricter enforcement, industrial pollution is likely to continue to worsen in the coming years as industrialization is growing. The Indian government's ability to safeguard the country's environment will depend on its success in promoting policies that keep the industry growing while providing adequate implementation of pollution control programmes. It is observed that the declared polluting industries are equipping themselves to meet the pollution standards. However, it will be under control in the coming decades.

## NOTES

1. Planning Commission (2001a). *Approach to the Tenth Five Year Plan (2002-07)*. New Delhi. 49 pp.
2. World Bank (1996). *India's Environment: Taking Stock of Plans, Programmes and Policies.* World Bank: South Asia Regional Office. 317 pp.
3. *India: State of Environment*, 2001, published by United Nations Environment Programme, 2001.

# 9

# Trade Liberalization and Environmental Degradation

Today, the whole world is witnessing a paradigm shift in the way businesses have been carried over the years and the way in which they are being designed in the present scenario. After the Second World War, the whole world was divided into two regional blocks, one that was led by the USA and the other which was headed by the then USSR. During the cold war scenario, the trade and business related to the international trade was done with political interest being given more weightage than business development plans.[1] The last five decades have witnessed a profound evolution of economic policy in developing countries, particularly in the case of trade strategies.[2] Both internal as well as external factors have prompted the need for more outward-oriented (or liberalised) trade policy regimes. The creation of the General Agreement on Tariffs and Trade (GATT) in 1947 and the World Trade Organization (WTO) in 1995 have been important driving forces for free trade.[3] During India's economic growth oriented paradigm of the 1950s-1980s, natural resources and the environment were regarded as free goods (or factors of production) and the costs of using natural resources were not internalized into production costs.

Faced with a severe balance of payments or foreign exchange reserve crisis in 1991, India embarked on an economic liberalization programme that encompassed industrial and trade policy, financial sector reforms and privatization. Since then, the major quantitative barriers to trade, i.e. tariffs and non-tariff barriers (quotas, licences and technical specifications, among other restrictions) have substantially been reduced or dismantled. Although the economic reforms began in 1981, the need for openness was felt for quite some time. However, the magnitude of trade and investment reform was negligible during the 1980s. The changes brought about during the 1980s were not systematic and were never integrated into an overall framework. Also, the progress towards more liberalized trade regimes, mainly in India, has been manifested in the trade.

Within today's global economy, trade has become an increasingly important global economic activity, with annual trade volumes increasing sixteen fold over the last fifty years and the ratio of world exports to Gross Domestic Product (GDP) now approaching twenty. With this recent acceleration of global trade, countries throughout the world have benefited from more investment, industrial development, employment and income growth.[4] Nevertheless, trade liberalization elements of restructuring programmes have provided India with a wide range of trade related benefits. This has been reflected in the rapid generation of increased domestic employment, income growth, and foreign exchange earnings. Trade liberalization in India has also facilitated imports of strategic goods and services, and attracted foreign direct investment, yielding enhanced technology transfer, the development of endogenous capacities, and the establishment of basic infrastructure needed to support national objectives for industrial development.[5] Trade liberalization may also indirectly benefit a nation's natural and environmental resource bases, as increased trade-related fiscal revenues can provide government with new financial resources to support environmental protection, conservation and remediation efforts. Recently, however, there has been an increasing concern over the potential negative impacts of trade liberalization, particularly on the environmental and natural resources of developing countries and countries with economies in transition where trade has grown most rapidly. These countries have found that economic activities supporting, or supported by, rapidly expanded trade can result in serious environmental degradation when complementary environmental policies are not in place.

Trade liberalization can have both positive and negative impacts on the environment and the economy. Increased trade can lead to expansion of production, employment and consumption, which is associated with a rise in living standards and a reduction of poverty.[6] Trade liberalization, thus, can promote the efficient allocation of resources and therefore, can reduce pressure caused by over-exploitation of global natural resources. On the other hand, without appropriate environmental policies and regulations, increase in production and consumption as a result of trade can also increase demand for natural resources and increased generation of waste and emissions. The degradation of environment and increased pollution may likely be hastened and can also have major implications on poverty and economic development.[7] However, in India trade liberalization, driven by macroeconomic policies and economic reforms, including Structural Adjustment Programmes (SAPs), may have environmental impacts, both negative as well as positive. For India, which happens to be a dumping ground for old technologies, there is every reason to believe that trade liberalization's effect on pollution is disastrous. A clear analysis of these effects is needed. This chapter is an attempt to pinpoint the environmental implications of trade liberalization in India.

The studies on the relationship between trade and the environment have found varying results. Low and Yates (1992) examined trade shares of polluting and non-polluting industries to developing countries and found that the export share of polluting goods from industrialized countries tended to decrease over time. Levinson and Taylor (2001) used a 2SLS (Two-Stage Least Squares) procedure with instruments to measure stringency of environmental regulations across states in the US, to capture the endogenous nature of the trade-environment relationship. Using this method, they found that tighter environmental regulations are associated with larger net imports. Dean (2002) uses provincial level data on water pollution from China and found support for the idea that trade liberalization has both a direct and an indirect effect on emission growth.

In contrast, Grossman and Krueger (1993) examined the environmental impacts of NAFTA and found no evidence that a comparative advantage is being created by lax environmental regulations in Mexico. Using data across different countries from 1960 to 1995, Mani and Wheeler (1999) found that 'pollution haven effects' are insignificant in developing countries because production is mainly for domestic consumption, not for export. Tobey (1990) tested the impact of domestic environmental regulations on international trade pattern in five pollution intensive industries for 23 countries. He found no statistical significance of the environmental regulation measures on the net exports of these industries. Eskeland and Harrison (1997) examined industry level FDI in four developing countries (Mexico, Cote d`Ivoire, Venezuela and Morocco) and found no significant positive correlation between industry level FDI and measures of air and water emissions.

Some countries experience patterns of specialization into dirty activities following trade liberalization, e.g. Indonesia (Lee and Roland-Holst, 1997; Strutt and Anderson, 1999), China (Dean, 1999; Jha *et al.,* 1999; Dessus *et al.* forthcoming), Costa Rica (Dessus and Bussolo, 1998; Abler *et al.*, 1999), and Turkey (Jha *et al.*, 1999). These countries are expanding or specializing in activities that are harmful to the environment.

According to the study by Khan and Zahler (1985), trade liberalization will raise the growth of exports and imports but the implications for the trade balance and the balance of payments are uncertain because of the relative uncertain impact of liberalization on export and import growth and to the prices of traded goods. Trade liberalization may promote growth from the supply side but, if the balance of payments worsens, growth may be adversely affected from the demand side because the payments deficits resulting from liberalization are unsustainable and not easily rectified by relative price (real exchange rate) changes.

Grossman and Krueger (1993) analyzed the relationship between trade, growth and the environment by regressing measures of environmental quality for cities in various countries on per capita income, trade intensity and other site characteristics. This approach yielded two novel results. First, they discovered a U-shaped relationship between environmental quality and economic growth: at low per capita income levels, environmental quality falls with increases in per capita; however, beyond a certain level of per capita income somewhere between $4,000 to $5,000, increases in income per capita lead to improvement in environmental quality. Second, they found that a country's trade intensity (the sum of imports and exports as a share of GDP) is positively related to environmental quality, which indicates that more the degree of openness in the economy, the less it pollutes.

## THEORETICAL ISSUES OF TRADE LIBERALIZATION AND THE ENVIRONMENT

The neoclassical factor endowment model known as the Hecksher-Ohlin theory of trade postulates that trade arises because of the differences in labour productivity—which they assume to be fixed—for different commodities in different countries. According to this theory, the basis for trade arises not because of inherent technological differences in labour productivity for different commodities between different countries but because countries are endowed with different factor supplies. Given relative factor endowments, factor prices will differ (for instance, labour will be relatively cheap in labour-abundant countries) and so too will domestic commodity price ratios and factor combinations. The above theory, therefore, explains why resource-abundant (for instance, labour-abundant) LDCs are into the production and export of labour-intensive commodities in return for imports of capital-intensive goods because of their relative cost and price advantage enhanced by international specialization. Trade, therefore, serves as an engine for a nation to capitalize on its abundant resources through more intensive production. What this theory suggests is nothing short of free trade which was equally elicited in the Hecksher-Ohlin-Samuelson (H-O-S) model, which is a development of the H-O principle. This model shows how an increase in the price of a commodity can raise the income of the factors of production used most intensively in producing it. Samuelson's factor price equalization theorem postulates the conditions under which free trade in commodities narrows differences in commodity prices between countries, and in doing so the incomes of the factors of production are also brought in line. In other words, free trade offers a substitute for the free mobility of factors of production. Based on the H-O-S model, free mobility of factors can lead to national resource movement from places of excess to places of relative scarcity, and the movement of polluting industries from their home countries to developing countries where environmental regulation is a matter of formality (the pollution haven hypothesis).

Antweiler *et al.* (2001) made a much clearer extrapolation of the original H-O model of trade. They decomposed the full impact of openness or trade liberalization on environment into composition, scale and technique effects. Their approach involves both mathematical and geometrical illustrations. In their geometrical exposition, they derived the condition under which trade liberalization for a dirty good leads to less pollution, if the technique effect (which for them is always benicial to the environment) can overwhelm the combined scale and composition effects (which for them are always harmful to the environment). In this model, trade liberalization (or reduction in trade barriers) produces the three trade-induced effects which interact to determine the environmental effects of trade. When there is a decline in trade barriers, when prices are brought in line due to reduction in barriers, the H-O-S model applies. The result is that domestic price approaches the world price and production is enhanced as it moves to a point where revenue increases and real income rises and there is a change in the production techniques.

The issues raised by most theories of the linkages between trade and environment include the following: if trade openness improves income levels and improves the access of developing economies to less polluting/cleaner techniques, why is there such an overwhelming negative impact of trade on pollution in many countries with these conditions? What is the extent of the technique effects of trade and is this variable only determined by income growth? If the technique effects of trade openness on environment are real, then how do we explain the dumping of especially old and obsolete technology on developing economies? What determines the direction of the composition and scale effects of trade? Are their effects on pollution always the same irrespective of whether it is a developing economy or a developed economy? Lastly, what is the impact of trade liberalization on resource exhaustibility? Is the current wave of excessive trade openness good for the optimal utilization of non-renewable resources? In light of these issues, the present study investigates the impact of trade openness on pollution and resource depletion in India.

*Empirical Evidences:* There is empirical evidence that trade liberalization also stimulates economic growth and at a theoretical level, trade can alter the rate of growth if it spurs innovation or factor accumulation. An important implication of our analysis is that with existing pollution taxes or emissions intensities, the environmental effects of trade liberalization may be quite insignificant. But if pollution quotas are in place, the environmental effects of trade liberalization may be negligible. The welfare analysis of trade liberalization in the presence of environmental problems draws heavily on the theory of the second best (Lipsey and Lancaster, 1956).[8]

Other researchers, employing slightly different country groups and methods, corroborate these findings. Ratnayake (1998) in a study of New Zealand's trade patterns notes that in 1980, 96 per cent of its imports of dirty goods came from the OECD, but by 1993 this had dropped to 86 per cent. At the same time, the share of dirty goods imported from the developing countries increased from 3 per cent to 11 per cent; but their share in clean good imports only increased from 9 per cent to 13 per cent over this same period. Similarly, New

Zealand's exports of dirty goods to developing countries fell from 59 per cent of exports to only 46 per cent, while its exports of clean goods rose. Both scale and, possibly, specialization induces environmental degradation. There is no definite evidence on which effect is dominant. Evidence reviewed by Beghin and Potier (1997) suggests that the scale effect is the most important. The countries are facing more domestic pollution after trade liberalization mainly because of the expansion of aggregate activities and not necessarily because of their involvement in specializing in dirty activities. However, new numerical evidence from a study by Ferrantino and Linkins (1999) suggests that specialization is a more important determinant of pollution compared to the scale. These authors provide estimates of the output effects of trade liberalization (the Uruguay Round and a hypothetical liberalization scenario in manufacturing) on toxic emissions using a multi-country, applied general equilibrium model.

Wheeler (2000) provides examples of the link between air pollution regulation and FDI in Mexico, Brazil, India, and the U.S. that illustrate the importance of community, or firm level efforts, to internalize the costs of pollution in developing countries. Feridun, Mete (2006) studied the impact of trade openness on pollution and resource depletion in Nigeria. The results indicate that pollution is positively related to trade intensity and real GDP per square kilometre, while capital to labour ratio and GNP are negatively related to pollution. In addition, strong evidence suggests that trade intensity, real GDP per square kilometre and GNP are positively related to environmental degradation indicating that the technique, scale, and total effects of liberalization are detrimental to the environment. The composition effect of trade liberalization on natural resource utilization, on the other hand, is beneficial. A number of policy implications emerge from the study for Nigeria as well as other developing economies. There is thus a need to investigate the impact of trade liberalization on environment in India.

Over the last 60 years, India's foreign trade has undergone a complete change in terms of composition and direction. The exports cover a wide range of traditional and non-traditional items while imports consist mainly of capital goods, petroleum products, raw materials, and chemicals to meet the ever-increasing needs of a developing and diversifying economy. For about 40 years (1950-90), foreign trade of India suffered from strict bureaucratic and discretionary controls. Similarly, the Government and the Reserve Bank of India have tightly controlled foreign exchange transactions. From 1947 till mid-1990s, India, with some exceptions, always faced deficit in its balance of payments, i.e. imports always exceeded exports. Imports galloped because of increasing requirements of capital goods, defence equipment, petroleum products, and raw materials. Exports remained relatively sluggish owing to lack of exportable surplus, competition in the international market, inflation at home, and increasing protectionist policies of the developed countries. The deficit in trade balance was the deliberate policy of the government to increase the inflow of foreign capital in the economy.

## Environmental Issues as Non-Tariff Barriers

In the era of liberalization, the developed economies are resorting to the alternate trade restricting measures. These new age barriers include the non-tariff barriers (NTBs) such as environment standards, food safety regulation, labelling requirement and quality standards. At the global level, 185 products have been identified, which face environment-related trade barriers in at least one importing country. These environmental based issues are of great concern for India because these are largely affecting the vibrant export sectors of the Indian economy. They are mainly leather and leather products, textiles, chemicals, marine products, tea and other agricultural products and are mostly concentrated in SME sector. The nature of NTBs faced by these sectors ranges from technical standards and product content requirements to mandatory labelling, eco-labelling, packaging requirements and other SPS-related measures.

The nature of environmental barriers are to eliminate use of toxic substances chemicals and heavy metals in particular, recycle waste and packaging, protect wildlife, raise food safety standards and promote organic food and oppose genetically modified organisms (GMOs). Environmental and health-related standards and regulations in developed-country markets are creating hurdles for the exports of products from developing countries like India. The environment-related non-tariff barriers (ETBs) generally cover all barriers that have been introduced by the importing country to protect the environment, as well as the health and safety of wildlife, plants, animals and humans. Developing countries like India have to adjust their production processes in response to changing environmental regulations in developed countries. Developed economy markets are applying measures such as pesticide Maximum Residue Levels (MRL) permitted in foodstuffs, emission standards for machines, and packaging /eco-labelling requirements have created operational hurdles for our exporters. These barriers mainly have deforming effects on the small sector exporters of developing economies because the costs involved in holding on to the standards set by the developed countries are huge in figure.

Another major issue of concern is that of the food sector as quality standard for food may also fall in the category of environmental standards. The developed countries put these environment related measures with any of the two motives, i.e. either as precautionary measure due to increasing consumer awareness with respect to quality and environmental friendliness of the product which compels the governments to put precautionary measures or as protectionist measure that is non-tariff measure. However, it is very important to distinguish between precautionary and protectionist ETBs. This is done by observing the frequency of repetition of the barrier in the list of notifications by member countries (Primary Survey of Industries 2001-02). This means, the greater is the number of countries notifying a particular ETB for a same product, the greater is the probability of this being a precautionary measure rather than a trade-restrictive measure.[9] It is assumed that when a single country or a limited number of countries enforce an ETB it is more likely that these countries have simply enforced a non-tariff barrier. Such trade restrictive measures are bigger threat for the trading environment.

## Critical Environmental Issues Affecting India's Exports

1. *Eco-labelling*: It is a voluntary method of environmental performance certification and labelling that is practiced around the world. According to the definition given by the International Standard Organization (Type 1) an "eco-label" identifies overall environmental preference of a product or service within a specific product/service category based on life cycle considerations. In contrast to "green" symbols or claim statements developed by manufacturers and service providers, an eco-label is awarded by an impartial third–party in relation to certain products or services that are independently determined to meet environmental leadership criteria.

2. *Effluent Emission Norms*: These are the norms regarding the disposal of waste/residues left after production of final product in a company. Under this, the company is required to process the waste in the effluent emission plant before disposing it, so that the negative effect of it on environment can be minimized.
3. *Standards Regulating (maximum residue) Levels of Toxic Substances in Products*: Regulations setting levels for toxicity and residues of certain substances in products impose trade barriers by either banning substances or products, or setting very low levels of tolerances for prescribed substances. In some cases these levels are even set below international standards. In other cases it is considered necessary to apply these as "precautionary approach". For example, the EU regulations limiting aflatoxin levels in foods are more stringent than International Codex standards and stricter than US standards. EU bans on the use of certain antibiotics in food products are also based on standards that are higher than those set in other industrialized economies. EU and EU-member state restrictions on the use of azo dyes in textile products have also come under scrutiny from developing countries for prohibiting or mandating very low tolerance levels for chemical substances.
4. *Standards for Product Harvesting*: Discriminatory trade barriers are imposed where products are banned from sale because the means in which they are harvested does not meet certain environmental standards or where the product harvesting or processing must meet certain environmental criteria as a condition for being placed on the market.
5. *Packaging and Labeling Requirements*: Packaging and labelling requirements restrict products from sale by banning products with certain packaging or mandating that they meet certain environmental requirements evidenced through labelling. Some impose obligations on producers to collect and recycle packaging. Some mandated environmental requirements are based on processes and production methods of products. In certain cases the packaging material used should be bio-degradable. Several EU regulations pertaining

to the labelling of wine impose labelling requirements pertaining to quality and geographical origin; also they restrict the import of product for which polythene is used as packaging material.

6. *Standards Mandating Energy Efficiency/Emissions Reductions*: Some regulations impose trade barriers where, as a condition for sale in the market, they mandate products meet certain environmental efficiency standards.

## Trends of Exports of Major Polluting Products

The policies of trade liberalization have changed the growth pattern of imports but there are not many changes in the pattern of growth of exports. We, therefore, have examined the growth rate of some of the most polluted exports from India. We know that leather tanning has been ranked as one of the most polluting activities compared to other manufacturing sector activities. It also has one of the highest toxic intensity per unit of output.[10] Converting hides into leather is a heavily chemical intensive process utilizing roughly 130 chemicals. Pollution or wastes resulting from these processes are air, solid and primarily liquid. Hydrogen sulphide and ammonia are the major gases released into the atmosphere.[11] Parikh *et al.* (1995) also mention several other environmental effects in their report on the Indian leather industry. These include the overgrazing by cattle, the smell of rotting flesh near the tanneries, the odour of sulphide emissions from the dehairing and the ammonia emissions and flue gas emissions from the unhairing and fleshing.

Our result shows that leather exports is growing at the rate of 11.88 before the trade liberalization. It has declined to 3.93 during the period between 1990-91 and 2004-05. It is explained in Table 9.1. All the coefficients are statistically significant at 1 level of significance. The coefficient of semi log quadratic function for the period of 1980-2005 is negative and significant at 1 level of significance. This shows that the growth of leather exports has been decelerated in this period. It is also found that the trade liberalization has reduced the rate of growth of exports of leather products. The coefficient of dummy variable ($b_4$) is negative and statistically significant at 1 level of significance. This clearly indicates that there is break through in the trend of leather exports due to trade liberalization in India.

**Table 9.1:** Growth of Exports of Leather and Leather Products (US Dollar)

| *Sl. No* | *Year* | *Function* | *Intercept* | $\beta_2$ | $\beta_3$ | $\beta_4$ | $R^2$ | *Growth Rate (%)* |
|---|---|---|---|---|---|---|---|---|
| 1. | 1980-1990 | Log linear | 2.529637* (0.05421) | 0.048762* (0.00873) | — | — | 0.79565 | 11.8825 |
| 2. | 1991-2005 | Log linear | 3.090946* (0.01880) | 0.016757* (0.00206) | — | — | 0.83465 | 3.93388 |
| 3. | 1980-2005 | Log Quadratic | 2.515277* (0.04172) | 0.060533* (0.00739) | -0.0012* (0.0003) | — | 0.93712 | — |
| 4. | 1980-2005 (1990-91) | Log linear with dummy | 2.52963* (0.0383) | 0.04876* (0.0061) | 0.3937* (0.0728) | -0.0320* (0.0070) | 0.95405 | — |

*Note*: Value in parenthesis is standard error of the coefficient.
* denotes significant at 1% level.

*Source*: Directorate General of Commercial Intelligence and Statistics.

Chemical industry is other and the oldest polluting industries in India. According to KPMG-CHEMTECH (2003) in the year 2002, the chemical industry constituted 6.7 per cent of India's GDP and 10 per cent of total exports. The Indian chemical exports accounted for 1.9 per cent of the global chemicals market. The growth of chemical industry will bestow directly or indirectly in the form of water and air pollution, land degradation and hazardous waste generation. The study of growth, acceleration and shift in the growth of chemical exports are interpreted in Table 9.2.

**Table 9.2:** Growth of Exports of Chemicals (US Dollar)

| Sl. No | Year | Function | Intercept | $\beta_2$ | $\beta_3$ | $\beta_4$ | $R^2$ | Growth Rate (%) |
|---|---|---|---|---|---|---|---|---|
| 1. | 1980-1990 | Log linear | 2.323961* (0.10544) | 0.067971* (0.016993) | — | — | 0.66666 | 16.94 |
| 2. | 1991-2005 | Log linear | 3.153975* (0.02735) | 0.057298* (0.057298) | — | — | 0.96541 | 14.1 |
| 3. | 1980-2005 | Log Quadratic | 2.285* (0.07143) | 0.0824* (0.012659) | -0.0005 (0.0004) | — | 0.9595 | — |
| 4. | 1980-2005 (1990-91) | Log linear with dummy | 2.3241* (0.0704) | 0.0679* (0.0114) | 0.257*** (0.1342) | -0.011 (0.0129) | 0.9658 | — |

*Note*: Value in parenthesis is standard error of the coefficient.
*,** and *** denotes significant at 1%, 5% and 10% levels respectively.

*Source*: Directorate General of Commercial Intelligence and Statistics.

It is found that the chemical export was growing at the rate of 16.94 per cent before the trade liberalization. It has declined to 14.1 per cent during the period 1990-91 and 2004-05. The coefficient of semi log quadratic function for the period of 1980-2005 is negative but statistically insignificant. This shows that the growth of chemical exports has not been showing any change before and after trade liberalization. The coefficient of dummy variable ($b_4$) is negative and statistically significant at 1 level of significance. This clearly indicates that there is break through in the trend of chemical exports due to trade liberalization in India.

Marine production is increasing tremendously in India. States like Andhra Pradesh, Orissa, Gujarat, etc. are mainly involved. Several studies point out that marine production is also causing environmental degradation in the form of water pollution and land degradation. This is a serious threat to the environment. We, therefore, have examined the growth of these polluting commodities and its share in the total exports. The story of exports of marine product is altogether different from the leather and chemical exports. Our result shows that the growth rate export of marine product was less before trade liberalization and it has increased after trade liberalization (Table 9.5). It was 4.4 per cent during 1980-81 to 1989-90, whereas it has increased to 6.69 per cent in post liberalization period. Our study also highlights that there is neither acceleration nor deceleration in the growth of exports of marine products in pre and post liberalization periods. It is also found that there is no shift in the trend of export of marine products during the same period.

**Table 9.3:** Growth of Exports of Marine Products (US Dollar)

| *Sl. No.* | *Year* | *Function* | *Intercept* | $\beta_2$ | $\beta_3$ | $\beta_4$ | $R^2$ | *Growth Rate (%)* |
|---|---|---|---|---|---|---|---|---|
| 1. | 1980-1990 | Log linear | 2.4521* (0.0263) | 0.0188* (0.004237) | — | — | 0.71246 | 4.439 |
| 2. | 1991-2005 | Log linear | 2.777* (0.0365) | 0.029* (0.004)1 | — | — | 0.80108 | 6.916 |
| 3. | 1980-2005 | Log Quadratic | 2.367* (0.0436) | 0.0388* (0.0077) | -0.0002 (0.00029) | — | 0.9371 | — |
| 4. | 1980-2005 (1990-91) | Log linear with dummy | 2.452* (0.0396) | 0.0188* (0.0064) | 0.0344 (0.0754) | 0.0102 (0.0073) | 0.9551 | — |

*Note*: Value in parenthesis is standard error of the coefficient.
*, ** and *** denote significant at 1%, 5% and 10% levels respectively.

*Source*: Directorate General of Commercial Intelligence and Statistics.

Economic activity and trade liberalization has affected the production and exports of various commodities. We, therefore, have examined the growth of exports of identified polluting industries in India. This is explained in the Appendix 13. The data show that the volume of exports of leather, chemicals and marine products are increasing. Leather export in 1990-91 was US$ 1419.47 million and reached at US$ 2379.44 million with slight deviations in between the years. However, there is a constant increase in exports from the year 1993-94 onwards. But it is very important to note here that the contribution of leather exports to total exports is constantly decreasing during post-trade liberalization period. It was 7.8 per cent of total export in 1990-91 and became only 2.8 per cent in 2004-05. There is thus a drastic change in the contribution of leather export in the total export of the country.

There is on the other hand a constant increase in the volume of exports of marine products. It was only US$ 535 million in 1990-91 and reached at US$ 1439 million during 2004-05. The contribution of marine exports to the total exports is fluctuating during post-trade liberalization period. Its share in the total exports is in between 1 to 3 per cent and showing decreasing tendency in the contribution to the total exports of the economy.

As far as the chemical export is concerned, there is a constant increase in the volume of its exports. It was US$ 1728 million in the year 1990-91 and became US$ 12443.7 million in the year 2004-05. However, the chemical exports bear a different story as compared to leather and marine products. It is found that the share of chemical products in the total exports is gradually increasing during the post-trade liberalization. It has increased from 9.5 per cent to 14.14 per cent during the period 1990-2005.

Thus, from the above analysis it is clear that the total export of India is growing at a constant rate. The interference of WTO and trade liberalization has widened the scope of trade. The volume of exports of polluting industries is growing but its share in the total exports has shown a decreasing tendency particularly after the emergence of trade liberalization. It is, therefore, very difficult to conclude that policies of globalization and trade liberalization have not promoted the trade of these products that generate more pollution in the country.

## Impact of Trade Liberalization on Environmental Issues

It is, thus, clear that the trade liberalization in India has increased the trade but not the trade of products that are generating pollution in the country. But still, we have evidence that the level of pollution and the degree of environmental degradation is increasing in the country. It is, therefore, important to examine the effect of various factors such as the degree of trade openness, percentage inflow of FDI and Real GNP on the level of pollution. We have estimated the degree of openness of capital inflow and technique effect in India for the period 1990-91 to 2004-05. The raw data are given in Appendix 14. It is very interesting to note here that all these estimates are massively increasing over the period. It is shown in Table 9.4.

**Table 9.4:** Trade Liberalization and Environmental Issues in India

| *Year* | *$CO_2$ (000' Metric Tons)* | *Degree of Openness* | *% Capital Inflow* | *Real GNP (Expansion Effect)* |
|---|---|---|---|---|
| 1990-91 | 185016 | 0.148253 | 0.496329 | 683670 |
| 1991-92 | 198499 | 0.155992 | 0.898631 | 691143 |
| 1992-93 | 211336 | 0.173885 | 2.785105 | 726375 |
| 1993-94 | 220346 | 0.182829 | 4.079866 | 769265 |
| 1994-95 | 234778 | 0.188259 | 7.61256 | 824816 |
| 1995-96 | 247689 | 0.213396 | 12.97498 | 886961 |
| 1996-97 | 273682 | 0.207259 | 16.43142 | 959359 |
| 1997-98 | 279873 | 0.204494 | 24.11749 | 1005946 |
| 1998-99 | 290412 | 0.199036 | 17.9184 | 1070773 |
| 1999-00 | 301294 | 0.212731 | 13.8133 | 1137185 |
| 2000-01 | 316335 | 0.228294 | 27.4883 | 1186438 |
| 2001-02 | 318030 | 0.218219 | 38.02299 | 1257636 |
| 2002-03 | 335662 | 0.244954 | 31.73534 | 1310471 |
| 2003-04 | 347577 | 0.258941 | 23.87602 | 1422479 |
| 2004-05 | 352312 | 0.309633 | 27.40126 | 1519749 |

*Source*: As computed by Author from indiastat.com

The trade intensity (openness) is increasing, which indicates that the openness in foreign trade is increasing in India. The increase in of capital inflow shows the massive use of foreign direct investment in the production activities. The real GNP of India is also increasing over the period. It is also found that the $CO_2$ emission is increasing highly in India.

It is, thus, achieved by running regression the level of air pollution on the degree of openness, percentage inflow of foreign capital and real GNP. The results are shown in Table 9.5. The interlinking model of environmental pollution and trade liberalization states that the overall explanatory power of the model is very impressive as $R^2$ is nearly about 97 per cent. We have used Durbin Watson test of autocorrelation for this estimation. But our 'd' statistics (Durbin-Watson Coefficient) is not showing the presence of autocorrelation. The calculated 'd' statistics falls under inconclusive area. However, the strong inspection about the data source suggests that there is absence of autocorrelation in the model. It is very remarkable to mention here that the intercept of the model is positive and statistically significant. The coefficient of openness (trade intensity) is negative but statistically insignificant. The coefficients of capital inflow and technique are positive and statistically significant at 10 per cent and 5 per cent level of significance respectively. It can thus be deduced that the degree of openness is not causing any effect on the emissions of $CO_2$ into the environment. It can be interpreted that the policies of WTO and trade liberalization have not endorsed the environmental pollution in India. The high rate of emission of $CO_2$ is due to capital inflow and expansion effect. The foreign direct investment and economic activity is encouraging the emission of $CO_2$ in India. The expansion effect is highly significant. This inferred that the economic development gives rise to environmental pollution and there exists a positive relation between economic development and emission of $CO_2$ in India.

**Table 9.5:** Impact of Trade Liberalization on the Environment

| | | | |
|---|---|---|---|
| $R^2$ | = 0.975154 | | |
| Adjusted $R^2$ | = 0.968378 | | |
| Standard Error | = 9830.312 | | |
| Durbin-Watson | d = 1.144 | | |
| Dependent Variable: | Pollution ($CO_2$ Emission) | | |
| Independent Variables: | Coefficient | Standard Error | T Stat. |
| Intercept ($\alpha_0$) | 88022.35 | 16916.44 | 5.20336 |
| Degree of Openness ($\alpha_1$) | -16600.1 | 189311.3 | -0.08769 |
| % of Capital Inflow ($\alpha_2$) | 861.0922 | 472.449 | 1.822614 |
| Expansion Effect ($\alpha_3$) | 0.170186 | 0.038065 | 4.470912 |

*Source*: As computed by the Author

However, there is a possibility of multicollinearity problem in the model because of the nature of two variables such as degree of openness and real GNP. We, thus, have transformed the model to make the model free from multicollinearity. We have transformed the model as:

$$\Delta POL_t = \alpha_0 + \alpha_1 \Delta [(EXP_t+IMP_t)/GDP_t] + \alpha_2 \Delta (Ft/TCF_t) + \alpha_3 \Delta RGNP_t + V_t$$

This equation has been evolved by taking successive difference of all the variables of the original equation $POL_t = \alpha_0 + \alpha_1 [(EXP_t+IMP_t)/GDP_t] + \alpha_2 (Ft/TCF_t) + \alpha_3 RGNP_t + \mu_t$. We have run the regression without intercept. Considering successive differences of the variables and regressing them from origin provide the estimates free from multicollinearity. The estimates are shown in Table 9.6.

**Table 9.6:** Impact of Trade Liberalization on the Environment (Transformed)

| | | | | |
|---|---|---|---|---|
| $R^2$ | | = 0.659 | | |
| Adjusted $R^2$ | | = 0 .567 | | |
| Standard Error | | = 8710.3051 | | |
| Durbin-Watson | d | = 1.712 | | |
| Dependent Variable: | | Pollution ($CO_2$ Emission) | | |
| Independent Variables: | | Coefficient | Standard Error | T Stat. |
| Change in Degree of Openness: ($\alpha_1$) | | 7440.212 | 154614.030 | .048 |
| Change in % of Capital Inflow: ($\alpha_2$) | | 62.790 | 367.793 | .171 |
| Change in Expansion Effect: ($\alpha_3$) | | .164 | .047 | 3.487 |

*Source*: As computed by the Author.

In the above table, it is seen that the overall explanatory power of the model is 0.659, which is lesser than that of the original equation. This transformed model is free from autocorrelation and multicollinearity. It is very important to note here that the coefficient of expansion effect is positive and statistically significant at 1 per cent level of significance. Other factors are playing insignificant role in environmental degradation in India. It can thus be inferred that the degree of openness and capital inflows are not causing any effect on the emissions of $CO_2$ into the environment. It can thus be concluded that the policies of WTO and trade liberalization have not endorsed the environmental pollution in India. The high rate of emission of $CO_2$ is due to expansion effect. The economic activity is encouraging the emission of $CO_2$ in India and thus polluting the environment.

After trade liberalization, India has been able to increase the volume of exports and imports. The growth rate of the trade is sound and accelerating. There is a shift in the trend of growth rate of import after the trade liberalization. The openness has given opportunities to export more in the world market. We could have managed the import very wisely. The balance of payment (BOP) crisis has been corrected and the foreign exchange reserve has become bulkier by the day. The exports of polluting industries have increased. The compound growth of leather exports has declined and decelerated in post liberalization period. There is a breakthrough in the trend line of leather exports. There is a slight decline in the growth rate of chemical products during post-liberalization. However, there is no shift in the trend of export of chemicals and marine products. The volume of these exports has increased but their percentage in total export has declined except in the case of chemical products.

It is found that there is no adverse impact of trade liberalization on emission of pollution ($CO_2$) and environmental degradation. The expansion effect (Real GNP) is causing environmental degradation in the form of emission of $CO_2$. Thus, it can be concluded that the trade liberalization and capital inflow in India are neither budding environmental pollution nor these are degrading the environment. There are other factors such as economic activities; maybe industrial activities are responsible for the bad environmental status in India. The links between trade and the environment are multiple, complex and important. Trade liberalization is itself neither necessarily good nor bad for the environment. Its effects on the environment in fact depend on the extent to which environment and trade goals can be made complementary and mutually supportive. A positive outcome requires appropriate economic and environmental policies.

India should examine carefully the challenges, opportunities and constraints they will face in participating in any further trade liberalization. In other words, India should be ready to participate actively in future negotiations so as to ensure that decisions on areas where India exhibits comparative advantage are not compromised. In addition, India should ensure that any trade agreement does not contain provisions that jeopardize its environment.

## NOTES

1. Joshi, G.N. and Shriniwas, V.A. (2006), *International Trade and Environmental Policy Issues: A Reference to India's position*; *Environmental Issues of Development,* The Associated Publisher, Ambala Cantt, 2006, xvi, 470 p.
2. For details please see Rodriguez, F. and Rodrick, D. (2000). 'Trade policy and economic growth: a skeptic's guide', in B. Bernanke and K. Rogoff, (eds.), *NBER Macroeconomics Annual 2000*, Cambridge MA.: MIT Press and *The Economic Journal*, 114 (February), F1–F3. Royal Economic Society 2004. Published by Blackwell Publishing, 9600 Garsington Road, Oxford OX4 2DQ, UK and 350 Main Street, Malden, MA 02148, USA.
3. World Bank, *Globalization, Growth and Poverty: Facts, Fears and Agenda for Action*, forthcoming.
4. *Trade Liberalization and the environment, lessons learned from Bangladesh, Chile, India, Philippines, Romania and Uganda; A synthesis Report*, United Nations, New York and Geneva, 1999.
5. See, for example, IMF, *World Economic Outlook*, May 1997; T.N. Srinivasan and Jagdish Bhagwati, "Outward Orientation and Development: Are the

Revisionists Right?", Yale University Economic Growth Center Discussion Paper No. 806, 1999; and Jeffrey Frankel and David Romer, "Does Trade Cause Growth", *American Economic Review*, June 1999.

6. Lundberg, M. and Squire, L. (2000). 'The simultaneous evolution of growth and inequality', mimeo, The World Bank.
7. For more details please refer "A study on the use of economic instruments in the pulp and paper industry", *Impacts of trade liberalization in Indonesia.* The Indonesian Research Bank, 2004.
8. The welfare effect of trade liberalization in the presence of environmental distortions has been a major theme of the literature: see Baumol (1971), Pethig (1976), Siebert (1977), Asako (1979), Copeland (1994).
9. Aserkar, R. and Vyas, R. "Environmental Policy Issues and Their Impact on Exports of India"; *Environmental Issues of Development,* The Associated Publisher, Ambala Cantt, 2006, xvi, 470 p.
10. WTO, (1997), p. 52.
11. Environmental Impacts and Mitigation Costs Associated with Cloth and Leather Exports from Pakistan; A Report on Trade and Sustainable Development submitted by Sustainable Development Policy Institute and IUCN-P to IISD Canada for the IISD/IUCN/IDRC Project on Building Capacity for Trade and Sustainable Development in Developing Countries, by Shahrukh Rafi Khan, Mahmood A. Khwaja, Abdul Matin Khan, Haider Ghani and Sajid Kazmi, Islamabad, June 1999.

# 10

# Conclusions and Suggestions

## CONCLUSIONS

In the pace of rapid economic development, we have exploited our natural resources at a rapid rate. It has disturbed the ecological balance and environment has become human unfriendly. With the process of development, the quality of environment is deteriorating. Economic reforms have taken place in 1991, in which the motto of privatization, liberalization and globalization was fixed, but no consideration has been given to protect the environment. There is no such consciousness, where economic development can be achieved at a faster rate without exploiting the environmental resources.

In order to achieve the objectives of planning, Indian planners formulated a strategy of planned economic development. The strategy in economic development means the utilization of the available resources to win the war against poverty. I.G. Patel advocates that strategy implies essentially a deliberate choice—a choice of the point and timing and manner of attack on the problems at hand. Thus, the major elements in development strategy are the size of the plan, the pattern of investment envisaged in the plan, i.e. the allocation of investment among the different sectors, the techniques or resource mobilization, the policy mix, i.e. fiscal policy, monetary policy, policy regarding controls and licensing, reliance on foreign aid, etc. Our development strategy has emphasized over the co-ordination of all these elements with some variations in emphasis from plan to plan.

India is facing a number of important challenges in terms of its environmental degradation. These include climate and atmospheric change, species loss, degradation of non-ecosystems and depletion of renewable natural resources. To a great extent, these challenges are driven by human activity in terms of consumption patterns, production processes and waste disposal. The assessments since 1987 show clearly that the forest cover in India had stabilized around 19.4 per cent of the total geographical area (i.e. around 64 million hectares). However, the 2001 assessment shows that only about 38 million hectares are dense forests (i.e. 12%) and the rest are open forests or degraded forests (about 8%) and mangroves. It is seen that the states like Uttar Pradesh, Andhra Pradesh, Jammu & Kashmir, Gujarat, Orissa and Maharashtra with lower forest cover are not able to protect their forests, but rather are keenly involved in the process of deforestation. But states like Manipur, Assam, Arunachal Pradesh, Meghalaya, Himachal Pradesh, Karnataka, Kerala and Tamil Nadu, which are rich in forest cover, have started the process of reforestation. This non-uniformity in protection of natural stock across Indian states is a matter of big amazement. There is a need to give more emphasis in protecting the natural resources.

After more than two decades of impressive economic growth and some important reforms as well as deregulation, the Indian economy is at the threshold of even higher growth. The annual compound growth rate of GDP was 5.8 during the period 1981-90, whereas it increased to 6.3 during 1990-2001. There is thus a shift in the trend of GDP growth due to globalization. Employment, and capital inflows increased tremendously in our country during post reforms period. The gap between export and import rose immensely over the period. Exports and imports of goods and services also grew during the period 1991-2005. There is no substantial change in land utilization pattern in India during 1990-2000. Only area sown more than once and total cropped area changed slightly. The area under forest, pastures and grazing lands, fallow lands and agricultural land did not change in the period 1991-2001. It is revealed that in between the share of agriculture in GDP declined, and as the process of industrialization and economic growth gathered momentum, the share of agriculture indicated a sharp decline and reached a level of 22 per cent in 2003-04. Industrial production grew at an average rate of 6.77 per cent per annum during the period from 1994-95 to 2004-05. This growth was mainly on account of the manufacturing sector, while electricity and mining and quarrying sectors witnessed much lower growth rates in production. The overall industrial growth path in the 1990s has been marked by cyclical fluctuations with the industrial growth rate increasing to a high of 13 per cent in 1995-96 before falling to 4.1 per cent in 1998-99. There was a significant improvement in overall growth in industrial value added to 6.7 per cent in 1999-2000 due to acceleration in growth rate of the manufacturing and construction sectors, which declined to 5 per cent in 2000-01. However, it has again increased to 8.4 per cent in 2004-05.

The interactions between economic development and environmental degradation were very clear and significant. It is found that both coefficient of PCCE is positive and statistically significant; coefficient of $(PCCE)^2$ is negative and statistically significant. This result shows that at the first stage, as per capita consumption of electricity increases, environmental degradation initially increases, but then eventually declines, once a threshold level of economic development is reached. It supports the EKC hypothesis of economic development and environmental degradation, providing the 'inverted-U' shaped curve propounded by Simon Kuznets. Thus, the level of economic development can explain the degree of environmental degradation in India. Later on, we have considered only those states which have shown substantial decrease in forest area and we have pooled the data for two time periods by using dummy variable technique. We found that the positive impact of PCI followed by negative of $PCI^2$ on deforestation supports the environmental Kuznet curve hypothesis on environmental degradation in India. Thus, it may be advocated that India can demand better quality of environment only after achieving certain level of growth. It is found that neither social factors like female literacy, decadal growth of population, etc., nor economic factors like per capita production of milk, urbanization rate, etc. explain the decay in the forest cover. Our regression analysis could identify only per capita consumption of electricity (PCCE), $(PCCE)^2$ and percentage of forest area as the factors that explain forest degradation. Our study also found that the per capita Consumption of Electricity (demand side factors) and the level of Forest Area (supply side factors) explain deforestation. When only those states which have shown substantial decrease in forest area are considered we found that level of PCI and rural poverty are important indicators to explain deforestation in the country.

The task of pollution control in India is complex due to the large number of heavy, large and small-scale industries involved. Further, the rise in the number of vehicles coupled with poverty and the large population puts tremendous pollution pressure on air, water and land. A comprehensive approach to pollution control is being undertaken based on certain principles such as preventing pollution at source, encouraging, developing and applying the best available practicable technical solution, ensuring that polluter pays for pollution and control arrangements, focusing on protection and revival of heavily polluted areas and river stretches and involving the public in decision making. The government aims to achieve these objectives with the use of a judicious mix of instruments in the form of legislation, fiscal incentives, voluntary agreements, educational programmes and information campaigns. The Central and State Pollution Control Boards are entrusted with the task of enforcing measures for pollution control. Environmental Impact Assessment has been made statutory for 30 categories of developmental projects under various sectors like industrial mining, irrigation, power, transport and others.

The process of development facilitated by industrialization and agricultural expansion has led to economic growth, but it has also increased the pressure on natural resources and resulted in pollution of air, water and land. The Government of India has over the years implemented a series of measures to protect the environment. In 1972, a Committee on Human Environment was created. The Central Department of Environment was set up in 1980, which was converted into Ministry of Environment and Forests in 1985. The Ministry is the nodal agency, which formulates environmental policies and legislations and implements the various programmes for environment management.

Our estimates show that a total of 2,155 large and medium industrial units have been identified in the country under the 17 highly polluting industrial sectors. The category-wise distribution of the 1,551 units reveals that sugar sector has the maximum number of (i.e. 392) industries, followed by pharmaceuticals, distillery, cement and fertilizer. It also indicates that agro-based and chemical industries have major shares of 47 per cent and 37 per cent of the total number of industries respectively. About 77 per cent and 15 per cent of the industries are predominantly water polluting and air polluting respectively, and 8 per cent of the industries are potentially both air and water polluting. It is very interesting to note here that at the first stage, as per capita industrial production increases, environmental degradation initially increases, but then eventually declines, once a threshold level of industrial development is reached. Therefore, it is supporting the EKC hypothesis of economic development and environmental degradation.

As far as agricultural growth and environment is concerned the estimates show that there exist a negative relationship between the agricultural prices and forest area. In other words, rise in the price index will give more return in cultivation. The farmer will prefer to go in for extensive cultivation by clearing the forest area. This, thus, shows that the increase in prices of jute and foodgrains is responsible for decay in forest area in India. It is also found that with increase in the price index of fertilizer, the farmer will not prefer to utilize more fertilizer. They prefer to go in for extensive cultivation by clearing the forest area. Therefore, the agricultural price has a vital role in forest clearings. It is also found that there is no adverse impact of trade liberalization on creation of pollution and environmental degradation. The coefficients of composition effect and scale of economic activity are negative, but only the coefficient of scale economic activity is statistically significant at 10 level of significance. That means the economic activities are zealously involved in environment degradation. But, there is no significant role of trade intensity on environmental degradation.

In the name of development, unfortunately the government has allowed landlords, private contractors, mine owners and industrialists to encroach upon public lands and pastures, and literally loot and destroy forests, water resources and mineral wealth. The rich and the more powerful have gradually but surely appropriated the country's natural resources in their favour. The bureaucrats actively collude with the more affluent in the destruction of India's environment. Neither the planners nor the bureaucrats gave any thought to the environmental degradation and the human suffering to the vast majority of poor people implied in our development process.

## SUGGESTIONS AND RECOMMENDATIONS

In India, these environmental issues of political economy cannot be resolved without a national consensus. The success of India's environmental programmes depends greatly on the awareness and consciousness of the people. Government and the people should sit together to discuss the policies for economic development and environmental conservation. One of the major fallacies of our times is the view that sitting in Delhi policies can be made for the entire country without the involvement of the State governments and the people. The major responsibility in this regard must be entrusted to the State governments, and through the agencies of civic bodies in urban areas and Panchayati Raj Institutions in rural areas, the people must participate in environmental protection. Women should be given a leading role; they are closer to earth and have an entirely different perspective on nature, on trees and animal life. In the initial process of economic growth, appropriate intervention is required by the government to protect the stock of natural resources. The Indian government's ability to safeguard the country's environment will depend on its success in promoting policies that keep industry growing while providing adequate implementation of pollution controlling programmes.

Environment and economy are inter-related and difficult to separate one from the other. Environmental pollution in India, as in the rest of the world, is increasingly becoming an important issue. Despite the regulations in place, enforcement has been weak. Government policies, in addition to regulatory mechanisms, incorporate a few market based economic instruments in economic and environmental planning. Hence, the development strategy ignores its repercussions on the environment that sustains life forms. For betterment of the economy and its people, the development strategy will have to take care of environmental protection and growth. There is, therefore, a need to make environment an integral part of development strategy.

Trade liberalization should be accompanied by government investments in education, skills, research and development so as to equip people to take advantage of new employment opportunities, and to create adequate safety nets to protect the poor and the environment during the period of trade liberalization. India should examine carefully the challenges, opportunities and constraints they will face in participating in any further trade liberalization. In other words, India should be ready to participate actively in future negotiations so as to ensure that decisions on areas where India exhibits comparative advantage are not compromised. In addition, India should ensure that any trade agreement does not contain provisions that make vulnerable its environment.

Last but not the least, there is little integration in the present set of economic and environmental policies in India. There is a strong need to assess integrated policies on environment and economy simultaneously. Therefore, it is high time that our planners review the entire position of development and environmental crisis and evolve a new process of balanced and rational development, which will also preserve the environment sustainably. It is also important to note here that government should be kind enough to encourage research and development in multi-fold so that future researchers will be attracted to conduct research in this thrust area and may be able to suggest a number of issues, which may help the planners to frame environment sustainable development policies accordingly.

# Appendices

## Appendix 1

### *Land Use Classification in India*

*(Thousand Hectares)*

| Year | Geographical Area | Reporting Area for Land Utilization Statistics | Forests | Not Available for Cultivation | | | Other Uncultivated Land Excluding Fallow Land | | | | Fallow Lands | | | Total Cropped Area | | |
|---|---|---|---|---|---|---|---|---|---|---|---|---|---|---|---|---|
| | | | | Area Under Non-agri Uses | Barren and Un-Cultural Land | Total | Permanent Pastures and Other Grazing Lands | Land under Misc. Tree Crops & Groves not included in Net Area Sown | Cultural Waste Land | Total | Fallow Lands Other than Current Fallows | Current Fallows | Total | Net Sown Area | Gross sown Area | Total |
| 1950-51 | 328726 | 284315 | 40482 | 9357 | 38160 | 47517 | 6675 | 19828 | 22943 | 49446 | 17445 | 10679 | 28124 | 118.75 | 131.89 | 118.75 |
| 1955-56 | 328726 | 291917 | 51343 | 13921 | 34475 | 48396 | 11473 | 5885 | 21537 | 38895 | 12544 | 11583 | 24127 | 129.16 | 147.31 | 129.16 |
| 1960-61 | 328726 | 298458 | 54052 | 14840 | 35911 | 50751 | 13966 | 4459 | 19212 | 37637 | 11180 | 11639 | 22819 | 133.2 | 152.77 | 133.2 |
| 1965-66 | 328726 | 305535 | 61543 | 15170 | 34327 | 49497 | 14810 | 4076 | 16965 | 35851 | 9262 | 13184 | 22446 | 136.2 | 155.28 | 136.2 |
| 1970-71 | 328726 | 303758 | 63830 | 16478 | 28161 | 44639 | 13261 | 4299 | 17500 | 35060 | 8759 | 11116 | 19875 | 140.27 | 165.79 | 140.27 |
| 1975-76 | 328726 | 304329 | 66699 | 18660 | 21578 | 40238 | 12592 | 3630 | 17743 | 33965 | 9229 | 12546 | 21775 | 141.65 | 171.3 | 141.65 |
| 1980-81 | 328726 | 304159 | 67473 | 19656 | 19962 | 39618 | 11974 | 3610 | 16744 | 32328 | 9916 | 14832 | 24748 | 140 | 172.63 | 140 |
| 1985-86 | 328726 | 304698 | 67067 | 20631 | 20090 | 40721 | 11783 | 3563 | 15718 | 31064 | 10051 | 14894 | 24945 | 140.9 | 178.46 | 140.9 |
| 1990-91 | 328726 | 304862 | 67805 | 21087 | 19389 | 40476 | 11404 | 3818 | 14995 | 30217 | 9662 | 13703 | 23365 | 143 | 185.74 | 143 |
| 1995-96 | 328726 | 304875 | 68817 | 22362 | 19009 | 41371 | 11064 | 3481 | 14098 | 28643 | 10016 | 13831 | 23847 | 142.2 | 187.47 | 142.2 |
| 2000-01 | 328726 | 305174 | 69529 | 23864 | 17598 | 41462 | 10656 | 3435 | 13611 | 27701 | 10309 | 14770 | 25079 | 141.16 | 185.71 | 141.16 |
| 2005-06 | 328726 | 305269 | 69785 | 25027 | 17476 | 42503 | 10415 | 3376 | 13123 | 26914 | 10504 | 13672 | 24176 | 140.88 (P) | 190.64 (P) | 140.88 (P) |

(P): Provisional except Geographical area.

*Source:* Ministry of Agriculture, Government of India.

# Appendix 2

## *Land Utilization Pattern, 1990-91, 2000-01 to 2005-06*

| Particulars | 1990-91 | | 2000-01 | | 2005-06 | |
|---|---|---|---|---|---|---|
| | Area (Million Hectares) | Per cent | Area (Million Hectares) | Per cent | Area (Million Hectares) | Per cent |
| (i) Total Geographical area | 329 | | 329 | | 329 | |
| (ii) Total reporting area | 305 | 100 | 306 | 100 | 306 | 100 |
| (iii) Barren land, not available for cultivation | 41 | 13 | 41.4 | 13.52 | 42.5 | 13.8 |
| (iv) Area under forests | 68 | 22 | 69.5 | 22.71 | 69.7 | 22.73 |
| (v) Permanent pastures and grazing land | 12 | 4 | 11 | 3.5 | 10.6 | 3.4 |
| (vi) Culturable waste lands, etc. | 19 | 6.2 | 17 | 5.5 | 16.5 | 5.3 |
| (vii) Fallow lands | 23 | 7.5 | 25 | 8 | 24 | 7.8 |
| (viii) Net area sown | 142 | 46 | 141 | 46 | 140 | 45.75 |
| (ix) Area sown more than once | 43 | 14 | 49 | 16 | 50 | 16.33 |
| (x) Total cropped area | 185 | 60 | 190 | 62 | 190 | 62.1 |

*Source:* Ministry of Agriculture, Government of India

# Appendix 3

*Compound Growth Rates of Land Utilization from 1950-51 to 2005-06*

| Source | Function | Intercept ($\beta_1$) | $\beta_2$ | $\beta_3$ | $R^2$ | Growth Rate |
|---|---|---|---|---|---|---|
| Barren | Log Linear | 4.692198* | -0.0018144* | — | 0.623554 | -0.4169 |
| and Un-Cultural Land | Log Quadratic | 4.724484* | -0.00515* | 0.00005859* | 0.759335 | — |
| Permanent Pastures | Log Linear | 4.095146* | -0.00081* | — | 0.04781 | -0.18736 |
| and Other Grazing Lands | Log Quadratic | 4.005856* | 0.008422* | -0.00016* | 0.44299 | — |
| Land under Misc. | Log Linear | 3.788739* | -0.00567* | — | 0.52235 | -1.2980 |
| Tree Crops & Groves not included in Net Area Sown | Log Quadratic | 3.925766 | -0.01985 | 0.000249 | 0.731847 | — |
| Cultural Waste Land | Log Linear | 4.337735* | -0.00407* | — | 0.89328 | -0.9323 |
| | Log Quadratic | 4.35959* | -0.00633* | 0.00003966* | 0.911017 | — |
| Net Sown Area | Log Linear | 2.112383* | 0.000928* | — | 0.55315 | 0.21399 |
| | Log Quadratic | 2.08726* | 0.00362* | -0.0000489* | 0.85157 | — |
| Gross sown Area | Log Linear | 2.151973* | 0.002621* | — | 0.91822 | 0.60543 |
| | Log Quadratic | 2.132067* | 0.004754* | -0.00003877* | 0.95723 | — |

*Denotes significant at 1% level.

*Source*: Ministry of Agriculture, Government of India, 2006.

# Appendix 4

## *Category-wise Total Registered Motor Vehicles in Metropolitan Cities of India (As on 31st March, 2004) (Provisional)*

| Metro Cities | Two Wheelers | Cars | Jeeps | Omni Buses | Tractors | Trailers | Others | Total Non-Transport | Grand Total (Transport+ Non- Transport) |
|---|---|---|---|---|---|---|---|---|---|
| Ahmedabad | 840285 | 137636 | 10969 | — | 109 | 172 | 1917 | 991088 | 1075213 |
| Bangalore | 1416317 | 257988 | 7161 | 17071 | 8877 | 7398 | 16549 | 1731361 | 1890692 |
| Bhopal | 317675 | 27886 | 3080 | — | 9756 | 3755 | 663 | 362815 | 391579 |
| Chennai | 1353177 | 341425 | 12114 | 8769 | 2317 | 11607 | 32306 | 1761715 | 2014776 |
| Coimbatore | 522441 | 60923 | 4295 | 303 | 5974 | 83 | 4126 | 598145 | 630094 |
| Delhi | 2665750 | 1192389 | 122283 | 8386 | 4851 | 99 | 9705 | 4003463 | 4236675 |
| Hyderabad | 1010536 | 167689 | 29287 | 10464 | 348 | — | 9252 | 1227576 | 1355700 |
| Indore | 502691 | 54023 | 4324 | — | 10903 | 7507 | 1669 | 581117 | 644771 |
| Jaipur | 617195 | 86332 | 25136 | — | 22655 | 2861 | 653 | 754832 | 823715 |
| Kanpur* | 352698 | 44094 | 4397 | 2040 | 4238 | 425 | 1192 | 409084 | 424652 |
| Kochi* | 81783 | 27630 | 5745 | 3817 | 403 | 159 | 235 | 119772 | 166481 |
| Kolkata | 391051 | 327337 | (a) | — | 4821 | (b) | 21075 | 744284 | 875156 |
| Lucknow* | 491012 | 66881 | 11185 | — | 11737 | 911 | 3029 | 584755 | 614794 |
| Ludhiana | 595768 | 85155 | 3852 | — | 45628 | 311 | 549 | 731263 | 770784 |
| Madurai | 252404 | 18825 | 1214 | 77 | 3841 | 1262 | 2612 | 280235 | 304039 |
| Mumbai | 584180 | 358742 | 21580 | 3936 | 1403 | 991 | 5996 | 976828 | 1199416 |
| Nagpur | 458353 | 32872 | 9429 | 497 | 3703 | 3841 | 774 | 509469 | 543322 |
| Patna* | 227572 | 36651 | — | — | 8143 | 6609 | 1589 | 280564 | 335623 |
| Pune | 561955 | 83357 | 11529 | 616 | 1142 | 1103 | 1392 | 661094 | 754902 |
| Surat | 582893 | 57603 | 4233 | — | 263 | 285 | 535 | 645812 | 692118 |
| Vadodara | 463268 | 55011 | 6189 | — | 1603 | 3275 | 2484 | 531830 | 586438 |
| Varanasi* | 304724 | 20694 | 2699 | — | 20705 | 1303 | 964 | 351089 | 365913 |
| Visakhapatnam | 340096 | 27731 | 3077 | 1204 | 2651 | 78 | 815 | 375652 | 411691 |
| India (P) | 14933824 | 3568874 | 303778 | 57180 | 176071 | 54035 | 120081 | 19213843 | 21108544 |

*Source:* Ministry of Shipping, Road Transport & Highways, Government of India.

## Appendix 5

### *State-wise Geographic Area, Recorded Forest Area and Actual Forest Cover in India (2001)*

| | *State/UT* | *Geographic Area (sq. km)* | *Recorded Forest* | | *Forest Cover* | |
|---|---|---|---|---|---|---|
| | | | *Area (sq. km)* | *Per cent* | *Area (sq km)* | |
| 1. | Andhra Pradesh | 275068 | 63814 | 23.2 | 43290 | 15.7 |
| 2. | Arunachal Pradesh | 83743 | 51540 | 61.54 | 68602 | 81.9 |
| 3. | Assam | 78438 | 30708 | 39.15 | 23824 | 30.4 |
| 4. | Bihar | 173877 | 29226 | 16.81 | 26524 | 15.3 |
| 5. | Delhi | 1483 | 42 | 2.83 | 26 | 1.7 |
| 6. | Goa | 3702 | 1424 | 38.46 | 1252 | 33.8 |
| 7. | Gujarat | 196024 | 19393 | 9.89 | 12578 | 6.4 |
| 8. | Haryana | 44212 | 1673 | 3.78 | 604 | 1.4 |
| 9. | Himachal Pradesh | 55673 | 35407 | 63.6 | 12521 | 22.5 |
| 10. | Jammu & Kashmir | 222235 | 20182 | 9.08 | 20440 | 9.2 |
| 11. | Karnataka | 191791 | 38724 | 20.19 | 32403 | 16.9 |
| 12. | Kerala | 38863 | 11221 | 28.87 | 10334 | 26.6 |
| 13. | Madhya Pradesh | 443446 | 154497 | 34.84 | 131195 | 29.6 |
| 14. | Maharashtra | 307690 | 63842 | 20.75 | 46143 | 15 |
| 15. | Manipur | 22327 | 15154 | 67.87 | 17418 | 78 |
| 16. | Meghalaya | 22429 | 9496 | 42.34 | 15657 | 69.8 |
| 17. | Mizoram | 21081 | 15935 | 75.59 | 18775 | 89.1 |
| 18. | Nagaland | 16579 | 8629 | 52.04 | 14221 | 85.8 |
| 19. | Orissa | 155707 | 57184 | 36.73 | 46941 | 30.1 |
| 20. | Punjab | 50362 | 2901 | 5.76 | 1387 | 2.8 |
| 21. | Rajasthan | 342239 | 31700 | 9.26 | 13353 | 3.9 |
| 22. | Sikkim | 7096 | 2650 | 37.34 | 3129 | 44.1 |
| 23. | Tamil Nadu | 130058 | 22628 | 17.4 | 17064 | 13.1 |
| 24. | Tripura | 10486 | 6292 | 60.01 | 5546 | 52.9 |
| 25. | Uttar Pradesh | 294411 | 51663 | 17.54 | 33994 | 11.5 |
| 26. | West Bengal | 88752 | 11879 | 13.38 | 8349 | 9.4 |
| 27. | Andaman & Nicobar Islands | 8249 | 7171 | 86.93 | 7613 | 82.3 |
| 28. | Chandigarh | 114 | 31 | 27.19 | 7 | 6.1 |
| 29. | Dadra & Nagar Haveli | 491 | 203 | 41.34 | 204 | 41.5 |
| 30. | Daman & Diu | 112 | N.A. | N.A | 3 | 2.7 |
| 31. | Lakshdweep | 32 | N.A. | N.A. | Nil | Nil |
| 32. | Pondicherry | 493 | N.A. | N.A. | Nil | Nil |
| | Total | 3287263 | 765210 | 23.28 | 633397 | 20.5 |

*Source:* http://www.Indiastat.com

# Appendix 6

## *State-wise Forest Land Diverted for Non-Forestry Purposes in India (upto 31-10-2002)*

| States/UTs | No. of proposals approved | Forest land diverted (ha) |
|---|---|---|
| Andhra Pradesh | 184 | 22626 |
| Arunachal Pradesh | 64 | 2491 |
| Assam | 119 | 1653 |
| Bihar | 102 | 5979 |
| Chhattisgarh | 176 | 15929 |
| Goa | 50 | 389 |
| Gujarat | 583 | 52657 |
| Haryana | 312 | 1582 |
| Himachal Pradesh | 356 | 4905 |
| Jammu & Kashmir | 8 | 1286 |
| Karnataka | 296 | 32408 |
| Kerala | 134 | 30993 |
| Madhya Pradesh | 518 | 228019 |
| Maharashtra | 1185 | 75650 |
| Manipur | 9 | 247 |
| Meghalaya | 61 | 356 |
| Mizoram | 42 | 8528 |
| Orissa | 265 | 27055 |
| Punjab | 437 | 2532 |
| Rajasthan | 268 | 12707 |
| Sikkim | 48 | 623 |
| Tamil Nadu | 225 | 4138 |
| Tripura | 91 | 2315 |
| Uttar Pradesh | 180 | 6484 |
| Uttarakhand | 2087 | 22930 |
| West Bengal | 77 | 9217 |
| Andaman & Nicobar Islands | 51 | 2223 |
| Dadra & Nagar Haveli | 87 | 168 |
| India | 8015 | 576090 |

*Source:* http://www.Indiastat.com

# Appendix 7

*Growth Rates of Production of Foodgrains, Non- Foodgrains and Principal Crops in India*

*(per cent)*

| Crops | 1994-95 | 1995-96 | 1996-97 | 1997-98 | 1998-99 | 1999-2000 | 2000-01 | 2001-02 | 2002-03 | 2003-04 | 2004-05 | 2005-06 | 2006-07* | Average Growth during 1994-95 to 2006-07 |
|---|---|---|---|---|---|---|---|---|---|---|---|---|---|---|
| Total Cereals | 3.68 | -5.51 | 9.37 | -2.29 | 5.1 | 4.24 | -5.57 | 7.83 | -18.71 | 21.04 | -6.48 | 6.27 | 3.16 | 1.7 |
| Total Pulses | 8.93 | -14.6 | 16.91 | -6.57 | 15.18 | -11.54 | -18.2 | 22.02 | 12.34 | 33.1 | -10.74 | 2.28 | 6.62 | 4.29 |
| Total Food-grains | 4.37 | -6.81 | 10.43 | -2.89 | 6.44 | 1.95 | -7.16 | 9.41 | -14.86 | 22.57 | -7.06 | 5.75 | 3.6 | 1.98 |
| Total Oilseeds | 1.88 | 2 | 8.96 | -12.99 | 14.07 | -15.54 | -7.99 | 9.98 | -23.25 | 53.74 | -0.59 | 14.34 | -11.86 | 2.52 |
| Total Fibres | 10.37 | 7.14 | 11.94 | -21.63 | 10.37 | -4.91 | -15.62 | 5.76 | -11.49 | 50.61 | -8 | 5.39 | 4.03 | 3.38 |
| Non-Foodgrains | 7.32 | 2.69 | 6.8 | -7.6 | 9.39 | -6.15 | -4.53 | 5.41 | -11.09 | 19.15 | 1.6 | 16.03 | 15.63 | 4.2 |
| All Principal Crops | 5.77 | -2.54 | 8.68 | -5.08 | 7.85 | -1.79 | -6 | 7.62 | -13.2 | 21 | -1.63 | 12.14 | 11.6 | 3.42 |

*Note*: *Based on Fourth advance estimates for 2006-07 except potato and tobacco for which final estimates for 2005-06 have been used.

*Source:* Ministry of Agriculture, Government of India.

# Appendix 8

## *Growth Rates of Area of Foodgrains, Non-Foodgrains and Principal Crops in India*

*( per cent)*

| *Crops* | *1994-95* | *1995-96* | *1996-97* | *1997-98* | *1998-99* | *1999-2000* | *2000-01* | *2001-02* | *2002-03* | *2003-04* | *2004-05* | *2005-06* | *2006-07** | *Average Growth during 1994-95 to 2006-07* |
|---|---|---|---|---|---|---|---|---|---|---|---|---|---|---|
| Total Cereals | 0.08 | -2.07 | 2.43 | -0.15 | 0.68 | 0.32 | -1.26 | 0.07 | -7.35 | 7.1 | -2.67 | 1.95 | 1.17 | 0.02 |
| Total Pulses | 5.62 | -5.16 | 2.16 | 2.11 | 2.43 | -10.15 | -3.64 | 8.16 | -6.87 | 14.45 | -2.96 | -1.77 | 3.36 | 0.6 |
| Total Foodgrains | 1.1 | -2.64 | 2.39 | 0.23 | 1 | -1.65 | -1.67 | 1.43 | -7.26 | 8.42 | -2.73 | 1.24 | 1.56 | 0.11 |
| Total Oilseeds | -2.68 | 5.6 | 1.39 | -1.37 | 1.6 | -7.28 | -4.69 | 1.61 | -7.75 | 6.8 | 15.21 | 0.63 | -3.49 | 0.43 |
| Non Foodgrains | 2.79 | 3.41 | 1.69 | -1.16 | 1.07 | -2.14 | -2.74 | 0.54 | -10.9 | 8.15 | 9.8 | 2.03 | -1.22 | 0.82 |
| All Principal Crops | 1.56 | -0.65 | 2.11 | -0.24 | 1.02 | -1.79 | -1.98 | 0.66 | -7.83 | 8.34 | 0.75 | 1.48 | 0.72 | 0.32 |

*Note*: * Based on fourth advance estimates for 2006-07 except potato and tobacco for which final estimates for 2005-06 have been used.

*Source:* Ministry of Agriculture, Government of India.

# Appendix 9

## *Growth Rates of Yield of Foodgrains, Non-Foodgrains and Principal Crops in India*

*(per cent)*

| *Crops* | *1994-95* | *1995-96* | *1996-97* | *1997-98* | *1998-99* | *1999-00* | *2000-01* | *2001-02* | *2002-03* | *2003-04* | *2004-05* | *2005-06* | *2006-07** | *Average Growth during 1994-95 to 2006-07* |
|---|---|---|---|---|---|---|---|---|---|---|---|---|---|---|
| Total Cereals | 3.58 | -3.45 | 6.69 | -2.12 | 4.39 | 3.91 | -4.36 | 7.75 | -12.26 | 13.02 | -3.91 | 4.25 | 1.98 | 1.5 |
| Total Pulses | 5.62 | -5.16 | 2.16 | 2.11 | 2.43 | -10.15 | -3.64 | 8.16 | -6.87 | 14.45 | -2.96 | -1.77 | 3.36 | 0.6 |
| Total Food-grains | 3.3 | -4.29 | 7.82 | -3.19 | 5.38 | 3.66 | -5.58 | 7.86 | -8.19 | 13.05 | -4.45 | 4.45 | 2.01 | 1.68 |
| Total Oilseeds | 4.76 | -3.47 | 7.47 | -11.76 | 12.27 | -8.91 | -3.45 | 8.24 | -16.8 | 43.95 | -13.72 | 13.62 | -8.67 | 1.81 |
| Total Fibres | 3.07 | -5.23 | 9.04 | -19.72 | 6.28 | 1.12 | -13.99 | -0.68 | 3.46 | 52.62 | -18.48 | 6.8 | -1.15 | 1.79 |
| Non-Food -grains | 4.42 | -0.67 | 5.04 | -6.46 | 8.24 | -4.1 | -1.84 | 4.85 | -0.25 | 10.18 | -7.47 | 13.71 | 17.05 | 3.29 |
| All Principal Crops | 3.96 | -1.81 | 6.4 | -4.83 | 6.76 | 0 | -4.1 | 6.91 | -5.83 | 11.68 | 2.37 | 10.5 | 10.81 | 2.93 |

*Note*: * Based on fourth advance estimates for 2006-07 except potato and tobacco for which final estimates for 2005-06 have been used.

*Source:* Ministry of Agriculture, Government of India

# Appendix 10

## Bivariate Correlations

| Pearson Correlation | Forest | Tea price index | Cotton price index | Fertilizer price index | Jute price index | Sugar price index | Groundnut seed price index | Food grain price index |
|---|---|---|---|---|---|---|---|---|
| Forest | 1.000 | .246 | -.122 | -.782** | -.428 | -.367 | -.525 | -.613* |
| Tea price index | .246 | 1.000 | .091 | .206 | -.540 | .659 | .113 | .411 |
| Cotton price index | -.122 | .091 | 1.000 | .312 | -.314 | .317 | .506 | .178 |
| Fertilizer price index | -.782** | .206 | .312 | 1.000 | .173 | .634* | .849** | .905** |
| Jute price index | -.428 | -.540 | -.314 | .173 | 1.000 | -.321 | .073 | -.003 |
| Sugar price index | -.367 | .659* | .317 | .634* | -.321 | 1.000 | .494 | .806** |
| Groundnut seed price index | -.525 | .113 | .506 | .849** | .073 | .494 | 1.000 | .699* |
| Foodgrain price index | -.613* | .411 | .178 | .905** | -.003 | .806** | .699* | 1.000 |

* Correlation is significant at the 0.05 level (2-tailed).

** Correlation is significant at the 0.01 level (2-tailed).

## Appendix 11

### *Year-wise Progress of Polluting Industries*

| *Period* | *Total* | *Closed* | *C** | *Defaulters*** |
|---|---|---|---|---|
| 1992-93 | 1551 | 51 | 960 | 540 |
| 1993-94 | 1547 | 74 | 1154 | 319 |
| 1994-95 | 1551 | 121 | 1178 | 252 |
| 1995-96 | 1551 | 111 | 1237 | 203 |
| 1996-97 | 1551 | 125 | 1260 | 166 |
| 1997-98 | 1551 | 125 | 1261 | 165 |
| 1998-99 | 1551 | 135 | 1269 | 147 |
| 1999-2000 | 1551 | 164 | 1320 | 67 |
| 2000-01 | 1551 | 172 | 1326 | 53 |
| 2001-02 | 1551 | 179 | 1349 | 23 |
| 2002-03 | 2155 | 225 | 1877 | 53 |

*Note*: * Having adequate facilities to comply with the standards
** Not having adequate facilities to comply with the standards
*Source*: Ministry of Environment and Forests.

## Appendix 12

### *Category-wise Distribution of Industries (as on 2001-02)*

| *Sl. No.* | *CATEGORY* | *Total No. of Units* | *Status ( No. of Units )* | | |
|---|---|---|---|---|---|
| | | | *Closed* | *C** | *Defaulters* |
| 01. | ALUMINIUM | 07 | 01 | 06 | 00 |
| 02. | CAUSTIC | 25 | 00 | 25 | 00 |
| 03. | CEMENT | 116 | 08 | 108 | 00 |
| 04. | COPPER | 02 | 00 | 01 | 01 |
| 05. | DISTILLERY | 177 | 32 | 134 | 11 |
| 06. | DYES & D.I. | 64 | 08 | 56 | 00 |
| 07. | FERTILIZER | 110 | 10 | 97 | 03 |
| 08. | IRON & STEEL | 08 | 00 | 02 | 06 |
| 09. | LEATHER | 70 | 11 | 59 | 00 |
| 10. | PESTICIDE | 71 | 07 | 63 | 01 |
| 11. | PETROCHEM | 49 | 00 | 49 | 00 |
| 12. | PHARMA | 251 | 26 | 225 | 00 |
| 13. | PULP & PAPER | 96 | 20 | 75 | 01 |
| 14. | REFINERY | 12 | 00 | 12 | 00 |
| 15. | SUGAR | 392 | 47 | 334 | 11 |
| 16. | TPP | 97 | 02 | 76 | 19 |
| 17. | ZINC | 04 | 00 | 04 | 00 |
| | TOTAL | 1551 | 172 | 1326 | 53 |

* Having adequate facilities to comply with the standards
*Source:* Ministry of Environment and Forests.

# Appendix 13

## *India's Polluting Products' Exports*

| Year | In US Dollar Million | | | % of Leather Export to Total Export | % of Chemical Export to Total Export | % of Marine Export to Total Export |
|---|---|---|---|---|---|---|
| | Leather Export | Chemical Export | Marine Export | | | |
| 1990-91 | 1419.47 | 1728 | 535 | 7.82284 | 9.52318 | 2.948438 |
| 1991-92 | 1247.88 | 1868.8 | 585.2 | 6.984898 | 10.46044 | 3.275605 |
| 1992-93 | 1290.09 | 1786.1 | 601.9 | 6.959465 | 9.63522 | 3.246984 |
| 1993-94 | 1339.54 | 2377.2 | 813.6 | 6.023572 | 10.68967 | 3.658553 |
| 1994-95 | 1627.22 | 3066.8 | 1126.4 | 6.179981 | 11.64733 | 4.277929 |
| 1995-96 | 1762.98 | 3597 | 1010.8 | 5.544852 | 11.31314 | 3.179126 |
| 1996-97 | 1618.27 | 3912.8 | 1128.9 | 4.83503 | 11.69057 | 3.372901 |
| 1997-98 | 1671.91 | 4396.3 | 1207.3 | 4.776012 | 12.55856 | 3.448798 |
| 1998-99 | 1654.89 | 4009.2 | 1038.4 | 4.981802 | 12.06911 | 3.12595 |
| 1999-00 | 1604.31 | 4706.5 | 1182.6 | 4.356886 | 12.78162 | 3.211632 |
| 2000-01 | 1963.54 | 5885.9 | 1393.8 | 4.406478 | 13.20884 | 3.127896 |
| 2001-02 | 1936.14 | 6051.8 | 1236.8 | 4.417718 | 13.80848 | 2.822024 |
| 2002-03 | 1875.21 | 7455.3 | 1431.6 | 3.556964 | 14.14147 | 2.715509 |
| 2003-04 | 2216.45 | 9445.9 | 1328.7 | 3.471741 | 14.79561 | 2.081212 |
| 2004-05 | 2379.44 | 12443.7 | 1439.8 | 2.848404 | 14.89623 | 1.72357 |

*Source*: Compiled from CLE Office, Chennai and A Hand book of Indian Economy, RBI, Mumbai.

# Appendix 14

## *Raw Data*

*(in million of Rs.)*

| Year | GDP at FC [Constant Price (Rs.)] | GDP at FC [Current Price (Rs.)] | Real GNP (Rs.) | Export (Rs.) | Import (Rs) | Total Capital Formation (Rs) | FDI (Rs) |
|---|---|---|---|---|---|---|---|
| 1990-91 | 692871 | 510954 | 683670 | 32557.63 | 43192.86 | 35057.4 | 174 |
| 1991-92 | 701863 | 589086 | 691143 | 44041.81 | 47850.84 | 35164.6 | 316 |
| 1992-93 | 737792 | 673221 | 726375 | 53688.25 | 63374.52 | 34648.6 | 965 |
| 1993-94 | 781345 | 781345 | 769265 | 69751.39 | 73101.01 | 45050.5 | 1838 |
| 1994-95 | 838031 | 917058 | 824816 | 82674.11 | 89970.66 | 54199.9 | 4126 |
| 1995-96 | 899563 | 1073271 | 886961 | 106353.3 | 122678.1 | 55275.6 | 7172 |
| 1996-97 | 970082 | 1243547 | 959359 | 118817.1 | 138919.7 | 60950.3 | 10015 |
| 1997-98 | 1016595 | 1390148 | 1005946 | 130100.6 | 154176.3 | 54815 | 13220 |
| 1998-99 | 1082747 | 1598127 | 1070773 | 139753.1 | 178331.9 | 57806.5 | 10358 |
| 1999-00 | 1148367 | 1761838 | 1137185 | 159561.4 | 215236.5 | 67601.5 | 9338 |
| 2000-01 | 1198592 | 1902999 | 1186438 | 203571 | 230872.8 | 66959.4 | 18406 |
| 2001-02 | 1267945 | 2081474 | 1257636 | 209018 | 245199.7 | 76887.7 | 29235 |
| 2002-03 | 1318362 | 2254888 | 1310471 | 255137.3 | 297205.9 | 76781.9 | 24367 |
| 2003-04 | 1430548 | 2519785 | 1422479 | 293366.8 | 359107.7 | 83179.7 | 19860 |
| 2004-05 | 1529408 | 2830465 | 1519749 | 375339.5 | 501064.5 | 99221.7 | 27188 |

*Source:* Compiled from CLE Office, Chennai and A Handbook of Indian Economy, RBI, Mumbai.

# Bibliography


A Report of Department of Environment and Climate Change, New South Wales Government-http://www.environment.nsw.gov.au/community/ethniccom.htm

Abler, D.G., A.G. Rodriguez, and J.S. Shortle. "Trade Liberalization and the Environment in Costa Rica," *Environment and Development Economics* 4 (3) July 1999: 357-73.

Agenda 21, United Nations, http://www.un.org/esa/sustdev

Ahluwalia, Isher Judge (1985). *Industrial Growth in India: Stagnation since the Mid-Sixties*, Oxford University Press, Delhi.

Albert B., Yanomami "Violence": Inclusive Fitness or Ethnographer's Representation? *Current Anthropology*, Vol. 30, No. 5 (Dec., 1989), pp. 637-640, The University of Chicago Press on behalf of Wenner-Gren Foundation for Anthropological Research.

Alison Dundes Renteln, "Environmental Rights vs. Cultural Rights" *Human Rights Dialogue*: "Environmental Rights" (Spring 2004) http://www.cceia.org/resources/publications/dialogue/2_11/section_2/4453.html

Allen, J.C. and Barnes, D.F. (1985). The Causes of Deforestation in Developing Countries. *Annals of the Association of American Geographers* 75, 163-184.

Amelung, T. and Diehl, M. (1992). *Deforestation of Tropical Rain Forests: Economic Causes and Impact on Development.* Tubingen (Germany). J.C.B. Mohr.

Ana S.L. Rodrigues, Sandy J. Andelman, Mohamed I. Bakarr *et al.* (2004). Effectiveness of the global protected area network in representing species diversity. *Nature* 428, 640-643.

Anderson, K. "The Standard Welfare Economics of Policies Affecting Trade and the Environment." In *The Greening of World Trade Issues,* K. Anderson and R. Blackhurst, (eds.), Chapter 2. Ann Arbor: The University of Michigan Press, 1992.

Angelsen, A. and D. Kaimowitz (1996). "Rethinking the causes of deforestation: lessons from economic models", in *The World Bank Research Observer,* Vol. 14, No 1.

Antle, J.M., and Heidebrink, G. (1999). Environment and Development: Theory and International Evidence, in: *Environmental Economics and Development.*

Antweiler, W., Copeland, R.B. and Taylor, M.S. (2001) 'Is Free Trade Good for the Environment?', *The American Economic Review* 4 (2): 877–908.

Archer, David (2005). "Fate of fossil fuel $CO_2$ in geologic time" (PDF). *Journal of Geophysical Research* 110 (C9): C09S05.1–C09S05.6. doi:10.1029/2004JC002625.

Arctic Monitoring and Assessment Program (AMAP) International Symposium on Environmental Pollution of the Arctic. Panel discussion highlights: are things getting better or worse? Available at: http://www.amap.no/.

Arrow, K., Bolin, B., Costanza, R., Dasgupta, P., Folke, C., Holling, C.S., Jansson, B.O., Levin, S., Mäler, K.G., Perings, C., and Pimental, D., (1995) Economic Growth, Carrying Capacity and the Environment, *Science* 268, 520-521.

Arunakumara, V.K. (1995). Externalities in the use of pesticides: An economic analysis in a Cole crop. MSc Thesis (Unpublished), UAS, Bangalore.

Aserkar, R. and Vyas, R. (2006). "Environmental Policy Issues and their impact on exports of India"; *Environmental Issues of Development*, The Associated Publisher, Ambala Cantt.

B.B. Vohra: Sardar Patel Memorial Lecture (1980), quoted in the *State of India's Environment 1982*, pp. 6-7.

Bailey, R., (ed.). *The True State of the Planet*. New York: The Free Press, 1995.

Barbier, E.B., and M. Rauscher (1994). "Trade, Tropical Deforestation and Policy Interventions," *Environment and Resource Economics* 4: 75-90.

Beckerman, W. (1992). Economic Growth and the Environment: Whose Growth? Whose Environment? *World Development* 20, 481-496.

Beghin J., and M. Potier (1997). "Effects of Trade Liberalisation on the Environment in the Manufacturing Sector," *The World Economy* 20 (4): 435-56.

Berkes, F. and Folke, C. (1993). 'A Systems Perspective on the Inter-relationship Between Natural, Human-made and Cultural Capital', *Ecological Economics*, Vol. 5, No. 1.

—— (1994), 'Investing in Cultural Capital for Sustainable Use of Natural Capital', in (eds) A. Jansson, M. Hammer, C. Folke and R. Constanza, *Investing in Natural Capital*, Island Press, Washington DC, pp. 128-49.

Bhagwati, J.N., and T.N. Srinivasan (1999). "Trade and the Environment: Does Environmental Diversity Detract from the Case for Free Trade?" In *Fair Trade and Harmonization*. J.N. Bhagwati and R.E. Hudec, (eds.), pp. 159-224.

Boyce, J.K. (1994). Inequality as a Cause of Environmental Degradation, *Ecological Economics,* 11, 169-178.

Brandon, C.; Hommann, K. and Kishore, N.M. (1995). "The Cost of inaction: Valuing the Economy wide Cost of Environmental Degradation in India" *Proceedings of the UNU Conference on the Sustainable Future of the Global System,* Tokyo, 16-18 October, 1995.

Brouzes, Raymond J.P., "Impact of Environmental Concerns on the Bauxite Industry and its Economic Significance", the book "Bauxite, Economic Outlook" chapter-42, http://www.onemine.org, 1984, ISBN 0-89520-422-3.

Bryant, D., D. Nielsen, and L.Tingley (1997) *The last frontier Forests: Ecosystems and Economies on the Edge"*. Washington DC; World Resources Institute.

Bryden, J.M. and Dawe, S.P. (1999), 'Development Strategies for Remote Rural Regions: What do we know so far?' *OECD*, pp. 1-23.

Capistrano, A.D. (1990). *Macro-Economic Influences on Tropical Forest Depletion:A cross country analysis*. University of Florida, Gainesville.

Cass, D., (1965) Optimum Growth in an Aggregate Model of Capital Accumulation, *Rev. Economic Studies* 32, 233-240.

Center for Science and Environment: *The State of India's Environment, 1982*, p. 35.

——: *The state of India's environment, 1984-85*, p. 13.

Central Pollution Control Board, Annual Report 2004-05.

Chand, Ramesh and Birthal, P.S. (1997). Pesticide use in Indian agriculture in relation to growth in area and production and technological change. *Indian Journal of Agricultural Economics,* 52(3): 488-498.

CII; SII. (1996) *India: An emerging environmental market—A handbook for trade and business opportunities.* New Delhi: Confederation of Indian Industry and Sanders International, Inc. 78 pp.

Cleveland, C.J., Costanza, R., Hall, C.A.S., and Kaufmann, R. (1984), Energy and the US Economy; a Biophysical Perspective, *Science* 225, 890-897.

Cole, M.A., Rayner, A.J. and Bates, J.M. (1997) The Environmental Kuznets Curve: An Empirical Analysis. *Environment and Development Economics,* 2, 401-416.

Conacher, Arthur; Conacher, Jeanette (1995). *Rural Land Degradation in Australia*. South Melbourne, Victoria: Oxford University Press Australia.

Constanza, R. & Daly, H. (1992), 'Natural Capital and Sustainable Development', *Conservation Biology*, Vol. 6, No. 1, pp. 37-46.

Copeland, B.R., and S.M. Taylor (1994). "North-South Trade and the Environment," *Quarterly Journal of Economics* 109: 755-87.

CPCB (Central Pollution Control Board) (1995) 'Air pollution and its control'. *Parivesh Newsletter* 2(1), June 1995. Delhi: Central Pollution Control Board. 20 pp.

—— (2000), *Management of Municipal Solid Waste*. Delhi: Central Pollution Control Board.

—— (2000a), 'Polluting Industries'. *Parivesh Newsletter* 2000, Delhi: Central Pollution Control Board.

—— (2001), Summary status of pollution control in 17 categories of industries. Accessed from http://envfor.nic.in/cpcb.

Cropper, M., and Griffiths, C. (1984). The Interaction of Population Growth and Environmental Quality, *Population Economics*.

D.B. Wake and V.T. Vredenburg. (2008). Are we in the midst of the sixth mass extinction? A view from the world of amphibians. *Proceedings of the National Academy of Sciences of the United States of America,* 105: 11466–11473.

Daly, H.E. (1994), 'Operationalising Sustainable Development by Investing in Natural Development', in (eds) A. Jansson, M. Hammer, C. Folke and R. Constanza, *Investing in Natural Capital*, Island Press, Washington DC, pp. 23-56.

—— (1973), *Towards a Steady State Economy.* San Francisco: Freeman.

—— (1991). *Steady-State Economics* (2nd ed.). Washington, D.C.: Island Press.

—— (1977), *Steady-State Economics*, San Francisco, Freeman & Co., 2nd. ed., Washington, D.C., Island Press.

Daniel, G. (2002). *Deforestation in Cameroon and Poverty in the Rural Zone.* Ethiopia. dgbetnkom2001@yahoo.fr

Dasgupta, Susmita and Wheeler, D. (1996). *Citizen Complaints about Environmental Indicators: Evidence from China.* World Bank, Policy Research Department Working Paper, December 1996.

Datt, R. and Sundharam, K.P.M. (2004). *Indian Economy,* S. Chand and Company Ltd., New Delhi.

Deacon, R., (1999). The Political Economy of Environmental Development Relationships, Santa Barbara, Preliminary Framework Working Paper, University of California.

Dean, J.M. (1999). "Testing the Impact of Trade Liberalization on the Environment: Theory and Evidence." In *Trade, Global Policy and the Environment*, P Fredrikksen, (ed.). World Bank Discussion Paper 402, 55-63, The World Bank, Washington, D.C.

Dean, Judith M. (2002) Does trade liberalization harm the environment? A new test", *Canadian Journal of Economics,* Vol. 35, No.4, 819-842.

Dessus, S., and M. Bussolo (1998). "Is There a Trade-off between Trade Liberalization and Pollution Abatement? A Computable General Equilibrium Assessment Applied to Costa Rica," *Journal of Policy Modeling* 20 (February): 11-31.

Diamond, P. (1965). National Debt in a Neoclassical Growth Model, *American Economic Review* 55, 1126-1150.

Ehrlich, P.R. and J.P. Holdren (1971). eds, *Global Ecology: Readings Toward a Rational Strategy for Man,* New York, Harcourt Brace Jovanovich.

—— (1973). *Human Ecology: Problems and Solutions,* San Francisco, W.H. Freeman.

Eleventh Finance Commission Report 2000.

Eskeland, S. Gunnar and Ann E. Harrison, (2003) "Moving to Greener Pastures? Multinationals and the Pollution Haven Hypothesis", *Journal of Development Economics,* 70(1), 1-23.

Fabayo, A. (1987) 'On the Scope for, and Direction of Capital-Labour Substitution in Nigerian Manufacturing Industries', *West African Economic Journal* 2(2): 78.

Feridun, Mete (2006): Impact of Trade Liberalization on the Environment in Developing Countries: The Case of Nigeria. Published in: *Journal of Developing Societies* 122: pp. 39-56.

Ferrantino, M.J., L.A. Linkins (1999). "The Effect of Global Trade Liberalization on Toxic Emissions in Industry," *Weltwirtschaftliches Archiv/Review of World Economics* 135 (1) 1999: 128-55.

G. Schmidt. (2005). "Ecology & Anthropology: A Field Without Future?" *Ecological and Environmental Anthropology.* 1(1): 13-15.

Galeotti, M. and Lanze, A., Richer and Cleaner (1999). A Study on Carbon Dioxide Emissions in Developing Countries, Rome, *Proceedings from the 22nd IAEE Annual International Conference,* June 9-12.

Gbetnkom, Daniel, *Determinants of Agricultural Exports: The Case of Cameroon,* African Economic Research Consortium.

George Foundation (1999) 'Project Lead Free: A study of Lead poisoning in Major Indian cities'. *International Conference on Lead Poisoning, Prevention and Treatment (Proceedings),* 8-9 February 1999, Bangalore.

Georgescu-Roegen, N. (1971). *The Entropy Law and the Economic Process,* Cambridge, Harvard University Press.

Ghosh, Arun (1997). "Budget 1997-98: Underlining NEP", *Economic and Political Weekly,* May 17-23/24-30, p.1139.

Government of India (1989). *National Accounts Statistics: Sources and Methods.* Central Statistical Organisation, Department of Statistics, Ministry of Planning, New Delhi.

—— (2003). *Forest Resources in India: An Overview* (http://envfor.nic.in/fsi/sfr99/chp2/t21b.html).

—— "Economic Survey, 2001-02".

Grossman, G., and Kreuger, A. (1995). Economic Growth and the Environment, *Quarterly Journal of Economics* 110 (2), 353-377.

—— (1993) 'Environmental Impacts of a North-American Free-Trade Agreement', in P.M. Garber (ed.) *The Mexico–US Free Trade Agreement,* pp. 13–56. Cambridge, MA: MIT Press.

Gulati, M. (1997) *Restructuring and modernisation of small medium enterprise clusters in India.*

Hasna, A.M. (2007). "Dimensions of Sustainability". *Journal of Engineering for Sustainable Development: Energy, Environment, and Health* 2 (1): 47–57.

Hettige, H., Mani M. (1997). "Industrial Pollution in Economic Development: Kuznets Revisited", David Wheeler Development Research Group World Bank.

Holtz-Eakin, D. and Selden, T.M. (1995), "Stroking the Fires? $CO_2$ Emissions and Economic growth", *Journal of Public Economics,* 57, 85-101.

http://en.wikipedia.org/wiki/United_Nations_Environment_Programme

http://geosci.uchicago.edu/~archer/reprints/archer.2005.fate_co2.pdf. Retrieved on 27 July 2007.

http://ipcc-wg1.ucar.edu/wg1/Report/AR4WG1_Print_SPM.pdf. Retrieved on 2 February 2007.

http://www.atmos.berkeley.edu/~jchiang/Class/Spr07/Geog257/Week10/Lu_Hadley06.pdf. Retrieved on 12/06/2008.

http://www.eia.doe.gov/emeu/cabs/indiaenv.html

http://www.indiastat.com

http://www.unep.org/

http://www.unep.org/themes/land/index.asp?page=programmes. Retrieved on 19 July 2008.

Human Development Report 2001.

*India Infrastructure Report (2002),* 3i Network, New Delhi: Oxford University Press.

India: Environmental Issues, (2001). http://www.eia.doe.gov/emeu/cabs/indiaenv.html

*India: State of Environment, 2001,* published by United Nations Environment Programme, 2001.

*Indian Agriculture in Brief,* (Ministry of Agriculture), 25th Edition, 1994.

J.I. Fisher, (1964). The Role of Natural Resources in *Economic Development: Principles and Patterns* (Eds). H. F. Williamson and J.A. Buttrick.

Jansson, A.M., Hammer, M., Folke, C. and Costanza, R. (1994) (eds), *Investing in Natural Capital - The Ecological Economics Approach to Sustainability,* Covelo, CA, ISEE Press/Island Press.

Jha, R., Chand, S. and A. Sharma (2003) "The Fiscal Constraint on India's Economic Growth" in R. Jha (ed.) *Indian Economic Reforms,* Basingstoke, Houndmills, Palgrave Macmillan

Jha, V., A. Markandya, and R. Vossenaar (1999). *Reconciling Trade and the Environment: Lessons from Case Studies in Developing Countries.* Cheltenham, UK: Edward Elgar Publishing Company.

Joshi, G.N. and Shriniwas, V.A. (2006). *"International Trade and Environmental Policy Issues: A Reference to India's position"*; The Book, *Environmental Issues of Development,* The Associated Publisher, Ambala Cantt, 2006, xvi, 470 p.

Kaimowitz, D. (1997). *Livestock and Deforestation in Central America in the 1980s and 1990s. A policy perspective.* Bogor, Indonesia: Center for International Forestry Research.

——, N. Byron, and W. Sunderlin (1998). Public policies to reduce inappropriate tropical deforestation. In Lutz, E. *et al.*, (eds), *Agriculture and the Environment: Perspective on Sustainable Rural Development.* A World Bank Symposium, Washington, DC.

Kawadia, G. and Ahuja, K.(2006) *Development and Environment Inter-relationship in MP,* in The Book "Environmental Issues of Development", The Associated Publisher, Amabala Cantt, xvi, 470 p.

Kelkar, V. (2004) "India: On the Growth Turnpike" Narayanan Oration, Australia South Asia Research Centre, Australian National University.

Keller, Wolfgang and Levinson, Arik, *(2002)* "Environmental Regulations and FDI to US States", *Review of Economics and Statistics,* 84(4).

Knack, S. and Keefer, P., Institutions and Economic Performance: Cross Country tests Using Alternative Institutional Measures, *Economics and Politics* 7 November 3, 207-227 (1995).

Koopmans, T.C. (1965). On the Concept of Optimal Economic Growth, *The Economic Approach to Development Planning.*

KPMG-CHEMTECH (2003). The Indian Chemical Industry: New directions, new hope. *A report by KPMG India-CHEMTECH foundation.* Retrieved on January 2, 2006 from http://www.kpmg.de /library/ pdf/ 030117_KPMG_Chemtech_Report_en.pdf

Kuznets, S., *(1965) Economic Growth and Structural Change,* New York, Norton.

——, (1966). *Modern Economic Growth,* New Haven, Yale University Press.

L. Watrud *et al.* (2004), "Evidence for landscape-level, pollen-mediated gene flow from genetically modified creeping bentgrass with CP4 EPSPS as a marker", *Proceedings of the National Academy of Sciences* 101, p.14533.

Lal, Anil K. and Clement; Ronald W. (2005). "Economic Development in India: The role of individual enterprise (and entrepreneurial spirit)", *Asia-Pacific Development Journal* Vol. 12, No. 2, December.

Lee, H., and D. Roland-Holst. (1997). "The Environment and Welfare Implications of Trade and Tax Policy," *Journal of Development Economics* 52: 65-82.

Levinson, Arik and M. Scott Taylor, (2001) "Trade and Environment: Unmasking the Pollution Haven Effect", Working Paper.

Lewis, W. A., *The Theory of Economic Growth,* Allen and Unwin.

Lloyd, P.J. "The Problem of Optimal Environmental Policy Choice." In *The Greening of World Trade Issues,* K. Anderson and R. Blackhurst, (eds.). 1992.

Lopez, R. (1994) 'The Environment as a Factor of Production: The Effects of Economic Growth and Trade Liberalization', *Journal of Environmental Economics and Management,* 27: 163–84.

Low, D. and A. Yeats, (1992) *"Do dirty industries migrate?. International Trade and Environment,"* World Bank, Discussion Paper No. 159.

Lu, Jian; Gabriel A. Vecchi, Thomas Reichler (2007). "Expansion of the Hadley cell under global warming". *Geophysical Research Letters* 34: L06805. doi:10.1029/2006GL028443.

Lundberg, M. and Squire, L. (2000). 'The simultaneous evolution of growth and inequality', mimeo, The World Bank.

Lutz, E., H. Binswanger, P. Hazell, and A. McCalla (1998). *"Agriculture and the environment: perspective on sustainable rural development".* A World Bank Symposium, Washington, DC.

Mani, Muthukumara, and David Wheeler, (1997) *"In search of pollution havens? Dirty Industry in the World Economy, 1960-1999",* PRDEI, April 1997.

McConnell, K.E. (1983) "An Econometric Model of Soil Conservation" *American Journal of Agricultural Economics,* 65: 83-89.

Meadows, D., Meadows, D. L., Randers, J., & Behrens, W. (1971). *The Limits to Growth.* New York: Universe Books

Meadows, D.H. Meadows, D.L., Randers, J. and Behrens, W.W., (1972). *The Limits to Growth,* London, Earth Island Limited.

Ministry of Rural Development, Department of Land Resources and National Remote Sensing Agency, (2000) *Wastelands*, Atlas of India.

Miranowski, J.A. (1984) "Impacts of Productivity Loss on Crop Production and Management in a Dynamic Economic Model", *American Journal of Agricultural Economics,* 66, 61-71.

*Modern Economic Growth,* New Haven, Yale University Press (1966).

MoEF. (2000) Draft on Status of Implementation of the Hazardous Waste Rules, 1989 New Delhi: Ministry of Environment and Forests, Government of India.

MoF (2000) *Economic Survey (1999-2000).* New Delhi: Economic Division, Ministry of Finance

MoF. (1999) Budget Speech 1999-2000, Ministry of Finance, Government of India. Accessed from http://finmin.nic.in/fub.htm.

MoF. (2000). Budget Speech 2000-01, Ministry of Finance, Government of India. Accessed from http://finmin.nic.in

MoF. (2002) *Economic Survey 2001/02,* New Delhi: Economic Division, Ministry of Finance.

MoF. (2002a) Budget Speech 2001-02, New Delhi: Ministry of Finance, Government of India. Accessed from http://finmin.nic.in

MoST (2000) *Handbook on transport statistics in India (1999).* New Delhi: Transport Research Wing, Ministry of Surface Transport.

Nagraj, R. (1997). "What Has Happened since 1991?: Assessment of India's Economic Reforms," *Economic and Political Weekly,* Nov. 8, IP: -2874.

Nayar, Baldev Raj, (2001). *Globalization and Nationalism: The Changing Balance in India's Economic Policy,* 1950-2000 London, Sage Publications.

Ninan, K.N. (2002) "Watershed Development Programmes in India: A Review", Paper Presented at the 12th ISCO Conference, Beijing.

Nordstrom, H., and S. Vaughan (1999). Trade and Environment. Special Studies No 4, The World Trade Organization, Geneva, CH.

Ostrom, E. (1990). *Governing the Commons: The Evolution of Institutions for Collective Action,* Cambridge, Cambridge University Press.

Pachauri, R.K.; Sridharan, P.V. (1998) *Looking Back to Think Ahead: growth with resource enhancement of environment and nature.* New Delhi: Tata Energy Research Institute. 346 pp.

Panayotou, T. (1993) *Empirical Test and Policy Analysis of Environmental Degradation at Different Stages of Economic Development.* Geneva: International Labour Office, Technology and Employment Programme.

—— (1995) *Environmental Degradation at Different Stages of Economic Development, Beyond Rio (The Environmental Crisis and Sustainable Livelihoods in the Third World)*

—— (1992) *Environmental Kuznets Curves: Empirical Tests and Policy Implications,* Cambridge: Harvard Institute for International Development, Harvard University.

——, Sachs, J., Peterson, A., (1999). Developing Countries and the Control of Climate Change: A Theoretical Perspective and Policy Implications, *CAER II Discussion Paper No. 45. August.*

Parikh, J.K., V.K. Sharma, U. Gosh and M.K. Panda, (1995), *Trade and Environment Linkages: A Case Study of India,* Indira Gandhi Institute of Development Research, Report prepared for UNCTAD.

—— (1989) "An Operational Measureable Definition of Sustainable Development", Indira Gandhi Institute of Development Research, Discussion paper No.21.

—— and Upal Ghosh (1991) "Natural Resource Accounting for Soils: Towards an Empirical Estimate of Costs of Soil Degradation in India", Indira Gandhi Institute of Development Research, Discussion Paper No.48.

——(1997) "India's Economy; Raised for take-off" *Economic and Political Weekly,* May 17-23, 124-30, p. 1151.

Patterson, C. "Cultural Capital and Development: The Dynamics of Change in a Small Coastal Community" Unpublished, School of Geography and Environmental Studies, University of Tasmania. (PhD candidate).

Paul Ehrlich and Anne Ehrlich, (1981). *Extinction,* Random House, New York.

Planning Commission. (2000) Mid-term Appraisal of Ninth Five-Year Plan (1997-2002) New Delhi: Planning Commission, Government of India. 510 pp.

Planning Commission (2001a). Approach to the Tenth Five Year Plan (2002-07), New Delhi: Planning Commission. 49 pp.

Planning Commission (2001b). *Indian planning experience: A statistical profile.* New Delhi: Planning Commission. 219 pp.

Planning Commission: Tenth Five Year Plan, 2002-07, Vol II, Ch. IX.

Ramsey, F.P. (1998). A Mathematical Theory of Saving, *Economic Journal* 38, 543-559.

Ratnayake, R. "Do Stringent Environmental Regulations Reduce International Competitiveness? Evidence from an Inter-Industry Analysis", *International Journal of the Economics of Business,* 5: 77-96.

Ravallion, M.H., and Jalan, J. (1997). A Less Poor World, but a Hotter One? Carbon Emissions, Economic Growth and Income Inequality, World Bank, October 15.

Repetto R., M. Wells, C. Beer and F. Rossini, (1987) *Natural Resource Accounting for Indonesia,* World Resource Institute, Washington D.C.

*Report on Indian Pesticide Industry,* Credit Analysis and Research LTD area Research, 4th Floor Godrej Coliseum, Off Eastern Express Highway, Somaiya Hospital Road, Sion (East), Mumbai.

Rodrik, Dani and Arvind Subramanian (2004). 'From 'Hindu Growth' to Productivity Surge: The Mystery of the Indian Growth Transition', unpublished manuscript, March.

Rohana Ulluwishewa, Adbul Aziz Kaloko and Dyhairuni Hj Mohammed Morican (1997) Indigenous Knowledge and Environmental Education. Paper presented at Environmental Education Workshop, University of Brunei Darussalam, pp. 3-4.

Romer, P.M. (1986). Increasing Returns and Long-run Growth, *Journal of Political Economy* 94, 1002-1037.

——., (1990). Endogenous Technological Change, *Journal of Political Economy* 71-101.

Rothman, D.S. (1998). Environmental Kuznets Curve - Real Progress or Passing the buck? A Case for Consumption Based Approaches. *Ecological Economics,* 25, 177-194.

Schmalensee, R., Stoker, T.M., and Judson, R.A., (1997). *World Carbon Dioxide Emissions: 1950-2050*.

Sehgal J. and Abrol, I.P. (1994) *Soil Degradation in India: Status and Impact,* Oxford and IBH Publishing Co.

Selden, T.M., and Song, D. (1994). Environmental Quality and Development: Is there a Kuznets Curve for Air Pollution Emissions? *Journal of Environmental Economics and Management* 27, 147-162.

Shafik, N. (1994), "Economic Development and Environmental Quality", *Oxford Economic Papers,* 46, 757-73.

—— and Bandhyopadhyay, S. (1992). *Economic Growth and Environmental Quality: Time Series and Cross Country Evidence.* Washington, D.C: World Bank.

——, (1977). Economic Growth and Environmental Resources, *Journal of Environmental Economics and Management* 4, 1-24.

Shah, Jayati (1998). "Liberalization Debates" in Terence Byres (ed.), *The Indian Economy – Major Debates since Independence* (Delhi).

Shaleen Singhal and Sunil Pandey, *Solid Waste Management in India, Status and Future Directions,* TERI, Darbari Seth Block, Habitat Place, Lodhi Road, New Delhi.

Singh Gurmel, Ram Babu, Pratap Narain, L.S. Bhushan and I.P. Abrol (1992) "Soil Erosion Rates in India", *Journal of Soil and Water Conservation* 47 (1), 97-99.

Srinivasa, D.K. (1993). *Environment and human health. Environmental problems and prospects in India,* Oxford and IBH Publications, New Delhi.

Stern, D.I., Common, M.S., and Barbier, E.B. (1996). Economic Growth and Environmental Degradation: the Environmental Kuznets Curve and Sustainable Development, *World Development* 24 (7) 1151-1160.

Stivers, R. (1976). *The Sustainable Society: Ethics and Economic Growth.* Philadelphia: Westminster Press.

Strutt, A., and K. Anderson (1999). "Will Trade Liberalization Harm the Environment?: The Case of Indonesia to 2020." In *Trade, Global Policy and the Environment,* P. Fredriksson, (ed.). World Bank Discussion Paper 402, pp. 13-34. The World Bank, Washington, D.C.

Subramanian, A. (1992). "Trade Measures for Environment: A Nearly Empty Box?," *The World Economy* 15: 135-52.

Tenth Five-Year Plan (2000-07), Vol. II, p.1071.

*The Hindu daily*, New Delhi, Online edition of India's National Newspaper, Thursday, February 17, 2005

Tobey, J.A. (1990) "The effects of domestic environmental policies on patterns of world trade", *Kyklos,* 43:191-160.

Torras, M. and Boyce, J.K. (1998). "Income Inequality and Pollution: A Reassessment of the Environmental Kuznets Curve", *Ecological Economics,* 25, 147-60.

Tuan, Nguyen Anh, (1999). Evidences of Environmental Kuznets Curve from CO2 Emissions in Six-Country Analysis, Working Paper, Institute d'Economie et de Polique de l'Energie (IEPE) BP 47, 38040 Grenoble Cedex 09.

UCN. (2006). The Future of Sustainability: Re-thinking Environment and Development in the Twenty-first Century. Report of the IUCN Renowned Thinkers Meeting, 29-31 January, 2006 http://cmsdata.iucn.org/downloads/iucn_future_of_sustanability.pdf

Ulph, A.M. *Trade and the Environment, Selected Essays of A.M. Ulph.* Northampton, MA, Cheltenham, UK: Edward Elgar Publishing Company, 1999.

United Nations Environment Programme (1997-12-11). *Industrialized countries to cut greenhouse gas emissions by 5.2%.* Press release. http://unfccc.int/cop3/fccc/info/indust.htm. Retrieved on 2007-08-06.

United Nations Industrial and Development Organisation. 221 pp. ILO. 2001 Country Objectives International Labour Organisation. New Delhi Area office. Accessed from http://www.ilo.org/public/english/region/asro/newdelhi/counobj.htm

United Nations (1987). "Report of the World Commission on Environment and Development", General Assembly Resolution 42/187, 11 December, Retrieved: 2007-04-12.

URL: http://www.eia.doe.gov/emeu/cabs/indiaenv.html

Vijesh, V.K.; Byju N.G. and Tamizheniyan (2006). *Integrated Pest Management In Indian Agriculture: A Developing Economy Perspective,* Radelife's IPM World Book, University of Minnesota.

Virmani, Arvind (2004a): 'India's Economic Growth: From Socialist Rate of Growth to Bharataya Rate of Growth', Working Paper No 122, Indian Council for Research on International Economic Relations, New Delhi, India.

—— (2004b): 'Sources of India's Economic Growth: Trends in Total Factor Productivity', Working Paper No 131, Indian Council for Research on International Economic Relations, New Delhi, India.

Wallack, Jessica Seddon (2003): 'Structural Breaks in Indian Macroeconomic Data', *Economic and Political Weekly,* October 11, pp. 4312-15.

Warren, D.M., Brokensha, D. and Slikkenveer, L.J., (eds.) (1996), *Indigenous Knowledge and Sustainable Development,* Sri Lanka Centre for Indigenous Knowledge, University of Sri Jayewardenapura, 1996, pp. vii-viii

Wheeler, D. (2000). Racing to the Bottom? Foreign Investment and Air Pollution in Developing Countries. Policy Research Working Paper #2524. Washington, D.C.: The World Bank.

Wiebelt, M. (1994). "Protecting Brazil's tropical Forest, A CGE Analysis of Macroeconomic, Sectoral, and Regional Policies". Kiel Working paper 638. Kiel Institute of World Economics. Kiel.

Wilcove, D.S., Wikelski, M. (2008). Going, Going, Gone: Is Animal Migration Disappearing. *PLoS Biol* 6 (7): e188 doi:10.1371/journal.pbio.0060188

Will, Allen (2007). "Learning for Sustainability: Sustainable Development."

William, D.S. and Resosudarmo, A.P. (1996). Rates and Causes of Deforestation in Indonesia: Towards a Resolution of the Ambiguities. Occasional Paper No.9, CIFOR, Indonesia.

World Bank (1992), *World Development Report: Development and the Environment,* Oxford University Press, New York.

——(1996) *India's Environment: Taking Stock of Plans, Programs and Policies.* World Bank: South Asia Regional Office. 317 pp.

——(2004) *India: Country Framework Report for the Private Participation In Infrastructure,* World Bank/Public-Private Infrastructure Facility, Washington, D.C.

# Index